The eBay Marketing Bible

The eBay Marketing Bible

EVERYTHING YOU NEED TO KNOW TO REACH MORE CUSTOMERS AND MAXIMIZE YOUR PROFITS

Cliff Ennico

and
Cindy Shebley

AMACOM

American Management Association
New York • Atlanta • Brussels • Chicago • Mexico City • San Francisco
Shanghai • Tokyo • Toronto • Washington, D.C.

Special discounts on bulk quantities of AMACOM books are available to corporations, professional associations, and other organizations. For details, contact Special Sales Department, AMACOM, a division of American Management Association, 1601 Broadway, New York, NY 10019.

Tel: 212-903-8316. Fax: 212-903-8083.

E-mail: specialsls@amanet.org

Website: www.amacombooks.org/go/specialsales

To view all AMACOM titles go to:
www.amacombooks.org

This publication is designed to provide accurate and authoritative information in regard to the subject matter covered. It is sold with the understanding that the publisher is not engaged in rendering legal, accounting, or other professional service. If legal advice or other expert assistance is required, the services of a competent professional person should be sought.

Library of Congress Cataloging-in-Publication Data

Ennico, Clifford R.
    The eBay marketing bible : everything you need to know to reach more customers and maximize your profits / Cliff Ennico and Cindy Shebley.
        p. cm.
    Includes index.
    ISBN-13: 978-0-8144-1440-8
    ISBN-10: 0-8144-1440-0
    1. Internet marketing.   2. Internet auctions.   3. eBay (Firm)   I. Shebley, Cindy.
    II. Title.

    HF5415.1265.E56 2009
    658.8'7—dc22   2009012582

Printing number

10 9 8 7 6 5 4 3 2 1

From Cliff: To Dolores Ennico, the toughest customer I ever sold ☺.

From Cindy: To Dany Byrne, who stood by me while I turned my hopes and dreams into reality, and to Buster, Rascal, and Shadow, who fearlessly helped by keeping the bad guys on the other side of the fence.

Contents

Acknowledgments

Any book is a team effort, and *The eBay Marketing Bible* would not have been possible without the support, friendship, inspiration, love, and occasional "noodging" of these individuals, among others. Our many thanks to:

- Janelle Elms, noted eBay author, mentor to both of us, and founder of the Online Success Institute (www.osirockstars.com), for being such a great resource on "all things eBay" and for having literally invented the field of eBay marketing.

- Jacquie Flynn, our editor at AMACOM Books, for believing that books for eBay sellers are indeed "business management books" worthy of the American Management Association.

- Jennifer Holder, our other editor at AMACOM Books, for going through the entire manuscript and at least two eyeglass prescriptions helping us blend two voices into a single harmony.

- The dozens of eBay sellers around the United States who allowed us access to their eBay marketing strategies and store designs, and shared with us "what worked and what didn't."

- Sharon Guldner, who oversees the eBay Education Specialist program and teaches us the stuff about eBay that we don't know.

- Skype, for making it possible for authors living on opposite coasts of the United States to collaborate on a book without running up thousands of dollars in telephone charges.

- Most important, Dolores Ennico and Dany Byrne, the people who share our lives, our frustrations, and our computers, and who tolerate all the craziness during those last couple of weeks before the manuscript is due ☺.

Introduction

If you own your own small business, marketing is the key to your success. It is hands down the most essential business skill. Without sales, without customers, without revenue, a small business cannot survive. And when you run your own business, on eBay or indeed anywhere else, you are the person responsible for making those sales happen, generating those customers, and bringing in that revenue.

Let us put it even more bluntly: If you are in business for yourself (whether on eBay or anywhere else) and you do not know how to market yourself, your products, or your services, you will fail. It is an absolute, 100 percent guarantee, with no exceptions. Whatever you call yourself in your business—whatever title you use, however you describe yourself at networking meetings and cocktail parties—you are the salesperson in chief.

If you don't make sales happen, nobody else will. This is one activity you *do not* delegate to your employees, your outside advisers, or your beleaguered spouse or life partner.

Without a doubt, this is the biggest difference between working for yourself and working for somebody else. When you work for somebody else—say, a giant Fortune 500 corporation—you can have a very exciting career indeed and not have to know a single thing about where your sales come from. You can pursue a career in finance, accounting, human resources (formerly known as "personnel"), or information technology, and climb quite far up the corporate ladder without having to sell anything to anybody at any time.

In the world of small business, that is a luxury you cannot afford. Marketing and selling are *the* most important things you do when you run your own business. Successful entrepreneurs and small business owners—however they may differ otherwise—are *always* very good at marketing, selling, advertising, and promoting whatever it is they have to sell.

A lot of people think that marketing is the easy part of business—they take courses in accounting, finance, and other more technical areas of business knowledge that require higher mathematics, but they leave the marketing part for last, figuring they can always pick it up as they go. As you will see in this book, that is a recipe for disaster. One of the dumbest things you can do in any business is build it first and then start looking for the people who will buy your merchandise.

Marketing is actually quite a challenge for most business owners. If you think about it, when you run any sort of business the one thing you *do not* have any control over whatsoever is your customers. You can control and manage your accounting records, your profit margins (by controlling costs), your employees, and other aspects of your internal operations to some extent, but you have no control over things that happen outside of your organization. And buying decisions are made by your customers, who by definition are outside of your organization.

You cannot force customers to buy something they don't want to buy—period. They decide where (and, in these tough economic times, whether) to spend their hard-earned money. Your job as a marketer is to persuade them that they should not only buy, but buy from *you*. There are literally hundreds of books on the market today teaching you how to sell—they wouldn't publish all those books if it were easy, folks.

Marketing and selling are scary for a lot of people. Let's say that you meet the authors at a cocktail party, and we point to someone you don't know and say, "That is one of the greatest salespeople we've ever known—that person could sell sand in Arabia, he or she is so good." Be honest: Are you going to run up to that person and introduce yourself? Probably not. All of us have had experiences with bad salespeople over the years—used-car salespeople, telemarketers who call you at dinnertime to sell you something you'll never need in a million years, people who show up at your doorstep while you're taking a shower to sell you magazine subscriptions, e-mail spammers, and so forth. The idea that we may have to become one of those people in order to survive is a tough one to swallow.

But, truth be told, you don't have to be a huckster or "slick" in any way to become very successful at marketing. In fact, the best marketers in the world are usually very sincere, honest, ethical people who would never tell a lie or put something over on anyone. That's the good news.

The bad news is that you just can't start listing stuff on eBay and then sit back and watch the money roll in. You've got to reach out to your customers, get your marketing message across, and keep them coming back for more on a fairly regular basis. You've got to be fairly aggressive about it—shrinking violets tend to be terrible marketers—and be prepared to devote to marketing-related activities at least 20 to 30 percent of the total time that you spend running your eBay business.

This book tells you how to market your eBay business, explains what to do (and what not to do), and teaches you some of the strategies that make eBay sellers successful in a challenging online marketplace.

The Internet: The Future of Small Business Retail

Drive down your local commercial strip or "miracle mile," and you will see lots of changes from a few years ago—new stores moving in, old stores shutting down. But one change you will almost certainly note: The mom-and-pop retail stores are disappearing.

Especially on the Atlantic and Pacific coasts, but increasingly in the heartland of America as well, mom-and-pop retail stores are slowly being replaced by chain stores, big box retailers, and franchises (yes, technically a franchise outlet is a small mom-and-pop business, but it doesn't act like one; it follows a uniform nationwide business plan and benefits from a national advertising budget, among other things, that enable most franchises to wipe their stand-alone competitors off the map).

However, don't lament the demise of small business retail—it really isn't disappearing at all. It's going online.

The mom-and-pop store you remember fondly from your childhood has found a new life as an eBay Store or a Yahoo! Store. The kindly old gentleman who sold you bubblegum cards and rang them up on his cash register is now poolside in Florida and making a fortune selling sports memorabilia on eBay from his laptop.

The Internet is the future of small business retail, and, with more than eighty million registered users worldwide and more than eight hundred thousand people in the United States alone registered as sellers, eBay is where the moms and pops are going to launch their e-commerce empires.

But if they are going to survive online, especially on eBay, the moms and pops are going to have to grow up a little.

Turning Your eBay Selling Hobby into a Real Business

As certified eBay Education Specialists (to find out what that means and how you can become one yourself, see Appendix A), the authors of this book give presentations around the United States teaching people how to build successful businesses on eBay. At these presentations somebody inevitably steps up to the microphone during the question-and-answer period and asks: "I've been selling on eBay for a while, but I don't know if I should treat it as a hobby or a business. Can you offer any advice on that?" It is without doubt the number one legal and tax question on the minds of eBay sellers nationwide.

Sooner or later, every eBay seller has to make the fateful decision: Should I do this only occasionally, for the fun of it, or should I consider making a part-time or full-time living doing this? Sometimes the decision is made for you, as when so many people are asking you to sell their stuff on eBay that before you know it you've made $50,000 or more in profits and you *have* to treat it as a business, whether you like it or not.

But the key difference between a hobby and a business is simply that people in business take themselves way more seriously than people with hobbies do. Businesspeople keep exquisite records of their sales, expenses, and income. They list items on eBay on a regular basis, at all times of the year, and often specialize in certain product categories where their superior knowledge of the merchandise gives them an advantage over their many competitors. They form corporations and limited liability companies (LLCs) to run their businesses. They keep regular hours for working on their businesses, and they sometimes burn the midnight oil to meet a tight deadline or get some key listings up on eBay in time for the holidays. Even the Internal Revenue Service (IRS) acknowledges, when it audits small businesses, that someone who appears to be having too much fun doing what he or she is doing is probably engaged in a hobby, not a business.

Most important, people with businesses (as opposed to hobbies) market their businesses to customers. They create e-mail newsletters and send them regularly to their eBay customers, they optimize their eBay Stores for the most popular search engines, they take out pay-per-click advertisements on those search engines, they put their eBay user IDs and Web addresses on their business cards and e-mail signature lines and paint them on the sides of their pickup trucks. They do everything they possibly can to attract and keep customers—all the time.

Today there are about nine hundred thousand people in the United States alone making a full-time or part-time living selling things on eBay, the world's largest online retailer, to eBay's more than eighty million unique registered users worldwide. Many people who started out selling on eBay as a hobby are branching out to Amazon, Yahoo!, uBid, and other e-commerce platforms, setting up their own e-commerce websites with virtual shopping carts and Web analytics software, and building e-commerce empires—all from the comfort of their own home offices.

Making the transition from an eBay selling hobby to a real online e-commerce business isn't easy—and it's getting harder. In order to create a viable business selling things online, you've got to start taking yourself seriously, pulling yourself up by the bootstraps, and thinking of yourself as a businessperson or entrepreneur.

Among other things, you are going to have to learn how to market your eBay selling presence, your products, your services, and yourself.

The Changing World of eBay

It's no secret. It's getting harder and harder to build a successful eBay selling business. Not only is the competition greater than ever before (remember those nine hundred thousand other sellers in the United States alone), but eBay itself is making it tougher for sellers to succeed by raising the bar for people it allows to sell on the site.

To understand the changes that have rocked the eBay community in recent years, it helps to understand the fundamental difference between *amateur* and *professional* retailers.

Cliff Ennico, one of the authors of this book, learned how to sell while he was literally in his diapers. His mother, Ruth, a child of the Great Depression of the 1930s, hated to throw anything away that she felt was worth a few pennies to somebody else. So she started selling her used household items several times a year at flea markets throughout Westchester County, New York, with her less-than-enthusiastic son in tow. Cliff grew up helping his mom at those flea markets, lugging the boxes, packing the merchandise (he jokes today that "Mom was the brains of the outfit; I was the muscle"), and watching or participating first-hand in thousands of retail sales transactions.

Whenever a customer would remark that Cliff's mother had the lowest prices of any vendor at the flea market, his mom would reply that she was "not a regular vendor" (in a thick New York City accent it comes out "nodda reguluh venduh"). This did not mean that she was not a frequent seller—Cliff's mom often rented tables at the same flea market venues year after year—but rather that she was not a *professional* seller. She was merely looking to clean out her house; she was not looking to her flea market sales as a source of income, nor did she treat it as a business (although once Cliff got his law degree, he made darn sure Mom paid her sales taxes).

When eBay was first launched in the mid-1990s, it developed a reputation (rightly or wrongly) as "the world's flea market." Anyone with twenty-five cents to spend and a few spare hours to create an eBay auction listing could sell anything on eBay to anyone in the world. Like Cliff's mom, these sellers did not have to be regular vendors: They did not have to follow rules of business etiquette; they did not have to keep careful books and records; they did not have to be disciplined about how they conducted their businesses or how they interacted with customers.

That was the great charm of eBay in the "good old days" of the late 1990s. It was more than just online commerce. It was a community of buyers and sellers interacting with each other on the site, and you never knew what would happen when you bid on something for sale there. You might make a personal friend for life. You might meet a world authority on a certain type of antique or collectible. You might even meet your future spouse or significant other on eBay—a special someone who shares your interest in tchotchkes (hey, it's happened).

Often you were buying from people who knew less about their merchandise than you did, and you picked up some amazing bargains that way because "these people on eBay don't know what they've got."

But eBay's charm was also its greatest handicap. Many times when bidding on eBay you found yourself dealing with the seller from hell—somebody who was trying to pass off fake antiques as genuine, somebody who was ripping you off on shipping and handling fees, somebody who shipped you an article different from the one you ordered (and wouldn't give you your money back), or somebody whose sole goal in life was to steal your personal identity online.

In short, eBay developed a reputation as the Wild West of online commerce—a place where anything could happen, and often did.

In recent years, eBay has taken some dramatic steps to move away from its Wild West image and become more respectable as an online commerce venue for serious sellers and buyers—steps that, in some cases, have alienated large sectors of their selling community. Among some of the more recent changes:

- The development of Detailed Seller Ratings (DSRs; see Figure I.1 for an example of feedback and DSR scores) that enable buyers to rate sellers on a variety of different aspects of the sale experience (for example, shipping speed, quality of merchandise, communications) rather than an overall rating

- Eliminating sellers' ability to leave negative feedback about buyers, while allowing buyers greater leverage to leave negative feedback about sellers

- Requiring eBay sellers to use an online payment system such as PayPal for all transactions, and prohibiting them from accepting checks, money orders, and other paper-based forms of payment

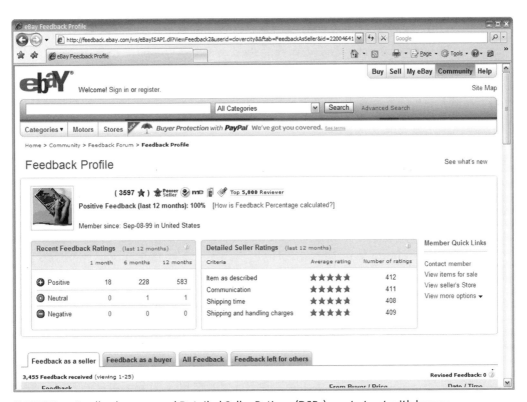

FIGURE I.1   Feedback scores and Detailed Seller Ratings (DSRs) create trust with buyers.

- Eliminating certain benefits (such as eBay's coveted PowerSeller status) for sellers whose DSRs fall below certain percentage levels

Many sellers complain that because of these changes "eBay isn't as much fun as it used to be," and numerous newspaper and magazine articles and online blogs have accused eBay of trying to eliminate mom-and-pop sellers from the site in favor of large corporate retailers.

However, the truth, as always, is a bit more complex than that; eBay continues to, and probably always will, welcome the small, mom-and-pop retailer on the site, especially in the antiques and collectibles and used/secondhand merchandise categories, where eBay still reigns supreme in the e-commerce world. Because the site is so easy to use, and because of the extensive support sellers receive there, eBay will probably, for some time, continue to be the first place small businesses go when venturing into e-commerce.

What will clearly no longer be tolerated on eBay, however, are amateur sellers—people who don't run their businesses in a professional, customer-friendly, and, well, *businesslike* manner.

Because of the changes occurring at eBay, sellers will have to learn to run their eBay presences like real businesses if they expect to survive, thrive, and grow on the site. Among other things, they will have to learn how to market, sell, advertise, and promote their wares just like the professionals do.

eBay Wants You to Succeed, So It Helps You with Your Marketing

It bears repeating because it is so important: The eBay platform is rapidly changing from a mom-and-pop retail site for amateur sellers into a more professional e-commerce venue. To survive in this new environment, eBay sellers have to take themselves more seriously as real entrepreneurs, give their buyers more of a professional retail experience, follow eBay's rules and regulations very closely, pay their taxes, keep good books and records, and learn how to run their businesses the way the "big boys" do.

The good news is that eBay recognizes the challenges many small business owners face in making the transition from being amateur sellers to becoming professional e-tailers and offers its sellers a variety of tools to help them market, sell, advertise, and promote their merchandise both within and outside the eBay community. Many longtime eBay sellers are unaware that some of these tools even exist and that most of them are available without charge to eBay sellers.

Chapters 2 and 3 of *The eBay Marketing Bible* offer a comprehensive checklist of eBay's marketing tools, with advice on how to use them.

The Two Faces of eBay

When it comes to its sellers and the merchandise they put up on the site, eBay has always had something of a split personality.

The site developed its reputation early on as a place for people to sell antiques, collectibles, jewelry, and used merchandise—one-of-a-kind items that are best sold in an auction-format listing. Rather than the seller trying to figure out what the best price for an item should be, he or she lists it as an auction on the site with a minimum price (say, $1.00), people bid on it, and the winning price—tah dah!—becomes the market price for that item.

However, soon another type of seller started working the site: "retail merchants" specializing in new consumer goods and merchandise including laptops, clothing, accessories such as handbags, housewares, and sporting goods. These people sold what are called *commodities*—items that are virtually identical to each other and are best sold in a fixed-price format (what eBay refers to as Buy It Now! sales).

Marketing an eBay selling business depends to a large extent on whether you are a one-of-a-kind seller or a commodity seller—a different strategy is called for when selling antiques and collectibles than when selling handbags and housewares.

Many newbie eBay sellers make the mistake of selling both kinds of merchandise from a single user ID or eBay Store—for example, antique toys and power tools—and soon find that customers aren't flocking to their listings.

Building a successful business on eBay, or anywhere else, means sending a clear marketing message to a particular group of customers, and that's really hard to do if your merchandise categories are all over the place. Your odds of selling successfully on eBay and building a recognizable brand for your business improve dramatically once you focus on a specialized niche of merchandise or customers and stick with that.

But what if you've found some great places nobody else knows about where you can buy both Barbie dolls and power tools at incredible discounts? Well, you can certainly offer different kinds of merchandise on eBay, but we wouldn't put these in the same eBay Store; the Barbie dolls should be separated from the power tools, and you should develop and execute two different marketing strategies for these two very different types of merchandise.

Individual Listings Versus an eBay Store

One of the most difficult marketing decisions eBay sellers have to make has little if anything to do with the actual marketing and selling process: Should they focus their eBay selling on individual listings or should they set up an eBay Store?

When people first start selling on eBay, they tend to post listings for individual items, using either an *auction* format (where buyers bid against each other and the highest bid wins when the auction closes), a *fixed-price* format (which eBay calls Buy It Now!), or some combination of the two.

Many eBay sellers—including some highly successful ones—never move beyond individual listings and do quite well indeed, because eBay makes it easy for buyers to search the site regularly to find merchandise from their favorite sellers. Buyers can easily search the site by a seller's user ID and see on a single page everything that seller is offering at the time. Buyers can also list sellers as Favorite Sellers on their My eBay pages, which authorizes eBay to send them e-mail bulletins or notices whenever those sellers list new items.

There's nothing wrong with using individual listings, but it can be difficult to build and market a viable *brand* on eBay this way. For one thing, most eBay listings are posted for periods ranging from only one to ten days—even if you optimize an eBay listing for search engines, the listing is likely to close before the search engine spiders even know it's there (although eBay has recently created a thirty-day Buy It Now! listing that, while a bit more expensive, may be easier to optimize for search engines). Also, if your listings are spread over several eBay categories, it is difficult for buyers to pin a brand label on you that helps you sell additional merchandise to them. It's okay to sell a one-of-a-kind item every now and then, but in order to build repeat traffic it is necessary to specialize in a product category (for example, topaz jewelry or antique mechanical banks) that is popular with one or more segments of the eBay community. Going forward, even eBay Trading Assistants (people who have been trained and certified by eBay to take consignments of merchandise for sale on the site) may need to focus on a specialized niche and/or serve a narrowly defined category to build a brand and create customer loyalty.

To build a viable brand on eBay, you should consider building an eBay Store—a miniature website within the eBay site that ties together all of your individual eBay listings and enables buyers to see everything you're offering in a single place. For a price beginning at about $15.95 a month, you can set up a basic eBay Store and customize it to achieve the look and feel your buyers are seeking. People can search for your eBay Store address within the eBay site or they can search for your individual listings, each of which features a link to your eBay Store so buyers can see "what else Cliff has this week."

Why should you build an eBay Store when buyers are already aware of your individual listings on eBay? The main reason is that eBay offers eBay Store owners access to many marketing tools that are not currently available to sellers who rely on individual listings, including:

- The ability to send e-mail newsletters to your regular buyers several times a month

- The ability, using eBay's Markdown Manager tool, to create excitement and buzz by offering sales and promotions

- Content pages where you can post articles demonstrating knowledge and expertise about your merchandise

FIGURE I.2   A search on Google brings up top rankings for eBay sellers.

Most important, eBay does a great deal to optimize your eBay Store for search engines so you don't have to. Have you ever searched for something using one of the major search engines—say, Google or Yahoo!—and an eBay Store address popped up on the first page of search results? (See Figure I.2 for an example.) If so, you are seeing the power of eBay at work. With an eBay Store it's much easier to find the people who love to buy the stuff you sell, keep them coming back for more on a regular basis, and build a community of repeat buyers who are passionate about the merchandise you're selling and who see you as the best source of that merchandise on eBay.

Online Marketing Versus Offline Marketing

Marketing an e-business, whether on eBay or anywhere else, involves a two-pronged strategy. One has to be familiar with both online and offline marketing techniques and strategies.

One of the great lessons we have learned about e-commerce in recent years is that "it's the search engines, stupid." Back in the 1990s, we all thought that banner ads and other advertising techniques that push vendors' messages into their customers' faces were the most effective way to market online businesses. We are much wiser today.

While some sites do base a significant portion of their marketing efforts on banner ads, the vast majority of sales on the Internet are generated by more passive marketing techniques that *pull* customers to a website, an eBay Store, or another online venue. Simply put, you cannot *push* your message into someone's face online. It won't work.

When your customers go online looking for information or to buy products, they, not you, are in control. They go only where *they* want to go, not where you want them to go—you cannot make people online look at something they don't want to look at, because they have too many tools at their disposal (such as spam filters and pop-up blockers) to prevent your message from getting through.

The most effective marketing strategy is to devise ways to seduce, or pull, them to your website, eBay Store, or other e-commerce venue—by matching your ad to keywords the users themselves type when they are looking for information, products, or services on the Web. Chapter 4 of *The eBay Marketing Bible* contains several sections detailing the many ways you can attract search engine spiders and drive Web traffic to your merchandise.

One aspect of e-commerce is just as true today as it was a dozen years ago: Often the best way to promote a website or e-commerce venue is to advertise offline, in the physical brick-and-mortar world. News stories about your business—distributed to the mass media in the form of press releases—can be an extremely effective way to get your website URL, eBay Store address, or other online address in front of millions of people nationwide. Using flyers, postcards, and other direct-mail methods of keeping in touch with regular customers can often be more effective than e-mail newsletters and other online means of communication, while billboards and television and radio advertising may actually be quite effective in promoting certain types of online businesses. If we're driving down an interstate highway and see a billboard with just the website URL www.renegadelawyers.com and nothing more, we're just a little bit curious, aren't we? You *are,* aren't you? You are likely to check out that URL the next time you're online, just out of sheer curiosity.

Chapter 5 of *The eBay Marketing Bible* discusses a number of offline strategies that may work effectively for an eBay business.

Four Things You Need to Know About Internet Marketing, or, Learning to Drive a Car in 1918

Selling merchandise on the Internet today is a lot like driving a car in 1918. Back then, the automobile was slowly beginning to replace the horse and buggy as the principal means of local transportation. Everyone at the time knew that—the news media were full of stories about how the "automobile age" was inevitable and how it was only a matter of time before everyone in the United States would be driving cars to and from work every day. But people weren't selling or shooting their horses in mass numbers quite yet in 1918.

Why? Because the infrastructure necessary to make the automobile an essential part of everyday living was not ready in 1918. There were very few paved roads in 1918. There were no gas stations on every street corner if you ran out of fuel. There was no AAA if your car broke down on a lonely country road. Go to a local museum and look at any automobile from that era—one of the first things you will notice is the large toolbox and gasoline tank strapped to the running boards on either side of the car. They were necessary in 1918.

If you drive a car today, you don't need to know anything about the internal combustion engine or the physics behind the car's turning circle. If you owned a car in 1918, you needed to know how the stuff under the hood worked. There was no automatic transmission or ignition—you had to walk in front of the car and crank the bloody thing into life, hoping the thing wouldn't run you over when it did start up. Windshields were nonexistent; you needed goggles to see what you were doing, and if you didn't wear a duster (a long, yellow smock that resembled a trenchcoat) to protect your clothing, you were soon filthy from dirt and mud churned up from the road by your ever-so-easy-to-puncture tires.

As we said, e-commerce today is a lot like driving a car in 1918. We all know—and the news media keep beating it into us—that this is the way we're going to be buying things ten or twenty years from now. Looking at the way younger people can live their entire lives online, we take for granted that online shopping will completely overtake brick-and-mortar retail during our lifetimes. But when we drive down the local suburban shopping strip, we don't see a whole lot of boarded-up storefronts (at least not any that were caused by competition from the Internet).

This is because the tools and infrastructure to enable anyone to sell things on-line with a minimum of effort either have not yet been developed or are only in their infancy. To sell online today you need to know what the available software can and cannot do, and it helps if you know a little bit of Web programming. It will be years or decades before selling merchandise online is as easy as driving a car is today.

Having said that, though, there are four things we know about marketing on the Internet today that we did not know twelve years ago, when the Web first burst into our collective consciousness.

1. **No one knows anything, really.** Not even the authors of this book. Internet marketing is still in its early stages, and hardly a month goes by when we don't learn something new about what works on the Web and what doesn't. The Internet is an extremely dynamic medium, and its limits are nowhere in sight. Marketing on the Internet requires staying up to date on the latest developments, tools, and strategies, knowing when to adopt new ones and when to abandon old ones.

2. **The Internet is a pull medium, not a push medium.** When Cliff was an eight-year-old boy, his favorite television sitcom was *The Beverly Hillbillies* (okay, Cliff is a lawyer and so is easily entertained). Every few minutes, the show was interrupted by several minutes of commercial messages

from companies offering products and services that an eight-year-old boy could barely comprehend, much less purchase—products such as Geritol, a tonic for "tired blood" (we challenge you to show us an eight-year-old boy with tired blood), various tablets for excess stomach acid, and (this was the early 1960s) liquor and cigarettes.

Much of this advertising was wasted on the youthful audience who watched the show regularly, and yet these viewers had to sit through these advertisements if they wanted to watch the entire half-hour episode of *The Beverly Hillbillies* unfold.

Television commercials are a form of push advertising: The advertiser pushes the message in your face, and you are forced to watch it if you want to receive another benefit. Most traditional advertising media are push media.

The Internet is not a push medium. It is actually the first commercially viable pull medium—the user or viewer is in total control of what happens in that medium. When we log on to our personal computers, laptops, or personal digital assistants (PDAs), we are in total control of what we see and don't see there. On the Internet no one can make us look at something we don't want to see.

To attract buyers online, you have to pull them to your website, your eBay Store, and your other online venues. They have to want to go there. Your job is not to push your product but to seduce them into wanting to buy what you have to offer. Chapter 1 of *The eBay Marketing Bible* is a basic lesson in the art of seducing customers—knowing what they're all about and tailoring your e-commerce presence to those emotional triggers that arouse their curiosity and make them find you, rather than the other way around.

3. **The Internet is unforgiving if you don't know what you're doing.** Anyone who has ever made a marketing mistake on the Internet knows how brutal people online can be. To put it mildly, the Internet is not a place where courteous, politically correct, highly polished, and polite communication takes place. It is frequently a snake pit where people, emboldened by the anonymity the Internet gives them, say things about other people they would never dare say to their faces for fear of physical violence. If you don't believe us, go to eBay's Community section and dip into any of the online chat rooms, where sellers and buyers communicate with each other about their frustrations.

Do something bad on eBay, and the next thing you know, you will be "flamed" by your buyers—not only in eBay's Feedback Forum (and remember that due to recent changes you can't fight back against negative feedback you get from buyers), but in eBay's community chat rooms, discussion boards, help centers, and so forth. An eBay buyer who thinks you have cheated in a transaction can suddenly turn into a monstrous vigilante whose sole purpose in life is to destroy you and bring your business down, whatever it takes. Even outside eBay there are numerous websites (such as www.uradeadbeat.com) where unhappy people can tell the whole world what a miserable, lousy, cheating, malodorous pervert you are . . . and get away with it.

The Internet can be an unforgiving place, and eBay is no exception. When marketing merchandise on the site, it is very important to make sure you are not doing anything that will arouse the wrath of the sleeping Behemoth that is the eBay community.

4. **The Internet is time consuming and labor intensive.** When you are selling on eBay, or indeed anywhere else on the Internet, remember that you are driving a car in 1918, not 2009. It takes time, effort, knowledge, and maybe some serious money to get your message across.

As you read this book, you will pick up on the lingo, but here are some ways you can free up more time for marketing:

- Automate as many of your eBay listings as possible using eBay software tools such as Turbo Lister 2, Auctiva, Blackthorne, or Selling Manager Pro (SMP).

- Hire a student intern for $10 to $20 an hour to help you with your listings.

- Go to Elance.com or Craigslist.org and advertise for a freelance writer who can write your blog, your Squidoo lens, and other online marketing material for you. Just be sure whoever you hire signs a copyright assignment, so that when you pay the person, you own all the content that appears on those pages.

- Repurpose your content as much as possible. Write an article for your blog, then change a few words and post it on your Squidoo lens, then change a few words and put it on one of your eBay Store content pages, so that you don't have to reinvent the wheel each time you sit down at the word processor.

One of the most important factors in deciding which Internet marketing strategies to pursue is the value of your time. There are lots of things you can do to market your eBay business online, but many of them require hours and hours of your time, with no assurance that you will receive even a minimum return on your investment. The average blog posting, for example, takes anywhere from fifteen to sixty minutes to create, and you have to post new ones at least every week so your blog doesn't become stale. Creating an *avatar* (or virtual person) on the popular alternative reality site www.secondlife.com can take several hours, and you have to spend countless hours more monitoring your avatar's every move on the site. Marketing on the Internet takes time and a steady, continuous dedication to make sure your marketing message is fresh and up to date.

When choosing among the marketing tools described in this book, you need to ask yourself some very serious questions:

- Will this marketing method reach the customers I actually want to reach?

- Will the investment of time required to keep this up to date be justified by the number of new or repeat customers it will generate for my business each month?

- When measured against the amount of new business generated each month, am I working for less than the U.S. minimum wage by using this method?

A Word About Legal and Tax Information

This book is primarily about marketing strategies and tactics for eBay sellers, but we will occasionally delve into some legal and tax issues that might arise when you use one or more of these strategies and tactics. For example, when setting up an e-mail newsletter it is essential to avoid violating the federal anti-spam laws. Cliff has discussed most of these issues at greater length in another book, *The eBay Seller's Tax and Legal Answer Book* and we suggest that readers look there for more detailed and thorough answers than are possible in a book like this one.

Any legal and tax information in this book is strictly for educational purposes and is not to be relied on as legal or tax advice, which can be given only by a lawyer or tax professional who is licensed to practice in your state.

A Final Word Before We Launch

This is a book about marketing an eBay business; this is not a book by eBay nor is it an official guide to anything. The authors of this book are not eBay employees—although we are certified by eBay to teach educational classes and offer business consulting services to eBay sellers, we do so purely as independent contractors of eBay and eBay is not responsible for our activities. Neither eBay, PayPal (an eBay company), nor any of their employees has reviewed, vetted, approved, or authorized anything in this book. *The eBay Marketing Bible* is entirely the authors' doing, and we are solely responsible for its contents.

Cliff Ennico, Fairfield, Connecticut, crennico@gmail.com
Cindy Shebley, Everett, Washington, cindy@clovercity.com
March 5, 2009

Step 2: The idea becomes an obsession—it's all the founder can think about, day and night.

Step 3: The founder begins doing research: She buys a couple of *For Dummies* books, attends some evening classes at the local community college, and (fatal error) starts talking about her idea with friends, family members, and neighbors, all of whom tell her it's a fantastic idea and that she should go for it! (meanwhile failing to realize that the idea is a truly terrible one, that the founder is totally bonkers, and that the founder's house will be on the market in the next few months if she's really serious about pursuing this crazy fantasy).

Step 4: The founder starts spending some serious money:

- She rents retail space in the downtown shopping district at $60 a square foot, signing an unbreakable five-year lease and paying a three-month up-front security deposit.

- She then hires a contractor to build out the space and install all of her trade fixtures—a construction project that ends up taking twice as long as anticipated and costing twice as much as was originally estimated. (Seriously, when was the last time a contractor finished a job on time and under budget for you?)

- She then has to buy inventory to stock the store; since her business is brand new and hasn't established credit with suppliers, she has to pay for everything in advance and out of her own pocket by cash or certified check.

- Her credit card balances are now in the six figures, she's taken out a home equity line of credit, and she's placed a third mortgage on her house.

Step 5: Finally, she has her grand opening. The town mayor cuts the ribbon to officially open the store, while a local newspaper photographer takes a picture of the scene (town mayors always make themselves available to do this, especially in election years).

Step 6: Six months later, the founder closes her store and begs the landlord to let her out of her lease because either (a) no one is coming to the store to buy anything, or (b) even worse, people *are* stopping by to rummage through the merchandise but are then going home and buying it at a discount on the Internet because everyone knows small retailers can't offer deep discounts the way major retailers do.

You would not believe how many times the authors of this book have seen this six-step scenario play out. It's a disaster when it happens, especially because it is so avoidable. All this founder had to do was some basic marketing research, and she could have avoided a catastrophe that will probably end up putting her and her family deeply in debt, if not in outright bankruptcy.

The time to come up with your marketing strategy is not after you have built the business—by then it's too late. You've got a basement full of dead fish that are rotting away by the minute, and you're running around like crazy trying to convince people they're really in the mood for a seafood dinner that night. That's not marketing—that's cold calling or desperation selling at its worst, and it never works.

The Four Essential Marketing Questions

The best time to create a marketing strategy for your small business is before you launch the business.

In fact, the best time to do your marketing strategy is before you *even have the idea* for the business.

Now, we can hear some of you saying, "Hey, wait a minute, that doesn't make sense. What you're saying here is that you should be doing your marketing strategy before you even know what it is you wish to sell."

Uh-huh.

"But don't you have to know what it is you're selling before you can identify the people who will want to buy it?"

Nope. Not at all.

Building a marketing strategy involves asking yourself four very specific questions, and these questions must be asked in a very specific order. Most people who start small businesses begin by asking the right questions but then get the order all fouled up, which ends up confusing them and making the start-up process all the more difficult. When asking these questions, it's extremely important to ask them in the correct order.

Here are the four questions, and the order in which they should be asked:

1. Who are my customers?

2. Why will they buy anything from me?

3. What merchandise can I develop that will have a *direct and immediate appeal* to them?

4. How do I get the word to my customers that I'm out there?

You begin by thinking about the people you want to sell to—the "natural" customers who have always bought from you (or who simply "get" who you are) and who will probably buy anything from you if it's you who's selling it. Once you've identified these folks, you go on to identify the two reasons—there are only two reasons anyone buys anything, as it turns out—they will buy anything from you. Once you've done that, you identify merchandise that will have a direct and immediate appeal to these folks, so that the minute they see it on eBay they will buy it. Last but not least, you decide how to communicate your business to your customers.

Oh, and one more thing: This isn't the SAT exams.

Huh?

Many of you probably remember cramming for the college entrance exam—the dreaded SAT—when you were a student in high school. One of your teachers offered a short "cram course" on how to take the SAT, and, of course, you took that course because you wanted to ace the test the first time you took it.

Remember what that teacher told you about what to do when you got stuck on one of the exam questions? "Skip over it, move on to the next question, and then when you've reached the end of the test go back and work through the questions you got stuck on."

That was great advice for taking the SAT, but it's terrible advice for building a successful marketing strategy. If you get stuck on one of these four questions, the absolute *worst* thing you can do is move on to the next question without getting the answer you need to the question you are stuck on.

Why? Because most of the time, if you get stuck on one of these questions, the problem isn't with you, your lack of knowledge, or your inability to grasp the finer points of marketing. The problem is *with the business.* There is no solution to the question you are stuck on, and because the question cannot be solved, the business is likely to fail. Skip over a question too quickly, and you may be overlooking the biggest problem the business will have—and neglecting to find a solution to the problem *before* you launch the business and it's too late to do anything about it.

The next few sections tackle each of the four marketing strategy questions and offer advice on how to find the answers you need to build a successful eBay business.

Step #1: Who Are Your Customers Going to Be?

It is impossible to sell everything to everybody.

Everybody knows that's true, but they tend to forget it when they start an eBay business. Probably because they're not really in business at all but are merely trying to clean out an attic or garage full of all kinds of different stuff, they begin by listing individual items in the Housewares, Toys, Jewelry, and Collectibles categories on eBay and are shocked when items actually sell in all four categories.

If your goal on eBay is simply to clean out your attic, then it doesn't matter that your merchandise is all over the place, but it's a terrible way to build a real business on eBay, even if you limit your selling activities to a single eBay category. The people who buy antique mechanical banks from the 1800s, for example, are very different from the people who collect baseball cards from the 1950s. If you are offering both lines of merchandise on eBay, you have to use radically different strategies to reach these two groups of collectors.

Trying to be all things to all people simply makes you crazy. The most effective marketers know the specific customer niches they are looking for and let that knowledge guide them throughout the marketing process.

So how do you decide *whom to sell to* when you haven't yet decided *what to sell*? Isn't thinking about the customer before you think of the merchandise putting the cart before the horse?

Not at all—in fact, it's the only way to successfully market anything to anybody.

Your Natural Customers

When you look back on your life, you will realize at some point that you do not appeal to everybody. At all points in your life there have been certain types of people who have understood who you are, and there are others who just don't, no matter how hard you try.

Think we're joking? We're not. Take down your dusty old high school or college yearbook, flip through the pages, and when you see one of your old friends from those bygone days, try to describe him or her in writing. Do this a few times, and you probably will see that your friends had more in common with each other—and with you—than you think. This shouldn't surprise you— social psychologists tell us that the old saying about opposites attracting is entirely baloney. Although our friends, lovers, and close acquaintances often look superficially very different from us, they tend—at least according to the available research—to share our deepest fundamental values, interests, and needs. That's what attracts us to each other.

Every small business, when you get right down to it, is a service business—you are in the business of serving a certain slice of humanity. And, in the immortal words of Bob Dylan, you've "gotta serve somebody."

To find the customers you are most likely to succeed in serving on eBay, it's a good idea to find out who your natural customers are—the people who have always bought what you had to offer, the people who have always understood you, the people who always have been attracted to you as a person. Now, those aren't the only people you can sell to (more on that later), but they're a great place to begin.

The Two Characteristics of the Natural Customer

A natural customer is someone who meets two basic criteria:

1. He or she is someone you know a lot about.

2. He or she is someone you care at least a little about.

People You Know

It is extremely difficult, if not impossible, to sell to people you don't know well. Try selling stuff to people you don't really know, and you end up not selling to a real person at all but rather to a stereotype or caricature of those people that may bear no relation whatsoever to reality.

Cliff Ennico is a lawyer by profession. A lot of people have opinions about lawyers, but how well do they really know them?

In one of his many presentations on small business marketing, Cliff offers an autographed copy of one of his books to anyone who can answer the following question: What is the biggest thing that keeps lawyers awake at night? In other words, what is a lawyer's biggest fear or anxiety?

Believe it or not, there is an answer to that question. Every year, one of the major bar associations publishes the results of a lawyer satisfaction survey, in which lawyers around the United States and Canada answer a detailed questionnaire about their practices. One of the questions in this survey is: "When you think about your practice, what is the biggest thing that keeps you awake at night?" Anybody in Cliff's audience who can correctly guess the number one answer to the survey question gets a free autographed copy of Cliff's book.

Cliff doesn't give out too many books, because in the vast majority of cases no one gets the answer right. Sounds surprising, doesn't it? If we were asking you to answer this question, most of you would probably come up with the following answers:

- Getting sued for malpractice

- Losing a key client

- Not getting paid by a client who files for bankruptcy

- Saying or doing something dumb that generates adverse publicity in the local press

And you would not be entirely wrong—these *are* some of the answers lawyers give to the survey question. But none of them is the number one anxiety lawyers feel when thinking about their practices.

Okay, give up? The number one thing that keeps lawyers in the United States and Canada lying awake at night, at least according to this survey, is . . .

"Not having enough time with my family."

If you know anything at all about the practice of law (the *real* practice of law, not what you see on television programs like *Boston Legal*), you know that lawyers work incredibly long hours—fifteen hours a day or more, with frequent weekend work on top of that. Lawyers do worry about spending so much time on the job that they grow old without knowing who their children (or grandchildren) are, without having enough time for friends, hobbies, community service, and the other things that make living worthwhile.

Are you surprised by this answer? If you are, don't beat yourself up—it's only because you really don't know lawyers all that well. Which means you really shouldn't be selling stuff to lawyers, because you really don't know what they'll be willing to buy.

People You Care About

Of course, if you really do know a lot about lawyers but don't give a tinker's damn about them either as professionals or as human beings, you're probably not going to sell anything effectively to them either.

When you sell things to people, you do so at least in part because you want to improve their lives in some way (we will see exactly how in Step #2), and that's hard to do if you really hate them.

You have to be careful here. Some of the worst customers you can have are people you really like a lot—people with whom you feel a strong common bond or people you strongly identify with. Why? Because when you really identify strongly with someone, you tend to put on the proverbial rose-colored glasses—you see only the good things about them, not their imperfections, faults, or weaknesses. Love is blind, after all, isn't it?

Even if you do see the bad stuff along with the good stuff, being very close to someone also puts you in a position where they can take advantage of you. Please don't get us wrong—we are not saying you should be mean, nasty, or cruel to your customers. Not at all. It's just that if you are *too* nice to them they will walk all over you; they will want your merchandise for nothing and make you pay for the shipping and sales taxes as well. And you will do it, because you really like these people and care—perhaps a little too much—about their opinion of you.

What they're thinking, of course, is this: "What a pushover. I wonder what else he's got that I can steal?"

The best customers are those you know a lot about but don't really feel very strongly about either positively or negatively—as long as you care enough about them to want to improve their lives in some way by offering them merchandise they won't find any other way.

Identifying Your Natural Customers

Try the following challenge:

Go home tonight, take out a pad of paper, a pencil (not a pen, because you will need the eraser), and a bottle of your favorite brandy or other beverage of choice, and make a list of ten groups of people—try for as many as possible but at least ten—whom you feel you know so well you can crawl inside their heads and look at the world through their eyes, the way they do.

Sounds simple enough, right? Try it. It ain't easy. You will be sitting there chewing on that pencil for at least an hour or two before you put anything down on paper.

It's actually one of the hardest things anyone will ever ask you to do—identify the people you know better than anyone else. It requires a lot of self-examination and a decent memory.

Let's take Cliff as an example. If he were doing this exercise, the beginning of his list would look something like this:

- **Lawyers:** Well, duh! Cliff has been a lawyer for twenty-eight years.

- **Book publishers:** For ten years Cliff ran a small publishing company specializing in career management advice for lawyers.

- **Professional speakers:** Cliff gives at least thirty live presentations around the United States each year.

But you shouldn't limit this list to just business, occupational, or professional people. You also have to list people you know simply "as people." So Cliff's list would continue as follows:

- **Middle-aged men:** Cliff is currently fifty-four years old, and so he qualifies.

- **People of mixed Italian and German extraction.**

- **People who grew up in the New York City suburbs.**

- **People who cannot wear contact lenses.** Because of a childhood medical condition, Cliff must wear glasses if he is to see anything at all.

So far, so good. But now comes the tough part. Sometimes the people you know the most about—the people who will make your best natural customers—are people who don't resemble you in any way whatsoever. When doing this exercise, you need to list people with whom you have had lots of contact, even if you yourself will never be a member of that group.

So Cliff's list would include, without any hesitation or irony at all, women between the ages of 70 and 80.

Now, we're sure some of you are thinking, "This is more about Cliff Ennico than I think I care to know." But he's actually quite serious about that—Cliff really does know a lot about women in that age group.

When Cliff came home from grade school each day, he was greeted by two women who were then in their seventies: his maternal grandmother and her sister. They lived in the neighborhood, took the bus over to the apartment where

Cliff grew up, and basically took care of him until his mom came home from work.

Can you picture these two old ladies in your mind? Your picture would be 100 percent accurate.

Well, these babysitting chores got a little dull after a while, so to liven things up these women started inviting some of their friends in the neighborhood—all of them women in their seventies—to keep them company during these babysitting sessions.

While these ladies were playing their card games, what were they doing? Talking! About what? About what it's like to be a woman in your seventies! Cliff was exposed to probably one of the best focus groups of women in their seventies ever assembled while he sat on the living room floor, playing with his Tonka trucks and soaking up all of this information like a sponge.

As a result, Cliff can tell you a lot about women in their seventies that will make your hair curl—even though he never will be one himself.

Your Natural Customers on eBay

We can hear some of you saying, "Okay, I get the importance of knowing your customers, but does it really work that way on eBay? I mean, buyers don't look for sellers on eBay who are kindred spirits; they look for merchandise they want. As long as I've got stuff that people want, does it really matter who I am or whether the customers like me?"

Your eBay merchandise is definitely the biggest factor in attracting first-time customers. But what will make those people buy? And, more important, what will keep those customers coming back for more?

Have you ever visited an eBay Store, only to be turned off by the way it was set up or the image the seller had established for the business (maybe the site was a bit too masculine or a bit too feminine for your tastes)? Have you ever seen something in a seller's listing that interested you, clicked on the View Seller's Other Items button, and seen that the item you first clicked on is the only one of the seller's many items you would ever in a million years be interested in? Have you ever clicked on a listing that interested you, and then clicked off right away because you didn't like the casual tone (complete with misspelled words, undeleted expletives, and political commentary) with which the seller described the item?

Who you are and *who your customers are* are very important considerations when selling on eBay. They determine not only the brand image you establish for yourself (upscale versus flea market, masculine versus feminine, etc.), but also, to a large extent, the merchandise you carry. If your market is primarily suburban middle-aged women, you are not likely to be offering combat boots and camouflage gear. Although people are attracted to you initially by your merchandise, if they don't feel at least a little kinship with you and your business they will not experience the trust and confidence that leads to repeat purchases.

Your customers want to know that you understand them, that you know what's going on in their worlds, that you care at least a little about them, that you share their interests and collecting passions at least to some extent, and that, accordingly, you will always have things for sale on eBay that they will be interested in at least some of the time.

Why is it so important to know a lot about the customers you will be selling to on eBay? Because if you don't, you won't have a clue why these people would buy anything from you. And that is the next of the four strategic marketing questions.

Step #2: Why Are These People Going to Buy from You?

Now that you have identified at least several groups of people who will buy anything from you, *why* will those people buy anything from you? To phrase it slightly differently: What will motivate these buyers to push the Buy It Now! button or submit a bid on one of your eBay auctions?

Selling to Needs Is a Mistake

Here is one of the dirtiest little secrets of the marketing world—something that, to our knowledge, has never appeared in print in exactly this way . . . until now. Most business books teach that people are motivated by their needs and wants— people buy things because they either need them or want them. This is wrong, especially when it comes to people's needs. One of the surest ways to fail in your small business is to sell things to people because you perceive or think they need them.

People talk about their needs all the time, of course—whenever they see something in a store, or on eBay, that they really want to buy, the words that come out of their mouths are "Oh, I need that!" But the painful truth is that people seldom, if ever, buy things because they need them. When people say they need something, there's something else going on in their heads psychologically. As a marketer, your job is to grasp what's really going on and make sure your marketing strategy takes that reality into account.

In order to buy something you need, two things have to happen, and they seldom if ever happen in the real world of consumer behavior:

1. You have to know that you need that something.

2. You have to be willing to act on that knowledge.

Do You Always Know What You Need?

Before you can buy something you need, you have to know you need it. But do you know all the things you need? Of course not! That's why you bought this book in the first place—you need to sell more merchandise on eBay, and you haven't a clue how to go about it or what to do first.

Before we can sell you something you need, we must make you aware and make you accept that you need it; we have to educate and persuade you that your life will be better in some way if you buy this thing we're selling. It may be a difficult persuasion, one requiring lots of time and money that, frankly, neither of the authors of this book has much of.

For those readers who are old enough to remember 1978, the year that the first personal computers (PCs) came on the scene, think back and ask yourself: Who really needed a personal computer in 1978? Just about everything the personal computers of that time could do was already being done by lots of other competing technologies:

- If you needed to write a letter, you had electric typewriters, some of which (like the IBM Selectric—remember those?) were extremely fast and reliable.

- If you needed to do an arithmetical calculation, you had pocket calculators (such as the many Texas Instruments products and the Bowmar Brain) that would do the job extremely well.

- If you needed to put together a spreadsheet, you had those wonderful green analysis pads that all of the accountants used and that you could buy at any stationery store. (Does anyone have a stationery store in their community today?)

Also, do you remember how absolutely bug-ugly the first personal computers were? How much heat they generated, and how much noise they created while taking forever to boot up? Remember how slow (at least by today's standards) they were? And when you bought a computer, you had to also plunk down money for a very expensive printer so you could print out the work you created on the computer—after all, e-mail, the Internet, and personal computer networks did not exist in 1978.

Don't get us wrong—today personal computers are absolutely essential tools for any business. The authors of this book wouldn't be able to do what we do today without at least several personal computers, a laptop or two, and a personal digital assistant such as a BlackBerry or Treo.

But back in 1978 we didn't need any of these things. We managed just fine, thank you very much. The early personal computer marketers had one devil of a job convincing people that their lives would be better, faster, easier, sexier, or what have you if they would only put one of these smelly, noisy, ugly contraptions in their kitchen or den (oops, sorry, family room—we date ourselves sometimes).

Even If You Recognize You Need Something, Do You Always Buy It?

But here's the kicker, at least as far as we're concerned: Even if you know you need something, even if I don't have to spend a penny or a minute of my time convincing you that you need something because it's self-evident that you do, do you always buy it?

If our experience is any indication, seldom, if ever, do you do so.

We realize that sounds a bit cynical, so let us illustrate the point with two stories.

First, a silly example. Let's say that you are attending one of our presentations, and you become ravenously hungry. You skipped breakfast this morning in order to make it to the presentation on time, there's at least two more hours to go until the cocktail break, and you are ready to eat your socks right about now.

Recognizing your dilemma, we make the following announcement from the podium: "We really appreciate that you guys were willing to hang tough with us during lunch, and we know some of you are really hungry right now, so we've called down to the cafeteria on the first floor of this building and they're going to be coming up here in a few minutes with a big steaming bowlful of . . . broccoli, Brussels sprouts, carrots, and cauliflower!"

Now, I'm sure most readers aren't nutrition experts or health fanatics, but we think most of you would recognize these four vegetables as among the healthiest foods on the entire planet Earth. These four veggies have all the vitamins, minerals, antioxidants, and beta-carotene anyone could ever want. But most of you would be sitting there, mouth agape in shock, wondering whether we had taken leave of our senses by ordering up a snack like that.

Here's a situation in which you know your body needs something, but you're not wildly excited about the prospect of eating it—you probably wouldn't want to shell out much money to help pay for it if we asked you to.

People do have needs, of course, at a very abstract or metaphysical level: We need food in the sense that if we stop eating altogether, sooner or later we die. But when we're hungry, we can reach for a fast-food hamburger or a stalk of celery. Our specific buying choice depends to a very large extent on something deeper than our needs.

So What About People's Wants?

Wants is heading in the right direction, but doesn't go nearly far enough to help us understand why people buy certain things and not others.

Wants is a very vague and general term—we *want* a salad for lunch today, and we also *want* world peace. Those are two very different types of *want*.

Generally, when we say we want something we mean something much more specific than that, and understanding precisely what it is we want is the first step toward effective selling, on eBay or, indeed, anywhere else.

Offering things for sale because you think people will need or want them seldom, if ever, leads to a successful business. In order to sell anything to anybody, you've got to appeal to them in a different way.

Here's how.

The Four Reasons Anyone Buys Anything . . . And How You Can Profit from Them

Passions. If you've got merchandise that turns people on—that gets them excited in a positive way—they will buy it from you. Many entire industries are based on appeals to people's passions, among them:

- Sporting goods

- Antiques and collectibles

- Jewelry

- Gourmet food

- Sports cars

- Anything to do with movies, music, or entertainment

If you know your customers well enough, you will know what they are passionate about.

Problems. If your customers are having trouble sleeping at night or are worried about something, and you've got something for sale that will solve those problems, they will buy it from you. Some examples:

- An eBay Store specializing in costume jewelry that will "match any outfit you have . . . for that special occasion"

FINDING YOUR CUSTOMERS' PASSIONS

If you have difficulty identifying your customers' passions, you can begin by thinking about these seven passions that are shared (to some extent or other) by almost all people:

- **Pride:** Anything that makes people feel better about themselves.

- **Lust:** No explanation necessary—sex sells.

- **Greed:** For example, a book that tells people how to get rich by marketing effectively on eBay.

- **Anger:** For example, negative political ads—we all hate them, but they're unfortunately sometimes very effective.

- **Envy:** "I've got something you don't have . . ."

- **Sloth or laziness:** Any convenience-oriented product or service.

- **Gluttony:** Gourmet foods, luxury chocolates (you get the idea).

Enough said. Find such a product, and the world is your oyster.

- An electronic swimming pool cleaner that will not only save your customers tons of money on maintenance but reduces the risk of exposing family members to harmful chemical-based cleaning products

- An e-book or other information product (such as this book) that teaches your customers how to do something better or save them money in a difficult economy

Probably the most obvious problem sell on eBay is one you won't have to work hard at all to make: the fact that people can often buy surplus or liquidated inventory, factory remainders, or "slightly used" items on eBay for a fraction of the cost of buying the same items at full retail prices. As this book is being written, the United States (and perhaps the entire world) is heading into what is projected to be a long and deep recession. The customer who will be scouring the eBay site looking for a used leather briefcase for $25 that isn't too badly banged up for his one-and-only job interview next week won't be motivated by passions.

But be forewarned: Building your marketing strategy on your customers' problems must be done very carefully. If your marketing pitch is too obvious or heavy-handed, you will be accused of pandering to people's fears and anxieties and exploiting them for personal gain—exactly what "sleazy" salespeople are loathed for doing. Especially on eBay, whose emphasis has always been on the fun and passion of shopping aggressively, such an approach is not looked upon kindly, and you may find yourself the subject of some extremely unpleasant postings in eBay's Community section.

When marketing a solution to your customers' problems, remember the two E's:

- **Empathize** with your customers. Show that you care about them or that you've experienced the same problem and that's why you decided to do something about it.

- **Emphasize** the solution, not the problem.

Hopes and Dreams. As an eBay PowerSeller specializing in photographic, video, and related items of equipment, Cindy Shebley focuses her marketing approach on "sidewalk pilots," of whom there are many on eBay. Lots of people dream of becoming a pilot but never take the aviation course or the test to get the license. However, they continue to dream of being the next Amelia Earhart. They buy products that help them visualize their daydreams, such as magazines, luggage, or flight jackets.

Cindy believes that often the best way to sell on eBay is to market to your prospect's hopes and dreams. While it's true that photographers do worry that their cameras might be destroyed by rain, there is a product called a rain protector to address that concern. Cindy's approach is to sell the rain protector as an accessory for the photographer's next trip to a rain forest. Done right, this pitch helps the shutterbug visualize the *dream* of being sent out on assignment for *National Geographic.*

What do we mean by selling hopes and dreams to eBay buyers? Here are a couple of examples.

The first example involves selling a collectible. Let's say you just purchased a nifty old fire helmet. It's beat-up, scuffed from use, but you know there are buyers out there who collect fire memorabilia. Probably these collectors are wannabe firefighters or professionals who are active or retired. Good or bad, they all seem to have a little pyromaniac in them. How would you pitch this helmet to their hopes and dreams?

Of course, you'd want to state condition, size, age, and other characteristics in the listing. But how about an opening paragraph that reads like this:

> You can almost smell the smoke from the many fires this helmet has seen. From the age and condition of this vintage fireman's hat you can visualize the sites and sounds of the sirens as the fire truck and crew blazed a path toward danger. Feeling the rough edges and seeing the many nicks and scrapes on the helmet, you know it saw many harrowing rescues in the line of duty. This helmet is a testament to all those rescues, great and small.

Isn't that a lot more fun to read than "fire dept collectable . . . vintage helmet, very nice . . . old, will clean up like new"? Readers or collectors are taken to the heart of the action, and you are telling them that by owning the helmet they'll be closer to their dream.

What if you sell new things? Here's an example of selling hopes and dreams in the form of a regular household item that most people have—a blender. What sorts of hopes or dreams do people have about a blender? Well, perhaps they hope to have a healthy lifestyle or dream about being the life of the party or just want to have the best-tasting milk shakes money can buy. Your job as a marketer is to figure out whom you are selling to and what their hopes and dreams are. For this example let's take the milk shake connoisseur and see whether we can romance someone into buying a blender by selling to their dreams.

> Want a strawberry milk shake? These days you pull up to your nearest drive-through window and are served a concoction of something that may have been frozen once, is mixed with a squirt of something sort of pink, and is served to you in a paper cup by a surly minimum-wage worker. As you roll down the window to receive the shake, the fumes from the diesel truck in front of you waft into your car. So much for that long-awaited reward you promised yourself for a job well done. What ever happened to real ice cream shakes?
>
> Those days of the soda fountain along the wall of your local five-and-dime are long gone. But it's fun to imagine the young, handsome soda jerk scooping out real vanilla ice cream and adding beautiful, plump, fresh strawberries into a highly polished silver blending cup while you watch the blender gently mix the ingredients into a milk shake. The second it reaches perfection it's poured into a heavy glass soda goblet. The strawberry delight, with a dollop of whipped cream and a cherry on top, is served with a spoon and a straw. You choose your weapon of attack. Whichever you choose, the sweat rolls off the clear glass as you try to drink the shake before it melts.
>
> Wouldn't it be nice to make a real ice cream shake at home?
>
> We can't turn back time, but we can offer you the XYZ blender, complete with a silver mixing bowl to merge your favorite flavors into perfection. Included is a book filled with good, old-fashioned soda fountain recipes.

As you can see from this example, we spent more time writing about a dream than we did actually talking about the blender. That's what we mean by selling hopes and dreams. Now, don't get us wrong—of course, we would complete all the features and details in the listing as well, but starting out by romancing prospective buyers helps tell them what's in it for them.

Most stuff you sell on eBay can be hooked into a person's *hopes* and *dreams* for the future, especially in difficult economic times. After a daily barrage of bad news fed to your customers via TV or the Internet and their financial and business advisers, widespread job insecurity, and the general stress and unease most people feel daily, a little trip into dreamland is a welcome breath of fresh air. You might find your customer purchasing your product simply because you've offered a minute or two of relief from reality.

Which Works Best: Passions, Problems, Hopes, or Dreams?

All people have passions, problems, hopes, and dreams. Which of them works best for you?

The answer is this: If you know your customers well enough, you will know whether to focus your marketing efforts on their passions, problems, hopes, or dreams. It won't require much thought or analysis on your part.

To eBay sellers whose sales are declining or who are having difficulty adjusting their business models to the recent changes at eBay (discussed in the Introduction), this book is a *problem-solving* sell. To eBay sellers who love reading about marketing and selling generally, who have read some of the authors' other books, and who enjoy our sometimes bizarre and funky senses of humor, this book is a *passion* sell. To eBay sellers who fantasize about being Platinum PowerSellers someday and joining the eBay Hall of Fame, this book is a *hopes and dreams* sell.

If you don't know whom you're targeting with your marketing efforts, then you won't have any idea what strategy will work; instead, you will be stabbing in the dark, hoping that your marketing pitch will hit a nerve with someone, somewhere—and that can waste a lot of your precious time. Learn more about the people you're selling to and try to focus your marketing efforts on the people you know the most about (as we recommended in Step #1), and you will find yourself marketing more and more successfully on eBay.

Selling the Benefits, Not the Product

Most inexperienced salespeople make a critical mistake when they pitch a prospect for the first time: They start talking too soon about the product they've got to sell. A good salesperson spends lots of time getting prospects to open up and talk about those things that are most important to them.

And what might those things be?

Why, their passions, problems, hopes, and dreams, of course!

When you create your eBay Store content pages, or write articles for your weekly e-mail newsletter, or put content up on a blog, what do you write about?

Your prospects' passions, problems, hopes, and dreams—and how your products will benefit prospects by making their lives more fulfilling in some way.

Now that you know your customers and their passions, problems, hopes, and dreams, you are finally ready to begin thinking about *what you will sell on eBay*!

Step #3: What Should You Be Selling on eBay?

It's one of the first questions asked by any seller who has managed to build an eBay presence beyond the "attic and garage" stage: "Where can I find good stuff to sell on eBay?" Entire books have been written on the subject of product sourcing for online sales.

Certainly, the merchandise you offer for sale on eBay is a large part of your marketing strategy. The Internet, including eBay, is a pull medium—as we pointed out in the Introduction, you do not push your marketing message in people's faces the way you would do with more traditional media. It is the customer, not you, who is in control on the Internet. Buyers search for the things they want, and—wonder of wonders!—they find you. If you do not have stuff that people want, people will not be looking for you, and therefore they won't find you. It's that simple.

But who are these people? What are they looking for, and why? If you don't have the answers to these basic marketing questions, you really haven't a clue what you should stock in your eBay inventory.

Sell Stuff That Arouses Your Customers' Passions, Problems, Hopes, and Dreams

Any book on eBay will tell you that you should "sell what sells" on eBay. That's a correct answer so far as it goes, but it really is a bit more complicated than that. A lot of people think you just put stuff up on eBay, wait to see who bites, and if nobody bites within a certain reasonable period of time, you put some other stuff up. That might work occasionally, but it's really no way to build a successful eBay selling business. Your goal is to always have merchandise that will sell on a regular, consistent basis, with lots of repeat customers and the potential for building an online brand on eBay for that type of merchandise.

As we pointed out in Steps #1 and #2, before you can even know what to sell on eBay you have to have some idea of:

- The target customers, or natural customers, who will buy things from you because they know you understand them, and vice versa

- The passions, problems, hopes, and dreams that will motivate them to buy things

Once you know these two things, then picking the right merchandise for sale on eBay involves asking this question: "What merchandise can I sell on eBay that will have a *direct and immediate appeal* to the passions, problems, hopes, and dreams of the customers I've targeted for this business?"

Research shows that when deciding whether or not to buy something, the average person makes up his or her mind within the first thirty seconds of being exposed to the item (this information is based on sales data in the brick-and-mortar world; the time frame is probably a lot faster when people are making buying decisions on eBay or elsewhere on the Internet). If people need longer than thirty seconds to make up their minds, the odds are that they will talk themselves out of buying whatever it is they were considering.

Simply put, people rarely talk themselves *into* buying things; they are much more likely to talk themselves *out of* buying things. So if you're planning to get your customers to say yes, you've got to hit them where they live in the first few seconds after they see the merchandise you are selling. Your merchandise must *directly and immediately* respond to a passion, problem, hope, or dream those customers are feeling at the very moment they check out your eBay listing or eBay Store home page. The appeal must be obvious and instantaneous; if people have to think hard and long about why they need whatever it is you're selling, you will not have many successful sell-throughs on eBay.

As the Wall Street investment bankers used to say, "Time kills deals." The longer it takes someone to make up his or her mind to buy your item, the greater the odds that someone else will post a better item at a more reasonable price, and your customer will be "gone in thirty seconds."

Item descriptions, photos, prices, and other visual aids in your eBay listings and on your eBay Store pages should all be focused on reducing the amount of time a buyer needs to make up his or her mind to purchase the item. If it doesn't grab the person immediately, it probably won't grab the person at all.

Please don't misunderstand; we're not saying that all purchases on eBay are impulse purchases. We are saying only that the vast majority of purchases on eBay are ☺. Given the choice between a lengthy word description of an item and lots of photos that are well executed and quick and easy to look at, you know which way you should go.

Sell Stuff That Sells on eBay

Even though you have merchandise for sale on eBay that your customers want, they may not be willing to buy those items on eBay. As we pointed out in the Introduction, in the early years of its history eBay developed a reputation, rightly or wrongly, as the world's flea market. Today most people know you can get some wonderful merchandise on eBay that is every bit as good as the stuff you find in Fifth Avenue department stores, but old perceptions die hard, especially in the world of retail.

We confess that whenever we see a high-end antique selling on eBay with a minimum price of $5,000, a little part of us asks, "What is an item this good doing on eBay? There's got to be something wrong with it somewhere, or else this person would be selling it at Sotheby's."

Especially when selling high-end antiques, collectibles, or other merchandise on eBay, you sometimes have to go to considerable lengths to communicate to your buyers that the stuff is okay. Instead of posting individual listings for these types of items, we recommend opening an eBay Store with lots of similar high-end items, so that customers identify you as a high-end dealer in that type of merchandise. The *look and feel* of this eBay Store should be tony and upscale—you definitely should work with a Web designer rather than have one of your student interns build the store using an eBay template.

If you have a brick-and-mortar store specializing in high-end merchandise, you should definitely post a photo of your store on your About My Store page so people can see that you operate in a "high-rent district" and have a long history of selling high-end merchandise.

Sell Stuff You Know About

Most eBay experts agree that it's difficult to sell successfully on eBay if you don't know anything about the merchandise you are selling. Buyers are looking for sellers they can trust and depend on, and they are not going to get "warm fuzzies" about a seller who says, "I don't know nuthin' about this stuff; I just found it in the back of my closet, and I ain't takin' it back" in every one of his listings (especially if there are misspelled words and bad grammar in the item description as well).

"A lot of people say you should sell what you're passionate about, but I think you're better off selling what you know," says eBay Certified Education Specialist

Steve Lindhorst (www.genuineseller.com), who explains, "If I'm selling serpentine belts on eBay Motors, I can tell you why one brand of serpentine belt is better than another. Now, I'm not passionate about serpentine belts—I really don't know if anyone can be passionate about serpentine belts—but it gives my buyers a lot of confidence that I know what I'm doing and that they should buy from me rather than someone else."

Another danger of "selling what you love," says Lindhorst, is that "because you're a collector you're going to want to keep some of the stuff you source for sale on eBay."

Those eBay sellers who know their merchandise have three major advantages over those who don't:

1. They can source product more easily, because they know where the best deals are.

2. They can market their listings and eBay Store more effectively by making themselves experts on certain merchandise and displaying that expertise on eBay's blog pages, Reviews and Guides, and other content-rich pages that attract search engine spiders.

3. It's easier for them to stay out of legal, eBay policy, and "bad seller" hassles on eBay. If they have specialized knowledge about designer handbags, such as the different styles and models and how they're made, it's much more likely they'll be able to spot fakes and knockoffs and keep them out of their eBay listings.

Sell Stuff Your Competition Isn't Selling

Most eBay experts agree that the site is saturated with sellers and that it's getting tougher and tougher to find profitable niches. "When I first started selling on eBay more than a decade ago, there were only about a dozen people doing what I'm doing on eBay," says eBay PowerSeller Marcia Cooper (www .generalenterprises.net), "but today there are more than 1,000 people selling stuff similar to mine." Look for niches on eBay where there are a relatively large number of buyers, a high sell-through rate (the ratio of successful listings to total listings), and a relatively low number of competitors.

Sell Merchandise That Delivers Consistently Decent Profit Margins

You can sell a lot of bobble-head dolls on eBay, but if you're making only a $2 profit on each sale it will take you a long time to make enough to earn a decent living. Look at the profitability of the things you sell on eBay, and source only those products that give you a reasonable return on your investment. A useful tool for this is ProfitBuilderSoftware, a profitability analysis program developed by eBay PowerSeller Corey Kossack specifically for eBay sellers (www.profitbuildersoftware.com).

Stuff for Which There Is a Growing or Changing Market

The beautiful thing about people's passions, problems, hopes, and dreams is that they're constantly changing. People are experiencing problems today that they weren't even thinking about six months ago. And people are passionate today about things that didn't even exist in the early 1990s, when eBay was getting off the ground—including eBay itself!

When people's passions, problems, hopes, and dreams are in flux, they tend to look for new and different things in their online shopping. Knowing your customers well and being able to anticipate their shifts in mood (or perhaps shifts in how much money they have in their wallets) enables you to stay one step ahead of the competition by offering only those items for sale that you know your target customers are looking for *right here and now.*

Doing this also builds your credibility. Whenever I see that eBay sellers are adjusting their merchandise mix to account for changing times, I know these sellers know what they are doing. They are responding to their customers' changing environment before the customers ask them to—and well before their competitors do.

Now all you have to do is get your marketing message across to your customers. It is time to consider your advertising and promotion strategy.

How to Sell Anything to Anybody

A lot of people are intimidated by the selling process. All of us have had painful encounters with used-car salespeople, telemarketers, and people selling magazine subscriptions door-to-door, and the idea that we might have to become one of those people to succeed in the business world makes us want to gag.

But here's some good news. Although selling effectively is an absolutely essential skill for any small business owner, you do not have to become one of "those people" to become a very good salesperson.

What those people are doing really isn't selling at all. What they are doing is *cold calling.* You are cold calling whenever you try to talk a total stranger into buying some worthless inventory you've got lying around the store that you need to get rid of in a hurry. If you have a basement full of dead fish that are rotting away by the hour and you meet me on a street corner and try to convince me how wonderful it would be to have seafood for dinner tonight, you are cold calling.

Cold calling is not good marketing, nor is it good selling. Cold calling is a waste of time and an insult to your customers. Don't ever do it.

Having gotten that off of our chests, here's the right way to sell. Not only is it extremely customer friendly, but it will work almost every time.

Step 1: Get Your Customer Talking

One of the biggest mistakes salespeople make is to start talking too soon about the stuff they've got to sell. Smart salespeople say very little at the beginning of a sales meeting or presentation—they let the customer do all of the talking.

What do you get your customers talking about? Their passions, problems, hopes, and dreams, of course!

When you think about it a moment, this is one of the easiest things anyone has ever asked you to do. All of us, as human beings, love to talk about our passions, problems, hopes, and dreams. They are our absolute favorite topics of conversation. Whenever we get together with friends or neighbors for dinner or a backyard barbecue, we spend at least 90 percent of our time talking about things that turn us on and things that keep us awake at night.

Step 2: Direct the Conversation to a Passion, Problem, Hope, or Dream You Can Do Something About

We all have passions, problems, hopes, and dreams. But we're not feeling all of them right at this moment.

Your merchandise addresses certain passions, problems, hopes, and dreams that your customers feel. But they will not buy unless they are feeling those emotions right here and now. If your customers are not feeling the emotions they need to feel in order to buy something of yours, you have to arouse those emotions. Paint a picture in the customer's mind of that passion, problem, hope, or dream so that the customer visualizes how his or her life will be different by accepting your solution.

Consider perfume ads on television. We buy perfume (or men's cologne) in order to smell better. But do the television ads feature a "talking head" saying, "Buy our perfume; you'll smell great!"? Of course not! The television ads present beautiful—heck, extremely gorgeous, beautifully dressed and coiffed—people in lush surroundings acting incredibly confident, sexy, and desirable. Sometimes you don't even know it's a perfume ad until they show the bottle at the very end. We would all like to be gorgeous, sexually desirable people in lush, beautiful surroundings (at least to the extent our spouses and significant others will allow us), and the implied message is that by buying a particular brand of perfume we can get there.

When customers focus on a passion, problem, hope, or dream that you can do something about, or for which you have a product solution, steer the conversation in that direction and really rub in the desired emotion until you can see in the customers' eyes (or by the tone of their e-mail messages) that they're feeling it right now.

Step 3: Offer the Solution

Your customers are feeling passions, hopes, or dreams or recognizing problems that you can do something about, so *now* is the time to begin talking about the merchandise you have in stock that can help gratify their passions, hopes, or dreams or solve their problems. By prepping customers, you have a very interested and motivated listener, and the chances of a successful sale have just gotten far better for you.

Great salespeople know their customers well and want to help them solve their problems. They are convinced—often passionately so—that their merchandise is going to help people improve the quality of their lives. Not only do they not consider it an imposition to talk about their merchandise to prospective buyers, they feel they are actually doing customers a *favor* by pointing out solutions they might not be aware of. Think of it as educating, not selling, and pretty soon people will be saying about you that "this person is so good they could sell sand in Arabia."

Step #4: How Will You Get Your Message Across to Your Customers?

This is the last of the four strategic marketing questions you have to ask when putting together a marketing strategy for your eBay selling business.

It's important to stress, though, that to answer this question effectively you have to have answered the three questions we discussed in the preceding sections by:

1. Identifying the customers who are most likely to buy from you

2. Identifying their passions, problems, hopes, and dreams that will motivate them to buy from you

3. Identifying products that will have a direct and immediate appeal to those passions, problems, hopes, and dreams

Once you've done all that, deciding on the right advertising and promotional strategy to get your message across is fairly easy. If you truly know your customers well enough to know why they will buy and what they will buy, then you will also know how your customers receive information, where they are most likely to find out about your merchandise on eBay, and what type of sales pitch is most likely to attract their attention.

We've said it before, and we say it again here: *You do not decide what your marketing strategy will be; your customers decide that.*

You do not pick an advertising strategy based on what's convenient for you or what you think will work. You base your advertising strategy—in fact, your entire marketing strategy—on what customers want and how they think.

Here are two examples of advertising dos and don'ts when selling to particular markets.

Example #1: How to Sell to a Lawyer

There are two things you need to know when selling products to the legal community, at least in the United States and Canada (we can't vouch for lawyers in other countries).

First of all, you need to know that lawyers *hate* sales pitches; they absolutely *loathe* anything that smacks even remotely of Madison Avenue hype.

When lawyers advise their clients, they are taught to give a fair and balanced review of their clients' situations, pointing out the strengths and weaknesses of their case: "You've got an interesting case here, Mrs. Jones. It has a lot going for it, but, frankly, I don't see that you have an argument that X occurred. In my experience, the judges around here won't rule in your favor unless you can prove that X occurred, so my advice would be to settle this one, and fairly quickly."

Lawyers like to be sold the same way they "sell" their clients on their advice: They want to hear both the positive and the negative aspects of what you have to offer so that they can make a fair, balanced, reasoned decision. So, for example, if we were trying to sell software to a lawyer, we would do it as follows: "Mr. Lawyer, this software will help your firm perform tasks A, B, and C. We have to fully disclose that it doesn't do task D, at least in its current version, but if your firm is willing to pay us an hourly consulting fee, we should be able to customize the product so it will perform task D as well." If we are the recipient of the sales pitch, we are being given the opportunity to determine just how important task D is to us, and whether or not we should splurge for the extra consulting time. Lawyers love being in charge like that.

The second thing you need to know about selling to lawyers is that lawyers want to see *everything* in writing before they make a purchase decision on anything. Lawyers are creatures of the written word—they worship it, actually, to the point that no lawyer we know believes anything is real unless he or she sees it in print.

So, for example, if you've written a book you think lawyers will be interested in buying, you will need to print up a four-page glossy brochure featuring:

- The table of contents of the book

- A sample chapter

- The authors' detailed biographies and photographs

- A list of the forms that will be included in the book and whether or not they are available in CD format

and so forth. The more detail, the better! Trust us, your lawyer customers will read every word before they buy your book.

Example #2: How to Sell to a Teenager

Let's say you have a product—a CD by a local heavy metal band—that you want to promote to the nation's teenagers. Would you send them a detailed glossy brochure with information and photos about the band, their history, a list of all the song lyrics, and so forth?

Of course not.

So how do you sell something to an American teenager? Let's make it a little easier by asking the question in a slightly different way: To whom do American teenagers listen?

Their peers, of course—teenagers are the ultimate pack animals. They move in groups. Get to one member of the group, and you've got the entire group in the palm of your hand.

So in marketing this band's CD you should consider the following:

- A MySpace or Facebook page (heck, get 'em both)

- An instant messaging (IM) campaign to their cell phones

- "Buzz" marketing strategies, whereby you offer discounts to teenagers if they blog about the band and the CD to their friends

- Creating an avatar on the alternate reality website teen.secondlife.com (the teen version of the popular Second Life website for adults), which goes around the virtual world talking up the band and how great it is

Teenagers in general hate to be different, but they all want to be the first to pick up the new cool thing, whatever that might be. If you can persuade them that this band is that next thing, they will be all over it.

Deciding on the Right Promotional Strategy

You can advertise your presence on eBay both online and offline. Chapter 4 of this book describes several common methods of marketing an eBay business online and discusses the advantages and disadvantages of each. Chapter 5 describes several common methods of marketing an eBay business offline and discusses the advantages and disadvantages of each.

It's tempting to do a little bit of everything and see what works and what doesn't, but there are three factors that will put practical limits on your marketing activities:

1. **Your market:** You have to go where your customers are, not where they aren't, so if your marketing strategy targets senior citizens, a Facebook page won't be of much use.

2. **Your pocketbook:** Some marketing methods are fairly expensive, and you have to take your budget into account. Ask yourself how many new sales you will need to make on eBay before you recoup the cost of marketing using method X.

3. **Your time:** Marketing, especially on the Web, can be extremely time and labor intensive, and it isn't worthwhile spending fifty hours of your time each week if the result is only a $100-a-month increase in your eBay sales. (Do the math—at this rate you are working well below what a farmer in a developing country makes each month.)

Building a Market-Friendly eBay Presence

Creating an Experience for Your Buyers

Chapter 2 of *The eBay Marketing Bible* deals with your selling presence on eBay: your eBay user ID, your individual eBay listings, your eBay Store, your presence in eBay's Community section, and everywhere else on eBay that your buyers can see who you are and what you have for sale.

As we discussed in Chapter 1, marketing is more than just figuring out how to sell what you have. Marketing pervades the entire way you do business, including the merchandise you offer, the design of your store (see Figure 2.1), the image you present to your customers, even the name of your business!

When building a presence on eBay, it is important that everything be done with the customer in mind, because it is the customers who make an eBay business possible. In Chapter 2 of this book we show you how to build an eBay presence that is not only customer friendly but customercentric, designed with the customer—and only the customer—in mind.

How to Run Your Business Like a Candy Store

In the New York City metropolitan area, one of the largest urban areas on planet Earth, there are hundreds and hundreds of candy stores.

But there is only one Dylan's Candy Bar.

FIGURE 2.1 Wandering Creek Antiques invites you to come in and browse around a real old-fashioned store. You can visualize the cracker barrels, checkerboard, and potbellied stove.

Founded by Dylan (daughter of Ralph) Lauren, the store is located across the street from Bloomingdale's department store on Third Avenue and 60th Street in Manhattan—as well as five other shopping mall locations in Long Island, Florida (near Disney World, naturally), and Texas. There you will find all the candy classics, such as Necco Wafers, Charleston Chews, and many items you didn't think they made anymore, like Black Jack chewing gum. Dylan's Candy Bar also makes signature chocolates, candy creations, candy spa products such as hot-chocolate bath beads, and custom-made ice cream flavors.

They've got all the candy you could possibly want, but, hey, this is Ralph Lauren's daughter who founded this chain of stores! Walking into a Dylan's Candy Bar is like taking a trip back into childhood—bright primary colors that overwhelm the senses, multicolored fluorescent lighting that sometimes says "bar" more than it does "candy," and a layout that comes right out of *Babes in Toyland* (those older New Yorkers who fondly remember F.A.O. Schwarz's flagship store only a couple of blocks away on Fifth Avenue will recognize the effect Ms. Lauren is striving for). With things in the world the way they are today, who couldn't use a little retreat from reality now and then? Dylan's offers an affordable treat that takes us back to the days when life was safe and simple, "with Mommy and Daddy standing by," as Don Henley sings.

Dylan's Candy Bar is not just about candy; it's about giving buyers an unforgettable retro experience that will bring them back time and again.

It's All About Marketainment These Days

Here's a new word for your vocabulary: *marketainment*. It means marketing your business in a cool, fun, humorous, dramatic, or compelling way that entertains your customers or otherwise manipulates their emotions to make them buy stuff from you.

Marketainment, as perfectly illustrated by Dylan's Candy Bar, is the future of online retail. When you are marketing your merchandise on eBay, or anywhere else online or offline, you are in the entertainment business, whether you like it or not. There are a number of reasons for this.

First, because of extensive, prolonged, and sometimes overwhelming exposure to television, the Internet, video games, and other entertainment media, people's attention spans have gotten much shorter. Have you noticed lately how difficult it is to stay focused when reading a long magazine article, say, in *The Atlantic Monthly* or *The New Yorker*? Postings on the Internet tend to be short, concise, easy-to-read information bursts or sound bites as opposed to long, elaborate digressions. There is even some scientific evidence that exposure to the Internet actually changes the cognitive structure of our brains—the way our brains organize information to enable us to perceive and learn about things—so that we lose patience with messages that take too long to get across.

Second, people, at least in the United States, seem to be increasingly challenged by maturity and adulthood. In his best-selling book *Rejuvenile: Kickball, Cartoons, Cupcakes and the Reinvention of the American Grownup* (Crown, 2006)—required reading for anyone looking to market to the American consumer—Christopher Noxon points out the many ways in which Americans, especially the baby boom generation, are resisting the pull of gravity, for example:

- Parents who dress like their teenage children and download the same ringtones for their cell phones

- The "toyification" of practical devices (those cute little energy-efficient cars that look like Day-Glo ladybugs)

- Adults without kids who visit Disney World every year

We can lament this trend or we can praise it as liberating, but as marketers we really don't care one way or the other: Our job is to find ways of making use of this trend, and marketainment is the way to reach the Rejuvenile adults of America, as well as their kids.

Third, there is simply much more marketing information out there than ever before, and you've got to act crazier and go farther out on a limb just to stand out from the crowd and get people's attention. Teenagers applying to college know what this means. To get into an Ivy League college nowadays it isn't enough just to be the valedictorian of your high school class and captain of the debate team. To get the admissions officers' attention at Yale or Harvard you have to have argued—and won—a case before the U.S. Supreme Court (preferably one involving the environment), rescued your entire homeroom from a terrorist assault, and been personally congratulated by the president of the United States and at least three other world leaders (with supporting photos to prove it).

It has always been the case that to succeed in marketing, you have to stand out from your competition. But the bar has been significantly raised for the current generation of online businesses, including eBay folks—there are thousands of eBay Stores on the site now, and all of them are marketing on search engines, doing blogs, and otherwise trying to grab buyers' attention.

"You Gotta Have a Gimmick"

On eBay, it isn't enough anymore just to have great merchandise and a well-designed eBay Store. In the words of the old Broadway song (from the musical *Gypsy*), "You Gotta Have a Gimmick." There has to be something about your eBay presence, and your online and offline marketing scheme, that really stands out, grabs people by the throat, and demands that they stop doing what they're doing *right this minute* and look at you.

The amazing thing about marketainment is that the gimmick doesn't have to have anything to do with your merchandise:

- **It can be your expertise.** The fact that you can recognize an authentic Jimi Hendrix signature and your competition can't makes your rock-and-roll memorabilia that much more attractive to customers.

- **It can be your personality or online persona.** This refers to the way in which you speak to your customers in your listings, your eBay Store content pages, or your blog. (Many eBay sellers have done quite well using an "aw shucks, I'm just folks" tone in their communications with buyers, which is great as long as you're not selling high-end jewelry or other merchandise that requires a more sophisticated, urban persona.)

- **It can be your sense of humor.** As the lawyers say, "A laughing jury never convicts." It's impossible to dislike anyone who makes you laugh. People will always bookmark or subscribe to a website or blog that regularly and consistently makes them laugh.

- **It can be the look and feel of your presence on eBay.** Does your eBay Store look like a picket fence where farmwives can swap recipes, a barbershop where middle-aged men can swap sports stories, or an ebony bar where *Sex and the City*–type urban professionals can talk about their work colleagues and/or their latest conquests?

- **It can be your love of animals, your social conscience, or your commitment to the environment,** which shows through in everything you do on eBay.

- **It can be your effective use of tear-jerking stories combining pathos with an uplifting message.** We all like a good cry every once in a while, especially if there's an inspirational kicker at the end.

Your gimmick can be anything at all, as long as it gets people saying, "Wow, this seller is special," and gets them telling their friends and acquaintances to "check this out, you're not going to believe it!"

Just keep in mind that your gimmick isn't about you—it's about your customers. Whatever your gimmick is, remember that you are entertaining your customers, not yourself. The goal is to sell merchandise, not create a fan club of people who love what you do online but don't buy anything because they don't feel any of the passions, problems, hopes, and dreams you are trying to arouse through your marketainment strategy.

The Downside of Marketainment

Of course, there are disadvantages as well as advantages to a marketainment strategy.

Some people (perhaps many people) may see you as superficial and more interested in attracting attention to yourself than trying to solve their problems. If you sense this is the prevailing sentiment, by the way, it's because you are not doing a good enough job of arousing your customers' passions, problems, hopes, and dreams (see Chapter 1, "Step #2: Why Are These People Going to Buy from You?").

Marketainment requires a lot of creativity and can be physically exhausting—anyone who has ever done a one-hour stand-up comedy routine before a bunch of rowdy drunks in a comedy club will tell you they usually sleep for hours afterward, especially if their act was successful.

But most important, as anyone in the entertainment business can attest to, you've always got to keep the act fresh, alive, and current. Once people have seen your act a couple of times, they want to see something new and different the next time they come back. Amusement parks always have to have new rides or other themed entertainment tied to the most recent blockbuster movie and eliminate the old rides tied to movies nobody remembers anymore. Successful concert performers such as Madonna and Cher change their entire images every couple of years or so to adjust to changing times. Theme stores such as Dylan's Candy Bar have to constantly reinvent their décor, their layout, or their image, so that customers are constantly surprised and awed each time they walk in the door.

Marketainment is all about change and self-renewal—the ability to build an audience and keep them with you for a long period of time. You will be constantly reworking your gimmick, looking for fresh material, and doing everything you can to make sure the crowd doesn't get bored. It's a lot of fun, but it ain't easy.

Your eBay User ID and Store ID

One of the first things anyone does when visiting the eBay site is create a *user ID*—a unique user name that identifies the person each time he or she visits the site. When someone creates a user ID on eBay, eBay creates a My eBay page for that user ID, which tracks everything the person buys and sells on eBay, among other things. Similarly, when an eBay seller sets up an eBay Store, the first thing he or she does is create a *store ID* that uniquely identifies that store within the eBay website.

Most people don't give a lot of thought to their user IDs, and that can be a big marketing mistake. Your eBay user ID and store ID should be both memorable and relevant to the merchandise you offer for sale. The user ID *cliffennicolawyer* (not Cliff's actual user ID, by the way) is nice, but it's not going to help Cliff sell any of the wonderful antiques he wants to sell on eBay. Do people actually trust lawyers to know anything about antiques? Heck, do most people really trust lawyers, period?

Choosing Your eBay User ID

The first thing you must do to sell on eBay is create a user ID. First, decide who you want to be or what you want to do with eBay. If you are just going to sell a few things around the house, the user ID you choose can be pretty simple. Choose an ID that reflects something about you. You might collect old cars and trade a little to help fund your hobby, so a user ID like *theoldcarguy* would work for you (if it hasn't already been taken). Before you register, take a few minutes to think about your user ID and have a couple of different ideas, because with millions of users on the site the odds are good that your first choice has already been taken.

If you are starting fresh or expanding your business, create a user ID that uniquely brands your business. Your user ID should be easy to remember and define who and what your business is. If you choose the ID correctly, your moniker will help customers navigate back to your listings over and over again. If it's easy to remember, your customers are much more likely to tell their friends about you when recommending the product they just purchased. Because you've made it simple for them, they can easily Google you as well. You'd be surprised how many people navigate eBay via Google. If they type in your user ID, chances are very good that your About Me page or store landing page will rank very high in the Google search results. Customers can enter your listings through those access points, even if you have done no additional search engine optimization.

If you have a business name already, we recommend that you carry that name through to your user ID to build brand recognition.

Here are some things to remember when choosing an ID:

- You may not use any of these characters: @ & ' ( ) < or >.

- If your name is two or more words, there may not be a space between them. Use an underscore or hyphen to separate them or run them together.

- Be careful about running the words together; ask a few people to read it back to you before you settle on the mashed-together name.

- You may use your business name, but you cannot use *.com* or any element that would suggest your website outside of eBay, for example, *johndoedotcom.*

- Don't use the word *eBay* in your title. It's a copyright violation, and you'll have to hire Cliff to bail you out when the eBay lawyers come after you.

- While we're on copyright issues, don't use another company's brand name as part of your ID, either. *Cocacolaseller* will get you into trouble as well.

- Don't be negative or profane. It's not allowed, and it's just bad for your business.

- Remember to build your business around trust and safety. A weird name is going to put off potential customers.

Perhaps you registered on eBay as a buyer, and now that you've built your feedback up, you don't want to start over. There's good news! You can change your ID without losing your feedback score. After you change to a new ID, eBay will put the dreaded sunglass symbol after your name for thirty days. The sunglass symbol says to buyers, "Watch out; something has changed in this person's user profile in recent years," which sometimes—unfortunately—translates in the buyer's mind into "Don't buy from this person because you can't trust him."

To change your user ID:

1. Log in to your My eBay page.

2. Find the Personal Information link and click on it.

3. About halfway down the page is a link to change your user ID (right above the Change Password link).

Go on, change that user ID from *stupidoldgolfguy* to *proseller* now!

Your Store ID

Your eBay store name is another spot where you can brand your business and attract the search engine spiders that will draw lots of customers to your eBay store. You have a little more flexibility when creating a store name. You are allowed to put spaces between words, and some symbols are allowed ("&" is an allowed instance). Before you charge on over to eBay and set up that store name, there are a few things to consider.

Choosing your store name also helps Google and other search engines index your site. When a search engine spider (a robot that indexes the site) comes to your eBay store, it is gathering information about what your store is selling. The spider reads the clues (or words) throughout your site and ranks their relevance according to where they find the words and how often the word is repeated or matched with the site.

One prime place to optimize for best search engine results is the title or name of the store. What you name your store helps the search engines rank its contents for relevancy. When customers come to Google, MSN, Yahoo!, or any of the other search engines and type in what they are looking for, if your store name matches the search terms, the index will show your store in the results.

If your store is named Jane Doe's Collectibles, that's not going to be nearly as relevant to the spiders as a more specific name such as Jane Doe's Fused Art Glass. The more specific you can be, the better. Many sellers go so far as to completely drop their branding and stuff the store name with keywords matching what they sell. This is a viable strategy if you expect to get most buyers through searches. However, it makes it difficult to build customer loyalty because your store name will be difficult to recall. If you want repeat business, combine keywords with a memorable title.

Others believe that branding your store is equally important and that search engines constantly change their algorithms. Next month a keyword-only title may put off the spiders and rank you lower. You may have already built a strong brand, and you should feature that prominently in the store name. People who take consignments of goods for sale on eBay (known as eBay Trading Assistants) might want to highlight as many items as they specialize in when naming their eBay Stores and worry about branding their businesses in the brick-and-mortar world. In other words, they would brand their businesses to their hometown customers, who are more likely to find them in a newspaper or Yellow Pages ad, and create a keyword-stuffed store name for the eBay store only. Consider what would work best for your particular business.

Here are two sample types of store names:

1. Keyword stuffed for search engine optimization: *Silk Screened Hoodies Tank Tops Sweat Shirts*

2. Business Name Branded: *J&J Silk Screened T's*

Tying It All Together with a Unique E-Mail Domain URL

Now that you have your user ID and store name branded, the next step is to create an e-mail address that matches them. This helps build trust and confidence with your buyers. Although eBay sends most communications through the eBay e-mail system, there are still several points where buyers see your e-mail address: when there are outside questions about delivery of the item, during the PayPal checkout process, and when you send any follow-up e-mails.

You do not have to have your own website to sell on eBay, and you may think that getting a domain name is for the independent sellers only. If you want to build trust with your buyers, they are more likely to respond if you send them an e-mail from jane@theglasscollectorstore.com than they would from jane@hotmail.com. The first tells your buyers you are a professional; the latter says that you have a free e-mail account, which are a dime a dozen and may have been hacked into by some unscrupulous thief.

To get your own e-mail account you need to register a domain. Domain registration is inexpensive and pretty simple to set up. Go to Google and type in "domain registration"; you'll see dozens of companies ready to help you. Price-shop for the best deal. Many people use Godadddy.com. With a service like Godaddy you can register a domain and then set up your e-mail account. You can even have the e-mail forwarded to your AOL or Hotmail account if you desire. You never have to set up a website. (Although to complete the perfect marketing tri-

---

ADD A SIGNATURE LINE TO PROMOTE YOUR BUSINESS

Once you have that unique domain name, be sure to add a signature line to every e-mail you send or every time you post a comment on a blog or online bulletin board. This is the easiest way to get people into your store. If they see the signature line often enough, they will get curious and click on it to see what it is. If you make your signature line compelling enough, you'll find lots of hits coming into your store. And the best bonus yet: You'll get a rebate for driving your own traffic into your eBay store.

Here is a sample signature line:

Jane Doe
unique fused art glass collectibles
www.theglasscollectorstore.com

angle, we strongly suggest that you set up at least a simple website. More about setting up that website later.)

A Bonus: Use That Domain Name to Save Money

Did you know that if you drive traffic to your eBay store and a customer purchases an item, you receive 75 percent off the final value fee (the percentage of the purchase price) eBay charges for that sale? That discount alone makes your own unique domain even more desirable.

Using a service like Godaddy, you can redirect a domain to another website or page. That way, someone who typed in the URL would be forwarded to your eBay store and would never know the difference. When you set the URL to redirect to your store, you simply have to put in a little code at the end, which lets eBay know you are responsible for the traffic. That little snippet is:

?refid=store

This is how the setup process works: Let's say your store URL is http://stores.ebay.com/EnterYourStoreIdHere. If you add ?refid=store to the end of it, you'll get a URL that looks like this:

http://stores.ebay.com/EnterYourStoreIdHere?refid=store

This example uses the standard URL eBay assigns to your store. These eBay-assigned store addresses are clunky, and you'll never be able to tell customers how to find your store using them. You should create the unique domain name with which to brand your business and then *redirect* that domain to go to the URL that eBay assigned to you. The redirect would look like this:

http://www.theglasscollectorstore.com

It would then take people to your eBay store. (See Figure 2.2.) Don't worry—the redirect happens so quickly that most people don't even notice it.

Once you have the redirect in place, you can create business cards, flyers, and so forth, and print your unique URL on the material. When shoppers type it in they are automatically taken into your store. A unique URL is much easier to remember than the mumbo jumbo address eBay assigns. And by using the special ?refid=store code you'll automatically earn the 75 percent final value fee rebate.

FIGURE 2.2   A redirected, or forwarded, domain setup inside Godaddy.

Your About Me and My World Pages

Your About Me Page

Another place to market your business, build your brand, and and attract search engine spiders is the About Me page. When eBay users create an About Me page, they get a little blue-and-red "me" icon behind their user ID. When other community members click on the icon, they are taken to the About Me page. When done correctly, the About Me page transforms you from a nameless seller into someone with whom buyers can identify. The nameless eBay seller is transformed into a person. As a result, the buyer and seller form a human bond.

Originally, these pages were created as a way for members to express themselves. They were designed and used to tell others about hobbies or interests. In fact, many part-time sellers and buyers still use the About Me page to talk about their pets, children, or hobbies. Others have seen the potential to reach out to their customers and build professional relationships with them. (See Figure 2.3.)

If optimized correctly, the About Me page can act as a portal into your listings or store. Search engines rank these pages very highly. For example, Cindy is an eBay consultant. Many clients know her only by her name or user ID and look for her store by using Google. The first results from Google are links to her eBay About Me page. From there, customers can go directly into the store via a link.

FIGURE 2.3 Janieruth has done an excellent job of branding her business and personalizing her About Me page (http://stores.ebay.com/Janieruths-Fabulous-to-Funky-Finds).

How to Set Up the About Me Page

You can find a link for creating an About Me page on the Account tab inside your My eBay area. Click on the button and you will be guided through the process step-by-step.

About Me pages are not complicated to set up. Your designer can create one to match the theme of your store. If you don't have a store design (or designer) yet, eBay offers many easy-to-set-up templates. Using the templates provided, you can add links to your listing so buyers can find their way to the items you have for sale quickly. There is a drop-down menu from which to choose Adding Your Feedback and the number of recent comments from customers that you want to show. You can feature listings on your About Me page using the eBay-provided template. You can choose how many items to showcase on the page. These are simple ways to add the links and testimonials we cover later in this chapter. These templates don't build your brand identity, but they will work in a pinch if you are not familiar with Web design or HTML.

What do you put on an About Me page? Here are a few ways to build your brand, create security and confidence, and guide the search engines and customers to your listings.

The Basics

Basic store information that is quickly accessible is the key to good customer service. Include your contact information. (Read eBay's current policy to make sure which information you can include and how to format it.) It is important to double-check eBay's policies, because they are constantly changing. Once you know the current policy, add as much contact information as allowed so that your customers can easily find you. If you have a Skype connection that would enable buyers to call you and speak to you live to discuss an item, include your Skype button on the page. Skype is owned by eBay, so this is very easy to do.

If you have a brick-and-mortar store, be sure to include the street address and instructions for how customers can find you. Include your store hours. If you have a photo of the store, include that as well—it helps establish your credibility.

Customers love that personal touch. If there is a story behind opening the business or why you got into the business, tell it. What is your experience or background? Include any certification or business awards your company may have received.

Mission Statement

A mission statement may sound a little formal for an eBay page, but we can assure you it's not. If you have a mission statement already, congratulations—now post it. If not, it's time to create one. A mission statement helps your business stayed focused and gives your business a clear direction, especially when it comes to customer service. A mission statement is almost like a condensed version of a business plan.

A mission statement should include three main components.

1. **The purpose of the business.** For example, offer properly fitting clothes for larger women.

2. **How the business provides a solution.** For example, it has the most extensive selection of plus-size clothes on eBay.

3. **The values of the company.** For example, customers are our number one priority.

When we put those three ingredients together into a mission statement, it might read something like this:

> The mission of XYZ-Clothes-For-Women is to provide the largest selection of plus-size clothes for women of all shapes and ages. We value our customers and want them to be completely satisfied. Customers are our number one priority. We will do what it takes to make sure you are happy with your wardrobe.

In just a few sentences your mission statement should convey the essence of your company. It should be concise and factual.

Terms of Service

Your terms of service (TOS) are your own private contract with your buyers—specifying such important matters as when you will accept returns of merchandise, refund buyers' fees, and collect sales taxes from your buyers—and it should be included in every listing. Not only does this promote your buyer's confidence in the sale, it spells out what a customer can expect. So why should you also put a copy of the TOS on the About Me page? The simple answer is repetition. Give your buyers more than one opportunity to see important information. If you offer a money-back guarantee (which you should), positioning your TOS near your mission statement boosts the authority of the offer. Brag about both of them—be proud, and let your customers know.

Testimonials

You're asking yourself, "If I get good feedback, why should I include testimonials?" You are thinking: "Isn't it just bragging to add a testimonial?" Polite society has conditioned us to think we must not brag, or others will think we're egotistical. Well, that's true in normal interactions, but in business, testimonials are essential ingredients in building security and confidence. In fact, they play such an important role in e-commerce that most sites put them inside the product listings. You may have noticed the reviews on product pages. That's a form of testimonial for the product. Testimonials for products, people, and services have influenced buying decisions since trade began.

If you get customers who take the time to write you e-mail thanking you for the product or your outstanding service (and you will eventually), ask them if you can use their words. Once you have permission, post them along with the writers' names on your About Me page. Don't be tempted to change wording or correct spellings. Leave the text exactly as the author wrote it. Everyone's writing style is different, and if you try to alter it, no matter how insignificant the change, you run the risk of ruining the authenticity of the testimonial. Video and audio testimonials are wonderful additions as well.

A Link to Your eBay Store

Why provide a link to the store on the About Me page when eBay also provides links? This may seem a little odd to computer-savvy eBay sellers. But remember that you are not the buyer, and your potential customer may not be as computer literate as you. Remove buyer confusion as quickly as possible for those souls who might have stumbled onto your About Me page through Google or another search engine. If they can't figure out how to navigate their way off the page into your store within three seconds, they'll be heading out the door. A big, bold link or button that says "Click Here" for more information (or to enter the store) keeps them shopping with you.

Your My World Page

Have you ever stumbled upon the My World link and wondered what the heck it is? When eBay rolled it out with much ado a few years ago, some said it was going to replace the traditional feedback page and others felt it would move eBay into the more social world of Web 2.0. The general idea was that My World would be a lot like MySpace or Facebook, allowing sellers to post profiles of themselves, their stores, their merchandise, and their special areas of expertise, and try to build a community of like-minded people within the larger eBay community. (See Figure 2.4.)

The eBay community hasn't exactly warmed up to My World. Many sellers avoid the feature entirely, but that's a *big* mistake. Yes, the average eBay buyer isn't searching My World every day to hook up with new sellers, *but* the search engine spiders that crawl eBay looking for content crawl My World frequently. They read the content, index it, and follow the links on the page. A My World page is just one more place to put up content that will attract the search engine spiders—but, hey, you need all the help you can get when you're trying to get onto the first page of Google search engine results for the merchandise you're selling. If a spider sees sixteen different references to antique mechanical banks in your eBay store, it is certain to rank you highly on the keywords "antique mechanical banks." When it comes to optimizing your eBay Store for search engines, the more content you have, the better.

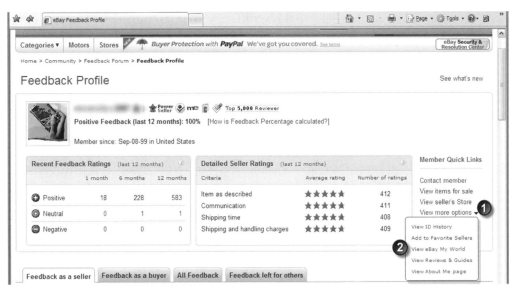

FIGURE 2.4   To access the My World pages, go to Members Feedback and click on the View Members My World Page link.

The My World page shouldn't take very long to set up. It won't take much maintenance. Check back and update it as your store inventory mix changes. Add it to your semiannual eBay tune-up.

What sort of things should you put on the My World page?

Layout

The layout you choose really doesn't matter that much—eBay provides you with a few different choices, so just pick one you like. Be sure that you pick colors and a style that are appropriate for your store. You can change the display order of the modules. The important assignment to build better search engine optimization (SEO) is to update your biographical field. Click on the Add Content link at the top of the form, then look for the bio module. Inside the bio module, you will find several fill-in-the-blank areas. (See Figure 2.5.) Let's take a look at them from an SEO standpoint.

What Everyone Should Know About Me

This doesn't have to be intensely personal. This is your business. However, it is important in business to be authentic, consistent, and transparent. Although this page is being written mostly for the search engine spiders, you never know when a human will stumble in and start reading it. Write these modules as if you were writing anything else that is written for your customers.

Things everyone should know about you can include awards you've won, certificates you've received, or any education or training you might have that makes you qualified to sell your product. Have you been going to garage and estate sales since you were old enough to drive? That would qualify you as a collector and give you more authority in your field.

Here are some other possibilities:

- If you are a Trading Assistant, you can write about past consignments you've done.

- Write about your favorite charity—why you contribute and what it means to you.

- Write about what you collect if it is related to your store inventory.

- Offer your favorite tips related to using your product or service.

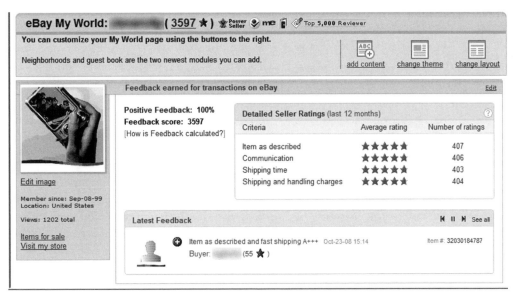

FIGURE 2.5   When logged in to your account, you can edit your My World page using the links at the top. To fill in bio information, look for the Add Content link.

Things I Sell

This one is pretty simple. Pull out that keyword list again. Include brand names as well as generic names of the products you sell, and fill up those 250 characters that are available here.

Things I Buy

One specific use of this area would be by collectors who buy items and are looking to expand their collections. Most of us, however, probably want to be a little more generic here. You could deliver a pitch about being a Trading Assistant and what you specialize in. Or you could fill in the names of products that relate to your items but that you might not necessarily carry. For instance, you might sell soccer balls. The "things that you buy" might be seat cushions, lap blankets, thermos bottles, or anything that could be used at a tailgate party or during a soccer game.

Things I Collect

This is your business page, so keep it focused on what you are selling. Perhaps you collect old cars if you sell vintage car parts.

Hobbies

Hobbies include the items related to your product. With a little imagination, everything someone sells can be associated with a hobby. Let's say you sell LED flashlights. You hobbies could include (1) walking the dog in the dark using a battery-powered torch, (2) stargazing while reading the star charts with a flashlight, (3) camping with a lantern, and so on.

Favorite Books

Favorite books should first include the title, author, and ISBN number of each of the books you carry in your store. If you don't carry any books, then include popular titles of books related to what you are selling. Go to a best-sellers list to find out what the trendy titles are.

Favorite Music/Bands

Favorite music, if you are a CD seller, should be simple. Read the preceding paragraph. If you are not selling music, how can you use this space creatively? Maybe here you could experiment with popular artists. Even if they aren't your favorites, you might get more hits to the site because your page is indexed as having a reference to a current artist. However, the truth is, that's a long shot. Try doing some free association and see if you can't come up with some titles that match your store theme.

Favorite TV Shows

The same advice goes for TV shows as for the favorite music category. Try to come up with shows that match your merchandise. However, if you don't have something relevant to put in either space, leave them blank. The idea here is to build keyword density, not create a bio full of nonsense that will only confuse potential buyers.

Use This Field to Make Your Own Category

Two "make your own category" areas are available to you. That's five hundred characters to describe in keyword-rich sentences more about the product or niche in which you are selling. Include trivia about your company or how your company lives up to its mission statement. This might be a good place to mention the charity work the company does or that your company uses recycled products in its packaging.

Business Information

Business information fields include History/background, Payment Methods, Shipping Information, and Return Policy & Contact Information. These fields should be easy to fill out if you've already created your terms of service information. You can just paste it in the appropriate fields.

Under business information you also have two customizable fields where you can say anything else relevant to your business. These fields allow one thousand characters each. Study your store keywords list and use this area to continue building your keyword density and your SEO.

History/Background

You may have provided this information on your About Me page. If not, here's a great place to let shoppers know how you started in this field. Another possibility is to write a blurb about the history of the products you are selling. For example, if you are selling scrapbook supplies, you could give a brief history of the evolution of scrapbooking through the last couple of centuries, from the advent of photography to digital scrapbooks.

The My World page may not see many human hits, but creating links with keywords helps boost your eBay SEO rankings. If you'd like to get people to your My World page and create a little marketing buzz, try having a company trivia contest. You've just put some trivia in the business information section on your My World page. Send out a newsletter offering a prize to the first person who can answer a question about that trivia. You'll have eBay users looking all over your site for the information. Everyone loves a contest.

Elements of an Attention-Getting Listing

Once you have your customers' attention it's time to close the sale by writing a compelling product listing for each item of merchandise you sell. For those new to eBay, a *listing* is a webpage within the eBay website offering to sell a particular product; it can be either an *auction* listing (the seller sets a starting price, such as $1, and buyers bid up the price until the auction closes) or a *fixed-price* listing (known on eBay as a Buy It Now! listing).

When it comes to ad copy, there are a number of different methods that marketers have followed successfully for years, and they all work on eBay. In this section we'll tell you how to use those techniques to improve your sales.

Long or Short?

There is a debate among copywriters, both on the Internet and off, about whether the sales pitch should be short or long. They can be equally successful, and this is where you should test, test, and test again to see what works for you. Try one written listing in the long style, usually eight to ten screens (many scrolls), and one in the short style to see which results in more purchases.

Generally, the style or length is determined by uniqueness and type of product. Something a buyer can find on the shelf at the local store doesn't need much ad copy written. For those types of items, keep the listing short and concise so your hurried buyer can click the Buy It Now! button quickly. For products and services that are unique and that buyers might never have heard of, a longer sales pitch is necessary.

Think of it as a TV commercial: A bar of soap gets a fifteen-second spot, but the latest gizmo you've never heard of might get an hour-long infomercial.

W-I-I-F-M

Regardless of whether it is short or long, there are some essential ingredients you need to include when writing your listing. Of course, you should add the properties of the product—things like height, weight, and dimensions—but there is more to a good listing than that. Always write to answer your customers' main question: "What's in it for me?" It doesn't matter what the product is, WIIFM is the number one question on all buyers' minds. This might sound jaded, but it's the truth. Your customers' whole motivation for considering the purchase is about them, not about you.

This is your USP (unique selling proposition). You must keep in the front of your mind the qualities that make your product or service stand out from the rest. Once you have the USP, it is easy to translate it into a benefit to buyers. Tell your buyers the benefits they will receive if they buy the product. You can save the features till later. Failing to emphasize benefits is one of the biggest mistakes eBay sellers make. They don't understand how important benefits are, so they just talk about the product's features.

What's the Difference Between a Benefit and a Feature?

A benefit tells your customers how the item can improve their lives, how it fills a need, or how it is a solution to their problem. A feature talks specifically about the product. Here's an example:

Fact or Feature: Mint-flavored toothpaste.

Benefit: Minty fresh flavor delights your taste buds and leaves your smile sparkling white.

Fact or Feature: Perfumed soap to clean your hands.

Benefit: Envelops your hands in a refreshing perfume of wildflowers while gently cleansing your skin so your hands are left feeling clean, soft, and freshly scented.

Tell your customers what is in it for them and how your product is a solution to their problem. Try to avoid this long-overused benefit line: "This is the perfect addition to your collection." Every eBay collector can tell you it's old and tired. But with knowledge of the item, you should be able to come up with a benefit-rich sentence or two.

Titles

There are two titles you should be aware of when creating your listing.

The first one is the eBay title section, the one that eBay uses to catalog the item. The eBay catalog title should be keyword rich, matching exactly what your buyer would type into the search box. It is important to fill all fifty-two available characters with good, keyword-rich words. This title doesn't have to be grammatically perfect. If you need to sacrifice an adjective to get another keyword in, do it!

Check completed items from other sellers to see what they are using effectively, and follow suit. Use research tools like Terapeak.com and HammerTap.com or BayEstimate (http://labs.ebay.com/raghavgupta/demoto/to) to help with keyword selection. Again, test different keywords in the title to make sure you are getting the most effective words to draw in traffic.

The second title is a subtitle, if you will, that appears within the listing page itself. Here's an opportunity to grab your buyers' attention with big letters as soon they scroll into the product description. Instead of repeating the same title used to grab the buyers' attention, create one that is benefit rich. Grab your buyers by stating clearly what the biggest benefit of buying your product is. Be direct and right to the point here—you've got only a spilt second to grab them. Here's an example:

> Wildflower Soap Leaves Your Hands Soft and Clean.

As you write the description, sell with benefits. Remember that buyers are motivated by passions, problems, hopes, and dreams. In the description remind them what they may lose, risk, or waste if they do not buy. Your job, when writing the description, is to spell out what they can gain or achieve or what problem will be solved if they purchase your product.

Pricing Strategy Is Marketing

Your pricing strategy is part of marketing as well. Fixed-priced items sell differently than auction items do. You need to consider that as part of the listing formula. A lot of decision making must go into this process. Are you going to sell low and go for volume or sell high and offer quality products? This, of course, is part of who you are on eBay. Once you determine who you are (or your store's persona), you can employ these pricing strategies.

Auction Pricing

In their paper "Seller Strategies on eBay," professors Steven Anderson, Daniel Friedman, Garrett Milan, and Nirvikar Singh analyzed more than a thousand handheld computer (or PDA) auctions to see whether there was any correlation between listing strategies and end-of-auction success. They evaluated auction length, starting prices, whether a reserve was used, Buy It Now! options, and information provided about the product. The study concluded that the most successful sellers consistently employed a combination of the following:

- Low starting bids (one penny)

- No reserve price

- Buy it Now! option

eBay has evolved since the 2004 study, and, with more competition, you should check completed items before you start all your listings out at a penny. Nevertheless, it is true that once people place bids on an item—even low bids—they start to take ownership of the item. When that happens, they forget their original limit and start contending with other bidders for the prize. The seller often sees higher final values as a result.

Reserve Pricing

Another two studies—one done by two economics professors at the University of Arizona and the other done by students at Vanderbilt University—reached two different conclusions about reserve-price auctions. The study done at UA concluded that (on lower-value) items, the number of no-reserve auctions resulting in a sale amounted to 72 percent, while only 46 percent of the listings with a reserve price sold. Additionally, they found that the no-reserve auctions earned, on average, a 90 percent higher final sale price than those with the reserve.

However, the study done by VU, which looked at higher-value items, concluded just the opposite. It found that on higher-ticket items, the "presence of a reserve price increases the auction price by about 15% on average."

Why are we telling you this and confusing the issue?

It goes back to the security and confidence issue. On the lower-value items, because the reserve is unknown, buyers don't know whether the seller is being reasonable or not. The uncertainty leaves buyers uncomfortable, and as a result they are more likely to move on to the next listing without bidding. However, that changes when the item is more valuable. Buyers are keenly aware that there are fraudsters everywhere. One way to assess legitimacy is to decide whether the auction seems just too good to be true. Would anyone in their right mind really auction off a diamond ring starting at a penny? If the item is high-value, buyers are reassured to see that there is a reserve. It tells them that the seller values the item. It also indicates that the seller is likely to really have the item available.

Fixed Price and Store Pricing

This type of pricing requires a different selling strategy than auctions. The fixed-price sector was the fastest-growing part of eBay in 2008. No longer just an auction site, eBay is evolving. To encourage more growth, eBay extended listing times and lowered listing fees for fixed-price items. With the new, extended fixed-price listings and the Best Match feature, competition among eBay sellers to have their merchandise appear at the top of the screen buyers see, without having to scroll down (called *above-the-fold* placement), is becoming increasingly brutal. If your title keywords are *not* spot-on, your DSRs *not* high, and sales record for the item sold is low, your fixed-price listing will appear *below the fold* (i.e., buyers will have to scroll down the results to find your listing) and thus will be less visible to potential buyers. To reach that above-the-fold placement, you need a spotless selling record.

The eBay website recently introduced a new feature that displays only ten items per listing, even if you have more in your listing inventory. That's to reinforce the perception of limited quantity and get people to act fast to purchase. The eBay algorithms includes a calculation of past sales. Before the item runs out of stock, revise the listing and add a few more. As part of your fixed-price strategy, keep the number of items available low to give the appearance of limited supply, but never let the listing run out of stock.

Pricing isn't fair. You'll find it is extremely difficult to compete on price alone. On eBay, there are big box sellers who get rock-bottom pricing by buying directly from the manufacturers, drop-ship sellers who don't mind that they make only pennies per transaction, and direct importers who can get the product at below wholesale price. If you want to compete here, you must offer buyers something more than price.

A simple way to get customers to pay more for your product or service is to add something of value to the product. Here are some examples of simple value-added products:

- A free e-book on how to use or get the most out of the product
- Follow-up consulting or customer care after the sale
- Bundling your product with another product, for example, a camera with a free camera bag as the bonus

Buy It Now!

Buy It Now! (BIN) is a call to action for your shoppers. Although you would never want to use this for an auction item for which you can't predict the final value—for example, a sought-after collectible—this pricing strategy works great for sellers' commodity-type items (things you can find new on store shelves around town). Commodities sellers can use BIN when listing items on auction. When the first few buyers enter the listing, they have a choice between bidding or simply purchasing the item outright. It turns out that, most times, anxious buyers really prefer to buy now and get the transaction under way instead of waiting.

Once the item has been purchased using BIN, the listing closes. That means the person who hesitates may lose out to a faster buyer. This gives your first few buyers a strong reason to act fast. It helps the seller with multiples to list one and, when it sells, list another—which keeps them from flooding the market. Yes, even on eBay you can flood the listings with too many of the same item.

Best Offer

Best Offer is a feature you can toggle on to attract buyers to your listings. This strategy involves you and your customers in a negotiation that is a win-win. Your buyers believe they are receiving a deal and, if you set your prices correctly, you receive the profit you need from the item.

To keep buyers from starting the offers too low, eBay allows buyers only three chances before they must purchase the item at the fixed price. Therefore, you don't have to worry about being bombarded with ridiculously low offers.

One seller we talked to recently uses the Best Offer feature to save time and promote buyer goodwill. When she lists an item, she sets the fixed price a little higher than the price she really wants for it. She then sets her Accept Offer point at the price she really wants to receive. Because she has set her eBay tools to automatically decline the Best Offer if it doesn't match what she wants, she doesn't receive any e-mails until the sale has been made.

Some buyers love to negotiate or dicker for prices. Best Offer gives them the chance to participate. They enjoy the thrill of the hunt for a bargain. That is the very essence of eBay, and using the Best Offer feature on your fixed-price and store listings attracts more buyers, especially in a competitive marketplace.

One service that makes the fixed-price, store, and Best Offer listings a lot more fun is a company called Deal4It. This company uses videos taped by actors to spice up the deal making. When buyers make offers that are too low, the actors prompt them to try again. Theses video shorts are designed to make buyers laugh and enjoy the process of buying. You can pick the actor you want as your spokesperson. Putting the interactive videos in your listings is easy. You simply push one button to insert the player. The price is modest for the returns, around twenty-five cents a listing, at the time of this writing. You can find out more about the video service at www.deal4it.com.

Setting Your Price to Sell

We're not talking about being the lowest-price seller on the site. Choosing to be the lowest-price seller is something most mom-and-pops can't realistically do. When sellers rely on the lowest price to bring in buyers, they must cut corners and sell obscenely high volumes of merchandise. If you go this route, you'll never have a life and your capital will be constantly tied up in inventory. When determining prices, the first concern is to establish the price point for your re-quired margin. After you set the initial price, continue to test and tweak it as you go along. Some manufacturers require that you adhere to a *minimum advertised price* (MAP), which means that you can't go lower than their recommended price or they may decide not to sell to you anymore. Generally, with the down-ward spiral of prices on eBay, using the MAP is a good thing. It requires sellers to compete for customers in other ways, and this is where you can outshine your competition.

Once you determine the price at which you will sell your product, marketing that price point kicks in. It may seem like a cliche, but it is a proven fact that the way you price your item does affect the sale. A number that ends in 9 or 7 will outsell a similar price nine times out of ten. So if you want to sell an item for around $50.00, offer it at $49.97 or $49.99.

Add a Sense of Urgency

Your buyers are interested in buying and you've brought them all this way, so it would be a shame if they decided to click out and do a little price-comparison shopping now, wouldn't it? You know it's likely that once they click out, they'll never return.

Your listing must have a *call to action,* and eBay does a pretty good job of this by sending out bid notices and featuring the BIN and Bid buttons in several prime locations throughout the listings. Your job is to get the buyer to click on one of those buttons instead of the Add to Watch List link.

One way to create a call to action is to give the appearance of limited stock. We are all concerned about the big box sellers on eBay, but when buyers click into a listing and see the seller is offering 542 of something of which most people are offering only one or two, they become doubtful. Does the seller really have that many of that item in stock? Limit the fixed-price listing to a few. If you really have that many more, put the rest into a few different listings inside your store.

Other calls to action are limited offers. You can bundle products together and offer only a fixed amount for sale. You can create limited editions from the bundles. Have you ever waited in line to be the first to receive the latest gadget or first in line to see a long-awaited blockbuster movie? People want to know they are special or unique. It creates an experience for them that they can share with friends. Steve Jobs has done wonders for Apple by using this strategy. Apple offers limited inventory, and when the company recently unveiled the new iPhone, people stood in line for days hoping to be among the first few to get one.

Put time limits on your offerings. With its one-, three-, five-, seven-, and ten-day listings, eBay does a wonderful job of this. When it comes to store and fixed-price listings, though, there is no time limit. There are sellers who have thousands of old, dusty listings that clutter up their stores and give buyers no sense of urgency or specialness when purchasing. Do some housecleaning and remove items that don't sell. Before you do, give your customers one more chance to purchase them by offering a "limited to stock on hand" sale.

Ask for the Sale

Don't forget to ask for the order. A simple statement like "Click the Buy It Now! button to get this delivered to your door ASAP" helps direct your buyer to the next step.

Incentives

One way to leverage all the work you've done to get customers into your listing is to give them a value-added bonus. Incentives and rewards, or loyalty programs, are used everywhere these days. Think of the local espresso stand. Any coffee stand that plans on being around for a while gives its customers a punch card for a free drink when the card is filled. Many supermarkets give customers cards that entitle them to discounts on items. Airlines give mileage points to frequent flyers. You can do something similar for your customers as well.

My Store Rewards: A Customer Loyalty Club

You can set up your own rebate incentive program or get a little help. One company found in the eBay Services Directory is MyStoreRewards. Using this application, it takes only a few minutes to set up and launch the buyer rewards program.

How does it work? Your buyers have the choice to join your MyStoreRewards (www.mystorerewards.com) program though an invitation link on your checkout page or in an e-mail in return for a cash reward (generally 1 to 2 percent of the payment total). When buyers return to make repeat purchases, they also get repeat rewards.

Another incentive might be a bonus report printed out on your home printer or burned onto a CD. If you want to really knock the socks off your buyers, offer them a how-to DVD. Production costs are minimal for burning DVDs with today's home computer and video technology.

Combined Shipping

Upselling or cross-selling is part of marketing as well. Offer combined shipping on more than one purchase. Buyers like to save on shipping and will oftentimes buy more than one item from you if you offer to reduce the total postage cost by shipping all items in one box.

THE PERSONAL TOUCH

Another, more personal, way to create an incentive is done by an eBayer at Joni's Red Onion. She sells sewing patterns and knows that buyers are likely to purchase many at a time if they are told they can combine shipping. Not only does she state that she'll combine shipping in every listing, if Joni is online and she sees a customer in her store and purchasing, she'll send the person an e-mail in which she tells them that she's at her computer and can answer questions. She invites them to look around and have a virtual cup of tea. If they find more patterns to purchase, she can fit up to fifty in one flat-rate box. She lets them know they have up to a week to fill the box, and when they're done shopping to just let her know. This tactic has been highly successful. Her post office can verify how many flat-rate boxes she sends out.

The suggestions outlined in this section motivate customers to purchase from you. When you sit down to write your listings, put a sticky note on your computer monitor to remind you to showcase benefits over features and always tell your buyers WIIFM. Then prompt them into the purchase by offering the best pricing strategy to get them to click the Buy It Now! button. Savvy sellers know that this recipe, along with a few incentives and rewards, gets buyers to not only make the first purchase but continue to look around your store to purchase more.

Building Your Brand in Five Easy Steps

Once upon a time, it was difficult to build a marketing brand on eBay because each product listing was unique and different. A seller would create listings in several different eBay product categories, and there was no effective way to tie them together in a single place so buyers could see everything you had to offer. Of course, sellers could adopt a recognizable template for their eBay listings, and buyers were free to search a seller's user ID to find everything the seller had listed at a given time (by bookmarking a favorite user ID in the Favorite Sellers section of their My eBay page, buyers could receive notices when these sellers put up new merchandise for sale), but this became cumbersome for sellers, who wanted to create individual brand identities within eBay. Thus, several years ago, the eBay Store was born.

An eBay Store is a webpage within the eBay site that is dedicated to the merchandise of a single seller. As such, an eBay Store serves two important functions: It ties together all of the seller's listings on eBay and it gives the seller the opportunity to offer merchandise in fixed-price (Buy It Now!) listings that are available only in the seller's eBay Store. These listings are commonly referred to as the seller's "eBay Store inventory" or just "store inventory."

The question is not "Why should I have an eBay Store"; it is "How can I make my buyers remember my eBay ID so they can buy from me again?" One of the best, most effective ways to do that is to have an eBay Store. The powerful eBay back end ensures that sellers receive top rankings from the search engines. However, you can do more to create a positive experience for your shoppers. Let's talk about building a brand that will make your customers stand up and take notice, while keeping your store at the top of search engine rankings.

Store Design

To get your buyers to stop and notice that your store is exceptional, you must brand it with a unique look. Janelle Elms, former eBay University instructor and visionary of membership site OSI Rock Stars, tells clients that it's about the experience.

She starts by asking them to visualize a coffee bean and how much it costs to make a cup of coffee at home.

"Take that same bean over to Starbucks; then how much does that cup of coffee cost?" she follows up.

Then: "And how much does it cost in a square in Venice, Italy?"

Her point is that while the price of the coffee bean is the same, what buyers pay extra for is an experience. Buyers will pay extra for an experience when shopping with you as well. Even on eBay you can create that unique experience by customizing your store.

Before we get into the mechanics of customizing a store, here's a quick primer on design and color.

Designs are best kept simple. Your logo should be a symbol that is quickly recognizable as yours. Everyone recognizes the Nike swoosh. It's not because it's intricate or colorful—it's simple. With most software programs it's easy to make beautiful, delicate patterns and flourishes, but they just don't render well on a monitor or business card. Look at your design—does it convey your brand at a glance?

What are the colors in your store telling customers? A bright yellow might be your favorite color, but it has a dark side. A negative connotation of the color yellow is the perception of cheapness. Colors play a very important role in design. Select your theme color carefully to create the right feel for your store.

Here is a list of colors and some examples of their associations:

Reds: positive—love and warmth; negative—danger and anger

Blues: positive—power and professionalism; negative—boredom and sadness

Greens: positive—nature and money; negative—decay and illness

Oranges: positive—creativity and fun; negative—cheap

Purples: positive—royalty and luxury; negative—craziness

Yellows: positive—creativity and fun; negative—cheap

Use colors that complement each other. Colors that work well together convey harmony to viewers and project confidence. If you are unsure about color matches, check out eBay's color wheel at http://pages.ebay.com/storefronts/designdodont.html#colorwheel.

Step #1: Create a Logo

The first step in customizing your store is to create a logo. You can select from a few predesigned logos available from eBay, which are simple clip art. They aren't very noteworthy, and few sellers profit from using one in their store. Do you want your customers to think of you as the corner barista or as the person selling coffee from the back of the snack truck? Replace that prefab logo! If you want to set your store apart, create a logo that represents who you are. You can use a graphics program, hire a designer, or use an online service like LogoYes.com, where you can create a logo for around $100 that will look professional and be sized perfectly for an eBay store.

Keep in mind the specific graphic size when you are creating the logo. It must be a maximum pixel size of 310 (width) by 90 (height). If your graphic does not fit or is not proportional to these dimensions, it will be resized or stretched.

The file must have one of the following extensions: .jpg, .jpeg, .gif, .bmp, or .png.

To add the logo to your store header:

1. Go to Manage My Store.

2. Navigate to Display Settings.

3. Click the Change link on the Basic Settings.

4. Upload your graphic to Picture Manager.

5. After it's put into Picture Manager, go back and click on Select from Picture Manager.

6. Click Save Settings.

Congratulations! You now have your logo in your store design.

Step #2: Choose Your Template

Choosing the correct eBay Store template is important for building a custom design and attracting the search engine spiders that drive traffic to your store (called *search engine optimization,* or SEO). When you sign up for a store, you are given several template choices. There are many to choose from, but not all give you the maximum flexibility and SEO you want on eBay. The good news is that if you have already picked a template, you may change it at any time without losing any of your customized work (e.g., custom pages and store title). Navigate to the display setting inside the eBay Store to change the store template. Click on the link Change to Another Theme.

The themes that are the best picks are those that allow you to describe your store, your merchandise inventory, and yourself, using keywords that will attract search engine traffic. Choose Classic Top, Classic Left, or Easy Customizable. There is a drop-down menu below each that allows you to choose a color theme. See Figure 2.6.

Step #3: Make a Custom Header

Another way to make your store stand out is to create a custom header for it. See Figure 2.7 for an example of a store designed with a customer header.

A custom header is simple to create and sets your store apart as a unique shop-

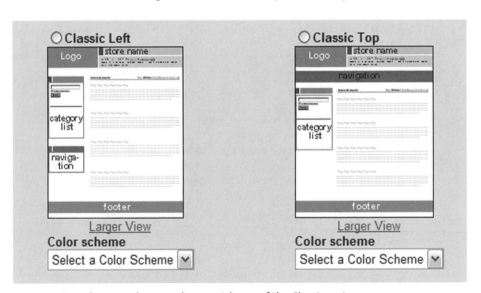

FIGURE 2.6   When you choose a theme, pick one of the Classic series.

FIGURE 2.7 Dandy Rubber Stamps and Crafts is a destination created by customizing the store header (http://stores.ebay.com/Dandy-Rubber-Stamps-and-Crafts).

ping destination. This is a powerful marketing and branding tool that most sellers never use. It is surprising because there are so few ways to set yourself apart from others on eBay, and this one is so simple.

There are several ways to create a custom header:

1. **Create your own HTML and add it to your store.** Use an editor like Front-Page or Dreamweaver, or use the eBay-provided HTML to create the design.

2. **Hire an eBay Stores Certified Designer.** You can find one at http://pages .ebay.com/storefronts/designdirectory.html. There are many designers who will work with you to customize your header, within a wide price range. Shop around, get a few quotes, and ask for samples of their work.

3. **Use an eBay-provided design template.** You can find one at http://pages .ebay.com/storefronts/headerdesign.html. These templates are designed to

feature products in the header. The designs showcase your products, items just in, best sellers, and so forth. The headers are simple to set up and customizable. When you are finished customizing the header, you cut and paste into the provided code.

Should you go below the fold? And what does that mean?

Above the fold and *below the fold* are old newspaper terms that are now equally applicable to websites and eBay stores. In newspaper lingo, *above the fold* refers to stories that appear above the fold when the newspaper is folded in half—these are the articles buyers see when they browse a newsstand. The most sensational articles and the biggest headlines appear above the fold to lure potential buyers into purchasing the newspaper. More mundane secondary articles appear below the fold.

To translate that into Web marketing terms, *above the fold* means the area that comes into view on a computer screen without having to scroll down. This is the prime real estate. On average, a visitor decides to either stay or click out of the page within three seconds, so what you place above the fold on your webpage is important because it might be all the visitor sees. It must be concise and eye-catching. You don't want your customers to have to scroll down to read the whole message because most people don't scroll.

Never create a custom header that either scrolls below the first fold or goes off the side of the monitor. If you are creating your own HTML header, preview it in different monitor resolutions. Check it on different browsers as well, because, for example, Firefox displays much differently than Internet Explorer.

Step #4: Set Up Your Promotion Boxes and Newsletter Sign-up

Each eBay Store gets four promotion boxes on the landing page. The promotion boxes are the little boxes on the top and sides of the page that say things like "newly listed" and "ending soonest." There are two spots for them above the fold, which are prime spots for grabbing your viewers' attention. The other two are on the left navigation bar.

To set up your promo boxes:

1. Navigate to Promotion Boxes inside Manage My Store.

2. Click on Create A New Promotion Box.

3. The guided setup walks you through setting up these boxes for landing pages as well as category-specific promo boxes.

If you want to design and customize the promo boxes, you can use your own HTML. When you use HTML, choose the Communicate with Your Buyers template option.

Set your store apart by customizing it ASAP. Those "newly listed" boxes are so common that they are just more white noise to your buyers. Promo boxes can be changed to highlight your store inventory and invite buyers to subscribe to your newsletter. Another promo box template that eBay provides is the countdown timer. This one gives your customers a *reason to act*—especially if they see that the auction on a particular item they want is ending within a few minutes.

One of the most attractive features of eBay Stores is the ability to publish e-newsletters and send them several times a month to your customers (e-newsletters are discussed in detail in Chapter 4). There are a few things to consider when you set up an eBay Store if you plan to offer your buyers an e-newsletter.

Give your newsletter sign-up top billing. On your landing page, be sure the Newsletter Sign-up promotional box is prominent and highlighted so people can't miss it. The promo boxes above the fold potentially get the most eyeballs, so use one to collect newsletter subscribers. (See Figure 2.8.) One of the most

FIGURE 2.8   Alice has an above-the-fold promo box set up to capture names of newsletter subscribers (http://stores.ebay.com/Stitches-Quilts-Fabrics-Gifts).

ONE OVERLOOKED MARKETING STRATEGY

If you are selling items in your eBay Store across several of eBay's product categories, did you know you can customize your promo boxes for each category? This is a great way to cross-promote and highlight new products, add information, or get customers to buy more stuff from you. How about a customized promo box with links to complementary items in other categories? For example, a promo box for a Bill Clinton mechanical bank in the Toys category could also reference a Bill Clinton political campaign button you have for sale under Political Americana. One eBay seller we noticed recently created a three-sentence tutorial about the product in the category. Other uses for the box could be to promote category-specific sales. For more information, go to the following webpage in eBay's Help section: http://pages.ebay.com/help/sell/promoting-your-store.html.

---

powerful tools a marketer has for building loyal customers is the newsletter. That's why you need to be sure the sign-up is prominent on this page. We know it's tempting to create one of those flashy scrolling item displays that eBay offers up at the top. However, you are better off getting customers to sign up for your newsletter. You must make it easy for them to find a Subscribe link. To encourage their participation and grant you access to their e-mail inboxes, offer them something special—for example: *Sign up and receive a free report on the history of blue willow china.*

Make the offer compelling enough that people will want to subscribe to your newsletter. Offer them a free report, a free membership, an interview, a podcast, or even just the chance to "be the first to know . . ." The better you can make the offer, the quicker you'll build your list. Marketers call this an *ethical bribe*. Tell them what's in it for them.

Step #5: Use a Listing Frame

To help your buyers navigate easily through your store, eBay provides a *listing frame*, also called a *banner* or *store banner*. By clicking on this, your buyers can see at a glance the merchandise you are offering in your store, along with a thumbnail directory of the store. A listing header includes the following items:

- Your eBay Store name
- Your eBay Store logo

- A link that allows buyers to add you to their Favorite Stores

- Up to fourteen category tabs, each one displaying up to five of your listings when clicked

- Your eBay Store search box

- A link that allows buyers to sign up for your newsletters

- A marketing message that you can customize for different types of buyers

An example of a store listing frame appears in Figure 2.9. You can insert your custom logo at the top of each listing along with links to sale items, custom pages, terms of service pages, or Frequently Asked Questions (FAQs). This gives your customers quick and easy access to other parts of your store while branding each listing.

The store listing frame allows you to include your store categories along the left side of each listing as well. This is a simple way to keep customers in your store as they search for more items, rather than losing them when they click out of a listing.

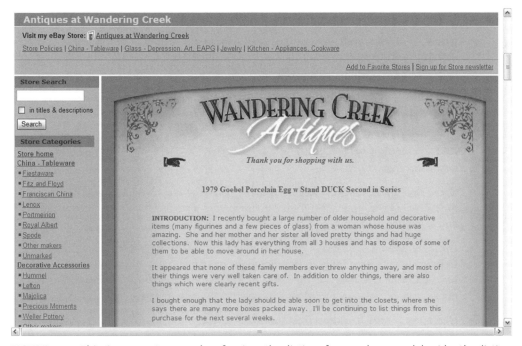

FIGURE 2.9 This is a great example of using the listing frame above and beside the listing (http://stores.ebay.com/Antiques-at-Wandering-Creek).

To set up the listing frame:

1. Navigate to the Manage My Store area.

2. On the left-hand side, under Store Marketing, look for the Listing Frame link.

3. Choose your options.

Select the links to pages you want to include in the listing header. These can be anything from custom pages about the products to popular store categories. It's always a good idea to also include a newsletter sign-up and a store search box. The easier and more convenient you can make it for your buyers, the better. In-

---

WHEN IT'S TIME TO HIRE AN eBAY STORE DESIGNER

Once you've decided to spruce up your landing page and brand your store with a unique look, it's time to hire a designer. Designers can create something that turns your eBay page into a "Wow!" experience. However, most designers are artists at heart. You'll have a much better partnership if you keep a few things in mind:

- **Know what you want.** A store designer can create a wonderful design for your store, but the more information you can provide about your desired look and feel, the closer they'll come to matching your idea.

- **Store designers are not business consultants.** There may be some crossover, but generally designers help brand your store, not list your items or advise you on the best selling strategy.

- **Store designers need time to be creative.** Don't expect them to come up with a design too fast.

- **Store designers love to design!** That's good—but rein them in if they sacrifice functionality for a pretty look. It's not going to improve sales if your customers can't find where to click to buy.

- **Store designers are always going to make things pretty, but they are not able to judge what's best for your business.** For example, if they suggest that the store newsletter link won't work in their design and you know the most effective place to put it is on top, negotiate. Business comes before appearance in most cases.

- **Use eBay Stores Certified Designers.** They'll know the specifics about what type of coding is allowed under eBay's policies.

clude the Add to Favorite Stores link, and buyers will automatically receive regular updates from eBay about your store. Of course, you should keep in touch with your mailing list directly, but it's nice to know that eBay is helping.

If you follow the five steps outlined here, you will have your own unique shopping destination. These steps can be completed by anyone. Devote a little time to it each day, and soon you'll have a unique, customized store that tells your customers you mean business.

Bonus Step

There is one more step that you might consider: creating a unique landing page. This can change your store from just another corner coffee shop to that romantic café in Italy.

This alternative takes extra work, or extra money, but it can result in a compelling experience for your buyers. A professionally designed landing page, combined with quality merchandise and service, creates an impression similar to that of a major retailing site—in short, it's not just another eBay Store.

To customize your store landing page, use HTML. Java and Flash are not allowed. If you don't have knowledge of HTML, hire a store designer. A poorly designed landing page can hurt sales, so if you are going to use one, do it right.

When customers click on the link to enter your store, they are directed to the store landing page. If you want your customers to feel like they are walking in the front door of a unique boutique, here is your chance to shine. Creating a custom store entry page is one of the simplest ways to give your customers that "showbiz" feeling. If you want your buyers to look at your eBay Store as a unique place to shop, you must provide them with a unique experience.

There is a downside to the customized store. The unique experience you strive to create may also cause confusion. On eBay, customers navigate through stores in a certain way, based on the standard setup. If you create a landing page that is too complex, you run the risk of losing buyers simply because they don't understand where to click. Make sure your custom design incorporates clickable links that are easy to find quickly and easy to use. You do not want to break buyer momentum. If they have to spend more than a few seconds searching for the category, shoppers will leave.

Information and templates designed to spruce up your store landing page can be found on eBay at http://pages.ebay.com/storefronts/designcenter.html. They are clean and simple designs, but they will display your items nicely.

The eBay award-winning store designers at Pixclinic have just released

Pronto, a simple-to-use way to create your own customized home page. For a one-time fee you can create as many store landing pages as you wish. Find them at http://www.pixclinic.com/pronto/.

To activate the new landing page once you have created the HTML, navigate to the Manage My Store area and you'll find Custom Pages under the Store Design area on the left. Create the custom page by clicking on the Create button. For the customized home page, elect the Text Selection/Html template, then cut and paste your design code into the dialog box under the HTML tab (see Figure 2.10).

To set it as the store landing page, use the drop-down menu next to the title of each custom page.

Once you have completed these steps, you will have set yourself apart from the crowd and come a long way toward building your brand. But don't stop there! Take advantage of some of the other marketing tools provided to you as an eBay Store owner. The next section looks at how to maximize your Web presence using the eBay Store.

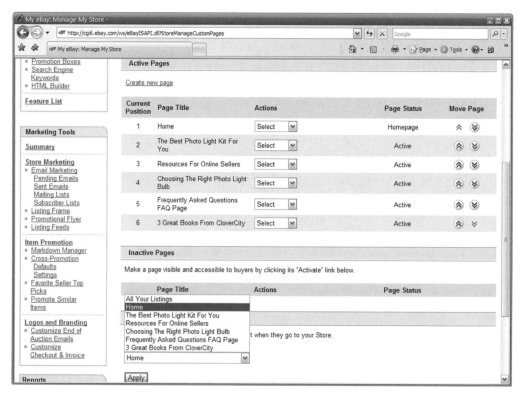

FIGURE 2.10   Use Custom Pages to activate your new store landing page.

eBay Listing Upgrades

A basic, no-frills eBay listing consists of just an item description, a photo of the item, the price at which the seller is offering the item, and one or two other details. To give eBay sellers the opportunity (for an additional fee) to make their listings stand out from other sellers' listings, eBay offers a host of listing upgrades (and charges for them). Perhaps the best-known (and most frequently used) listing upgrade is the option to have your listing appear in color in the eBay search engine results. Since most listings appear in black and white, a purple listing jumps or pops out at buyers. For a solid introduction to the currently available listing upgrades, go to the following page in eBay's Help section: http://pages.ebay.com/ help/sell/promoting_ov.html.

The various upgrades offer additional marketing value, but which ones bring maximum value for your marketing money? If you don't budget, the costs start to eat away at your profits. In this section, let's take a look at these extra features and determine which ones are best for you.

Before deciding which marketing upgrades to use, refer to your marketing budget. Consider these upgrades a part of your marketing strategy. When you determine how much to spend on the upgrades, consider the final value you expect to receive for the item. If the upgrade is 2 percent or less of the final value, the feature should be considered.

Subtitle

A subtitle goes under the main title on the search page. That little line gives your listing some extra visual real estate. However, the subtitle is not keyword searchable. Even though the subtitle has no search value, this marketing workhorse is a wonderful feature. There are a number of uses for the subtitle.

Branding your business with the subtitle gives you a lead on the competition. Let's say you are a consignment seller who specializes in a certain industry. You can make it easy for repeat purchasers to find you while scanning through the listings by using a simple subtitle like this:

Another great auction by ABC Trading Company

The subtitle can help qualify your item as well. If you are selling in a competitive market, use it to state a benefit or feature. Your competitors may have the same product with the same features, but remember that customers are time starved. If buyers notice your subtitle stating that your product includes XYZ, they will zero in on your listing first.

International Sales

Offering international shipping is a great marketing practice. Sellers in the United States can expect about a 13 percent increase in bidding activity or interest in items if offered internationally. If you make your products available to Canadian shoppers, you are likely to see an increased sell-through rate of about 6 percent.

It's estimated that about 44 percent of eBay users are outside the United States. The more countries you offer your products to, the higher your sell-through rate will be. In the United States, eBay offers sellers the ability to market their goods across international platforms. For instance, you can list your item directly on the United Kingdom's site for more exposure. Listing on international sites costs extra, but in some product categories you'll find a significant increase in sales.

Gallery Plus

When you use Gallery Plus, an Enlarge icon is displayed right below your Gallery image on search results pages. Buyers can click or hover over the icon with their mouse, and a larger version of the picture appears (up to 400 by 400 pixels, depending on the original size of the picture). This feature allows browsers to quickly see a clearer photo of the item to determine their interest.

Gift Icon

Add the little gift icon at the end of your listing title as a way to upsell your buyers. Rushed customers will happily pay a little extra to have you wrap their gifts and send them to the recipients.

You could build a whole group of services around this and offer customers a pick-and-choose service. For a price, they could customize their gift cards (you could print them out on your color printer), their gift wrapping, and the delivery method.

Buyers just might love shopping with you for all their gifts.

Bold Print

This feature displays your title in bold print. In theory it helps your listing to stand out from the rest, but this is not usually a recommended feature upgrade. However, if you use the highlight upgrade, you should make your headline bold as well to ensure that it's readable to viewers as they skim down the page.

Borders

This feature attracts buyers' attention by putting a purple frame around the title of your listing. This adds more visual real estate and draws a buyer's eye directly into your title.

Highlighting

A highlight displays your title as blue text against a purple (instead of white) background. It works to draw a viewer's eye; however, it is often overused. When everyone else in the category is using it, the highlight becomes more noise to screen out.

Featured Plus!

When a buyer searches for an item, the best match sort brings back the results. Depending on search algorithms to pinpoint your listings is chancy. For a really important product, you can pay extra to have your listing show at the top of the search results, above the best match items.

Gallery Featured

If you purchase this upgrade, your listing will periodically appear in the special Featured section above the gallery of search results (known as the General Gallery or Gallery), and your picture will be almost double the size of nonfeatured Gallery pictures. Your listing will also appear in the General Gallery.

Home Page Featured

This feature gives you eBay front-page exposure, displayed in a rotating sequence at the bottom of the page, below the fold, so buyers will have to scroll down to see the listings. Considering the high price, this upgrade seems worthless. The eBay home page is generally slow to load, and most people click right off it and onto the search box or into their My eBay listings. We've found no conversion rate data on this feature published on the Web. Your advertising dollar is better spent elsewhere.

All of the features we've discussed in this section are designed to make your listing stand out from the competition. Research your category and the completed listings before purchasing any upgrade. If all your competitors are using the same upgrade, then using it isn't going to make your item stand out. These features should make your listing stand out from the crowd, not disappear into it. And remember, any upgrade that costs more than 2 percent of the expected final value will probably fail to pay for itself. To justify the added expense, a feature upgrade has to boost profits as well as attract attention.

Using Your eBay Store Custom Pages to Generate Search Engine Traffic

An Introduction to Search Engine Optimization (SEO)

A lot of people are confused about search engine marketing, but it's really very simple. If you have ever searched for information or products online using any of the major search engines such as Google or Yahoo!, you were presented with a search results page that contained a list of webpages that matched your search inquiry (called the *organic* or *natural* search results). Why did the search engine pick those pages to show you and not any others?

The answer is that those webpages were *optimized* for the search engines. Twenty-four hours a day, seven days a week, the search engines send out little pieces of software called *bots* or *spiders* (because they "troll the Web"—get it?), that look for new pieces of information. When the spider looks at a webpage, it looks for specific text, known as *keywords*, and assigns the webpage to one or more *indexes* based on the keywords it sees. When you search one or more of the keywords, the search engine shows you the index with the most closely matched results that the spiders came up with.

Search engine optimization (SEO) is simply the process of selecting the right keywords that you want the search engine spiders to see and making sure those keywords appear in as many places in your eBay store as possible. Have you ever searched for something on the Web and an eBay store popped up in the first ten listings? If you've had that experience, you are dealing with an eBay seller who has mastered the art of SEO.

SEO is a pretty complicated topic, and picking the right keywords can often be as much an art as a science. Our two favorite books on SEO (other than ones we've written ourselves, of course) were written by Catherine Seda, the former Internet marketing columnist for *Entrepreneur* magazine; the titles are *Search Engine Advertising* and *How to Win Sales & Influence Spiders,* and they should be part of any basic library of books on Internet marketing.

Using Custom Pages

As a store owner, you can make use of a number of eBay-provided custom pages. The higher the store subscription you have, the more custom pages you are allotted. Sellers don't seem to know what to do with these gems. Let's talk about how you can take advantage of the hidden power of these pages.

There are two marketing reasons why you should make use of your custom pages.

1. **By providing solutions or answers to the questions buyers have about a product, you could win their purchase.** According to the May 2007 Harris Interactive Online Retail Report (http://www.rightnow.com/pdf/Online-Retail-Report.pdf), one attribute that stood out in delivering a successful online experience was fast access to information. The report found that 57 percent of consumers "always" or "often" research products or services online before they make a purchase. If you use your custom pages as an information point to drive researching customers into your store, they are just one button away from purchasing from you.

2. **A huge part of Web marketing is helping clients find you among the crowd by using SEO.** One place to do this is through the custom pages. Before creating a custom page, let's talk a little bit more about SEO. While the search engine algorithms are secret and change constantly and we can't say specifically how Google, Yahoo!, or MSN index sites work, we have noticed a few patterns. One pattern the indexing sites seem to follow when ranking a page is something called *keyword density.* The spiders come to the page and

crawl the site, reading the words in the text. They then match up the title and headers with incidences of words used throughout the article. If they find relevant words or phrases, the spiders conclude that the article has authority and gives it a higher ranking.

Don't confuse this with keyword stuffing. The search engine robots are programmed to catch cheating spammers who use certain words over and over again to rank higher. If you have a good, keyword-rich title and then write about your product or service using the keywords associated with it, you should rank well. If you try to game the system, the indexing sites will drop you like a stone.

Creating and Making the Most of Custom Pages

The custom pages offered by eBay come with several templates you can take advantage of if you aren't comfortable with design or Web authoring. There are highly customizable pages as well. Your imagination is the limit for these pages. Let's explore a few of the uses to help build your brand and market your store.

Store Landing Page

We discussed this feature previously. One of your store custom pages can be devoted to creating your unique store landing page. You should work with your designer to decide whether you prefer to use a custom header to brand your store or create a unique display of your items when a visitor lands in your store. Figure 2.11 shows how you can create a unique shopping experience by turning the landing page into a custom-designed layout.

Terms of Service

Sellers who don't have a store can put their terms of service (TOS) on their About Me page, which we discussed previously. The problem with trying to get all the information about your store onto one page is that it becomes cluttered and most buyers don't want to scroll down and wade through a lot of information. They just want to know whether you'll take a return and who will pay the shipping on returns. To make it easy for your shoppers, create a TOS page for them.

FIGURE 2.11 Worldwide Traders Online uses a custom page as its store landing page (http://stores .ebay.com/worldwide-traders-online).

Frequently Asked Questions

You can use an eBay-provided template for your frequently asked questions (FAQs) page. Use it to answer the most-asked questions you receive. Whether you use the template or create your own, this page is important. It instantly answers your customers' questions, and it helps build SEO. Because these FAQs pages have many instances of phrases relating to your store (keyword density), they do wonders for getting your store indexed. It's a good idea to make sure your listing frame is turned on and the category selection is placed on the left-hand side. If your FAQs page gets highly ranked, the rest of the links on the page will be boosted as well because they are linked to an authority page. An authority page, or site, is one that the indexing sites consider the best of the Web. These pages are the ones being pointed to as the experts in their niche, and thus they get top index ranking.

Do not just make up questions that you think customers might ask. You don't know—you are not a customer. Copy and paste the multitude of e-mailed questions received from bidders and buyers into a file. Remove any personal identifiers such as name or e-mail address, unless you get specific permission to use them. Use the questions exactly as they were asked—don't try to change them. (Okay, you can change spelling, but even that is iffy.) Your FAQs page should read as though the questions came from other shoppers, not from you. This gives your readers a sense that the questions are authentic. Guess what that does? It helps build your customers' confidence.

How-to Pages

If you have a product that requires more than the instruction manual provides, use a custom page as a guide for your customers. For instance, a camera manual is pretty comprehensive, but it really doesn't tell you how to get pretty pictures during your vacation. Custom pages with tips on photo composition, instructions for getting cute pictures of the grandchildren, or a list of the accessories all photographers need are all relevant, keyword-rich, and highly ranked subjects. Figure 2.12 is an example of how-to information on a custom page.

Product Comparison Pages

If you carry an item that comes in a variety of styles, a product comparison page will help confused customers. You can compare the products side-by-side and tell your customers which item works best for each purpose. This aids shoppers who may not know what to ask to get the appropriate style for them.

A comparison like this helps make the sale and keep returns to a minimum. It builds trust in your store as an authority. It does one more thing: It can help up-sell your customers. Telling them why they should pay for certain features by showing them the facts helps them make informed decisions. If shoppers know clearly why one product type is better than another, they will often choose the better one, regardless of the added cost. Buyers want the best they can afford. Have you ever heard someone say they would prefer a Ford Aspire to a BMW?

Size Charts

Clothing, shoes, backpacks, and car seat covers are all items that require sizing. Creating a size chart page gives your customers instant access to the information they need to find the correct size.

FIGURE 2.12   An instructional custom page for those who wonder how to tell whether they've got genuine Bakelite (http://stores.ebay.com/bakelite-johnny's/how-to-test-for-bakelite.html).

These size charts, if done via text rather than an image, are keyword searchable. So take the time to create an HTML table with clear labels and a keyword-rich title. If a customer is wondering what size widget to use for a project, it's very likely your custom page size chart will show in the search engine results.

Sale Pages

Pick one of the four templates available in the custom page section to highlight product sales. These custom pages can be turned on and off quickly. You can create a page to promote the latest items on sale so that customers are one click away from your biggest sale items. When the sale is over, turn off the custom page so that it is available for other uses and promotions in the future.

Glossary Pages

A list of the terms associated with your industry make a great custom page. Create a glossary to explain technical terms or jargon associated with your product. This keyword-rich page is solid gold in the search engines.

There are many ways to take advantage of the eBay custom pages. Don't let them go unused. When it comes to helping customers by having easily accessible answers to their questions, these are powerful pages. And, of course, these pages are SEO workhorses when you remember to use keywords and phrases that are relevant to your store.

Do You Need More Than One Store?

Sooner or later, you will be selling more than one type of merchandise on eBay. Sometimes the items will be related—for example, an antiques store might offer a selection of antique furniture, toys, and books. Each of these items would be listed in different product categories on eBay, but all fall under the general category of Antiques. In this situation, a single eBay Store might be a useful way to tie together the different offerings and cross-promote items from one category that buyers in another category might not see.

However, sometimes the items will not be related—they will be directed toward radically different markets. If you are selling Hummel figurines and hunting equipment, you are trying to reach very different folks, and by combining these items in a single store you are sending a very confused message to your marketplace. In this situation, it's probably best to have separate stores for the figurines and the crossbows.

Identifying Your Niches

Don't get us wrong—there is nothing illegal, immoral, or fattening about pursuing unrelated markets. It's similar to diversifying your investment portfolio. Diversification is important if you hope to retire to Hawaii instead of spending your retirement working at McDonald's.

Let's look at what a niche is. Most niches are *not* narrowly defined as *one or two products.* A niche can include a wide variety of items. Think of your local bicycle shop. Inside you'll find bikes and more. A really good bicycle store offers grease cleaner for your fingernails, spare parts, bags and backpacks for riders, clothes, shoes, energy bars and drinks, books on where to ride, magazines for enthusiasts, lights for night rides, and more. A niche is not necessarily as narrowly defined as, to extend our example, selling only bicycle fenders for rainy climates.

A really good niche keeps you constantly learning and growing. Every year new technology makes ascending a hill easier for bicyclists or introduces a new breathable material for clothing for long summer rides. Sellers who focus on one niche are able to answer customer questions knowledgably—customers flock to specialty shops for answers to questions about products. In order to buy massive inventory, the really big sellers, such as Target and Walmart, often cut corners when it comes to hiring help. Many customers abandon those big box stores in favor of smaller mom-and-pop stores where the staff is knowledgeable enough to answer simple questions about the merchandise they are selling.

Savvy sellers also understand trends in the marketplace—which items to avoid this season and which items will be hot for the next season. You might be able to drill down into research about what the trends were last month by using software programs provided by eBay and third-party vendors, but it's still the human element that makes a successful retail buyer.

Department stores have been successful for decades by selling across multiple product niches. Target, Walmart, Kmart, and others very effectively brand themselves. In fact, they are so successful that it has made competing against them nearly impossible. That's why specialty boutiques have become the best way to succeed in business if you are a small retailer. Performance Bike has successfully built its brand as the bicycle shop of choice in eleven states and online. Over the last twenty-five years Performance Bike has successfully sold in their niche, even though you can find plenty of bicycles at Walmart, Kmart, Toys "R" Us and other department stores. This is an example of why you should consider setting up multiple niche stores instead of a single store where everything is sold under one store name.

Consignment Sales (or "Whatever I Can Get I Sell")

Let's say that you don't have a niche. Like many eBay sellers, especially in the Antiques and Collectibles categories, you take consignments for sale on eBay (for example, as an eBay Trading Assistant) and have a variety of types of products for sale at any time that are constantly changing. Should you have a single eBay store or multiple stores?

The answer is . . . "it depends." We've seen many successful sellers who sell everything under the sun in a single eBay Store. They've branded their store as "Consignment Sellers," but their eBay customers tend not to be repeat customers—they search eBay for specific items (not the store) and buy only when the store has that particular item for sale.

But a new trend is emerging among consignment sellers: They too are specializing in a select few niche products. For example, author Cindy Shebley accepts only photo and camera equipment for consignment in her eBay Store. When she accepts consignments, they fit naturally into her store because she sells to that niche market; people looking for quality photo and camera equipment bookmark her store and check out her inventory frequently. This gives her repeat customers—not only eBay buyers who purchase that type of equipment, but also people looking to consign camera equipment for sale—these folks usually have more inventory to sell over time as they grow and expand their hobby or business. If you give them a good experience on eBay, they will be certain to come back for more.

If you happen to be in the lucky (or unlucky) situation of having an eclectic (or just plain weird) mix of inventory, you might benefit from having more than one store. It's a great idea to keep widely different products separate to help brand each eBay store. Chances are, though, you'll find that trying to purchase complete product lines for multiple stores eats up your time and capital. Although the focus of this book is on eBay, if you are considering multiple stores, perhaps instead you might consider selling more of the same product in more than one online venue. There are several alternative sites to sell on (such as Amazon and Yahoo!), and many buyers don't cross over. You'll reach more customers and be able to improve your purchasing power by ordering in larger quantities. You can rest assured that there is always more inventory that fits into your niche if you've chosen correctly.

Building Multiple Brands Versus a Single Brand

As an eBay seller, you should very carefully consider your business plan. Who exactly do you want to be and what exactly do you want to sell? There are many large businesses on eBay that have large staffs, tremendous buying power, and lots of storage room. They can blanket the listings on eBay with their deep-inventory strategy. But is that you? Most sellers start out with an idea, a computer, a little storage space (usually a spare bedroom or closet), and limited capital. Most eBay sellers start small and focus on one niche or product type.

Starting a store takes money. As you begin the process of opening your store and hiring a designer to create a brand, your capital starts to dwindle. It's a good idea to automate your eBay Store as much as possible, so you can focus on the other tasks of running a business; thus, it's better to have a featured store than a basic store. That's a $50 investment (per store, if you plan on multiples). The second or third $50 store could pay for a storage unit to hold more products—which would help you build depth of inventory.

When you start purchasing inventory, you'll quickly notice that most suppliers reward stores with lower prices for purchasing more of each stock-keeping unit (SKU). Here's where trying to purchase in multiple niches starts eating away at your overall brand. If you can't purchase at a competitive price, then it is very hard to resell at a competitive price. And even though you don't need to be the lowest-price seller on eBay, you do need to keep prices in line with those of other retailers. On an even more practical business level, the more you spend on inventory, the less capital you have to purchase other inventory. Unless you are a Rockefeller, you'll have no (or limited) credit. It is hard to purchase enough inventory to build one niche, let alone two or three.

You'll find that most lucrative niches have many branches that you can explore. A vitamin and supplement store may find that organic foods fit its niche well and work within the same branded store. The seller is also much more likely to be accepted by the supplier/distributor as a reseller if he or she demonstrates a history of selling similar items. Not only does this mean that the supplier will sell to this store owner, but if he or she can supply references in a similar industry, this seller is much more likely to get terms (or credit). This helps the seller build a niche and increase sales by bringing in new customers (now this seller has customers for the organic foods as well as for the supplements).

To find your perfect niche store, think "lifestyle" instead of a specific Google search term. You are much more likely to find repeat customers when you sell something that involves your client personally. A person who purchases organic products is much more likely to come back and purchase from you again than the buyer who is Googling the search term "acai berry." This is where branding truly comes into play. That Google searcher might be looking for acai berry juice because she's heard it's nutritious and wants to see whether it gives her more energy. If she lands in your store and sees you are an organic products retailer, that may or may not persuade her to purchase from you, depending on her view of organics. Some people still consider organic products to be akin to voodoo. That customer may decide to purchase from you this time, despite the association with voodoo. But unless she makes a real commitment to purchasing only organics, she may never return. However, a vegan customer who comes looking for organic acai berry juice, finds your store, and sees your wide array of products, logo, and branding built around the organics theme knows he's found a place to return again and again. That's the beauty of branding and niche marketing. It's about finding those customers who fit the products you are selling into their lifestyle choices.

Using Drop Shippers to Build an eBay Business

What if you are working exclusively with drop shippers to build your eBay business? For those new to eBay, *drop shippers* are those who allow you to sell their inventory on eBay—you list their merchandise, collect the purchase price or winning bid, keep your commission, and remit the rest to the drop shipper, who ships the item to the buyer directly from the warehouse.

You might have heard that by using drop-ship companies you can obtain an endless cash flow with a minimum outlay. Unfortunately, many gurus proclaim the easiest way to Internet riches is to use drop-ship programs. Here's the problem: It is very hard to just type "drop shipper," into a search engine and find a reliable one. Along the same line, it is very hard to buy a subscription to a wholesale or drop-ship resource that other eBay sellers haven't already tried. If you do find a reliable drop-ship source or a membership site, chances are that some unsophisticated sellers before you have diluted the market by using bad business practices. The earlier sellers might have decided they needed only a few pennies' profit instead of the more practical 30 to 40 percent markup that most retailers need to stay in business. Another scenario might be that the manufacturer's brand was sold below the minimum advertised price (MAP), and now the manufacturer has banned all eBay sales. This means that the drop shipper may still list the item for sale, but unbeknownst to you, the manufacturer will not stand behind the warranty if anything goes wrong with the product.

Don't be discouraged; drop shipping products can be done effectively. It's an old practice designed to help small businesses succeed. In many cases, the retailer purchases smaller items to keep in inventory, and the larger, more expensive items (or those that are too big for the showroom) are available for special order, should a customer so desire. Catalogs also use drop shipping as a viable alternative in retailing. They pay to produce a catalog and pay the postage to have it delivered to customers. They take the orders, and then the distributer ships the product. This is a winning situation for both businesses. It can be a win-win for eBay retailers as well. However, to make it work, you must drill down into your niche, make contact with suppliers, and build relationships with them. Once you have gotten to know your suppliers by talking to them or doing a little business with them, you can bring up the drop-shipping proposal. After the suppliers have gotten to know you and trust your reputation, they are much more likely to drop ship for you. Subscription services never find these kinds of special arrangements, and you won't be competing against the clueless sellers who undercut prices and dilute the brand.

With today's technology, uploading a catalog's worth of inventory to eBay via CSV file is quick. In no time at all you can have thousands of listings on eBay, and you may be on the prowl for a new line of inventory. The new line will require a new store and different branding. But does that business model really work for eBay sellers who have limited staff or knowledge of the product? Probably not. For instance, do you know if that specific part fits bicycle model XWY? Or can you explain the difference between wild and cultivated acai berries? Or the nutritional element that acai berries add to a diet? As a seller, you can take a guess, and if you guess wrong, you will watch those DSR ratings slip. Worse yet, you can say good-bye to repeat business.

So should you have multiple eBay Stores if you are dealing with drop shippers? The answer depends on the merchandise you are carrying. If you are carrying one line of merchandise (or related lines, such as both handbags and wallets) from several drop shippers, one eBay Store should be sufficient. If you are dealing with five drop shippers, each one offering a different type of merchandise, then multiple eBay Stores are probably the answer.

However, there are several obstacles to overcome when using drop shippers to build a recognizable brand on eBay:

- Some less-reputable drop shippers will use your relationship to market their wares directly to your customers (be sure your drop-shipping contract prohibits them from doing that—a useful form for the contract appears at the end of Cliff's book *The eBay Seller's Tax and Legal Answer Book*).

- Drop shippers frequently run out of inventory, change their inventory mix, or go out of business, and they sometimes don't tell you until *after* you've sold a ton of their merchandise on eBay. If a drop shipper can't commit to keeping your preferred inventory in stock for at least a couple of years, it's probably not a drop shipper you want to deal with.

- Drop shippers vary quite widely in the quality of their customer service. If customers complain that they haven't received their merchandise thirty days after your listing closed, you don't want to hear the drop shipper say that he or she is waiting for a new container load of items to arrive from China.

Should You Have More Than One eBay User ID?

A related question is whether you should have more than one eBay ID. This one is easier to answer: Yes, it's a good idea to have more than one eBay ID for multiple reasons. First, it enables you to keep your personal and business record keeping separate. You are allowed to have two PayPal accounts, and it is easy to have two eBay accounts if you buy items for personal use in addition to selling merchandise. That way you can keep your bookkeeping simple. One ID is for the business of selling; the second is for your personal purchases. Each ID has its corresponding PayPal account.

Another standard business practice on eBay is to purchase items directly on the site to resell in your store. You might find a local eBay Trading Assistant or a consignment seller selling box lots of products that fit your niche, or a seller who incorrectly listed an item and now you can get it at a good discount. It's a great idea to purchase those items using another ID. That way, buyers looking at your feedback won't see the discounted price at which you purchased the inventory and feel cheated by your markup. Although with the new privacy measures eBay has in place, even this is not as necessary as it once was.

3

Using eBay to Market Your Products

eBay's Policies and How They Affect
Your Online Marketing Activities

Rules? You mean there are rules?

As eBayers know, eBay has many rules, restrictions, and policies that limit what sellers can and cannot do on the site. Many of these rules affect how eBay sellers conduct their marketing and promotional activities, both on the eBay site and elsewhere on the Internet.

Some of the important eBay rules are covered elsewhere in *The eBay Marketing Bible,* but here is a short summary of the most important marketing-oriented rules and policies eBay requires of its sellers, with references to more information that is available on the eBay site itself.

Misrepresentation, Fraud, and Overly Aggressive Promotion

Here's a good general rule to remember when preparing your eBay marketing strategy: If eBay does not permit you to say or do something in your eBay listings or eBay Store, then you also are prohibited from saying or doing that something in your e-mail newsletter, your blog, or anywhere else you may be marketing your business on the eBay site.

So, for example, eBay sellers cannot:

- Make false or misleading statements about their merchandise

- Misrepresent the location from which their item will be shipped

- Include brand names or other inappropriate keywords in a marketing piece (a practice known as *keyword spamming*)

- Have misleading titles that do not accurately describe the items they have for sale

That's not just a violation of eBay rules and policies, folks. That's fraud—you can be sued for that, and you can even go to jail.

Legally, it's okay to talk up your merchandise when marketing your individual listings or eBay Store—this is called *puffery* and is generally considered harmless because everybody expects people to say good things about their stuff (although eBay probably will wrinkle its nose if you make the claim that your stuff is "the best on eBay" because there's really no way to verify that). But if you are making statements of fact about your merchandise (statements that are either true or false, not just opinions), they must be absolutely true "to the best of your knowledge and belief," as the lawyers say.

Using Other People's Material in Your Marketing Materials

Whenever you quote other people in your marketing materials, or use their photos, you must get their permission (preferably in writing) before doing so.

If you don't, there's the risk that if someone believes they've been misquoted or that the photo you've selected makes them look unattractive or silly, they will call you and ask to have their photo or quote removed—after you have sent your newsletter out to a gazillion customers. Because they own the copyright to the quote or photo, they have the absolute legal right to make you do that unless you get their permission up front.

We also recommend getting a signed release from them authorizing you to reprint their quote or photo and to use the quote or photo any way you like. If you don't, then you will have to go back to the person and get his or her permission each time you want to reuse the quote or photo in another place.

Regarding photos, not only do you have to get permission from the subject (the person appearing in the photo), but you must get the photographer's permission as well because he or she technically owns the copyright to that photo for legal purposes. You should also credit the photographer in your marketing piece, for example: "Photo Courtesy of Cliff Ennico. All rights reserved."

A lawyer can prepare a simple, one-paragraph release form for less than $100. It's a worthwhile investment for any serious eBay marketer, and you can use the same form over and over again.

The policy prohibiting sellers from "encouraging copyright infringement" on eBay can be found at pages.ebay.com/help/policies/encouraging.html.

Spamming Other eBay Members

When preparing any marketing promotion, such as an e-mail newsletter, that is directly targeting members of the eBay community, sellers must take into account eBay's antispam policy.

This policy is extremely strict and prohibits any communication that is both "unsolicited" and "commercial" in nature. By "unsolicited," eBay means that "the e-mail or Skype message has been sent without the permission of the person who received it." By "commercial," eBay means that "the e-mail or Skype message discusses buying, selling or trading of goods or services."

Here are some examples of spam:

- Unsolicited e-mail or Skype offers to potential buyers for items that are the same or similar to items a member is bidding on or has bid on in the past

- E-mail or Skype messages sent to a member from a mailing list without the member's explicit permission

- Direct or stand-alone invitations to join a mailing list

- E-mail sent using the Contact eBay Member link on the eBay site to send unsolicited commercial offers

The eBay antispam policy can be found in its entirety at pages.ebay.com/help/policies/rfe-spam-ov.html.

Circumventing eBay Fees

Sellers on eBay cannot use techniques to avoid eBay fees. So, for example, the following practices are prohibited:

- Offering customers a selection of completely different items, in an effort to circumvent eBay's prohibition on "choice listings"

- Mentioning one of your listings and informing customers you have additional items for sale at the same price (that are not also listed on eBay)

- Offering your customers a catalog through which they may order items directly from you (unless the catalog consists solely of links to your eBay listings)

- Listing your contact information (including home page URLs), which directly or indirectly promotes an outside-of-eBay website in your marketing materials

- Advertising your desire to buy or trade certain types of merchandise

The eBay fee circumvention policy can be found at pages.ebay.com/help/policies/listing-circumventing.html.

Creating a Playing Field That Is Not Level

There are a number of eBay rules that cannot be easily categorized except that they all have to do with preventing members from getting unfair advantages over other members.

Here are some examples:

- Describing a listed item in greater detail, or offering more information about the item, than is available in the actual item listing. If you do this, you are required to change your item description to make the additional information available to all potential bidders or buyers (pages.ebay.com/help/policies/listing-links-describe.html)

- Similarly, describing selling terms and conditions that are not included on the Terms and Conditions page your customers are allowed to see in your listing or eBay Store (pages.ebay.com/help/policies/listing-links-terms.html)

- Promoting giveaways, lotteries, sweepstakes, random drawings, raffles, contests, or prizes. This could also violate antigambling laws in several U.S. states (pages.ebay.com/help/policies/listing-bonus-prize-giveaway-raffle.html)

- Advertising a general desire to buy or trade items of a specific type, such as "wanted to buy" announcements, except for those permitted in eBay's Want It Now! section (pages.ebay.com/help/policies/listing-want-ads.html)

- Putting in your marketing materials third-party endorsements that appear to validate, verify, or claim trustworthiness of eBay members—for example, "Cliff Ennico says that Seller X is the most trustworthy seller of antique mechanical banks on eBay!" (pages.ebay.com/help/policies/third-party-endorsements-of-eBay-members.html)

- Using profanity in any marketing message, unless you are promoting a presence in eBay's Adults Only section (pages.ebay.com/help/policies/everyone-profanity.html)

- Giving credit to a third-party service provider (such as the designer of your eBay Store) that contains promotional material about additional services or other information about the company (pages.ebay.com/help/policies/listing-links-credits.html)

Directing eBay Traffic to Your Website or Other Site Outside of eBay

Offers to buy or sell merchandise outside of the eBay site are not permitted.

This can be the toughest rule to deal with when selling on eBay, especially if your goal is to create an e-commerce empire where people can buy your merchandise on multiple platforms. The bottom line is that if you are using the eBay site to sell your merchandise, eBay doesn't want you directing traffic elsewhere and depriving them of their fee revenue.

Here are some examples of offers outside of the eBay site:

- Using member contact information obtained from eBay or using any eBay system to offer to sell any listed item outside of eBay. (That's right, folks, even adding the e-mail address of an eBayer to the e-mail newsletter for your off-of-eBay website potentially violates this policy if eBay catches you doing it.)

- Looking up eBayers who bid in other sellers' auctions and sending them unsolicited e-mails or Skype messages informing them of your merchandise or inviting them to subscribe to your e-mail newsletter on the same or similar merchandise. (We note that this might also violate eBay's antispam policy.)

- Putting up any link from an individual listing to a webpage either within or outside the eBay site except for those expressly permitted by eBay's links policy (pages.ebay.com/help/policies/listing-links.html).

- Putting up any link from an eBay Store to a webpage either within or outside the eBay site except for those expressly permitted by eBay's Links from an eBay Store policy (pages.ebay.com/help/policies/listing-links-ebaystores.html).

The eBay policy prohibiting off-site sales can be found at pages.ebay.com/help/policies/rfe-spam-non-ebay-sale.html.

Linking Your About Me Page to Your Website

Historically, there was one exception to the rule that you couldn't direct eBay customers to your website or other e-commerce presence online: You were permitted to place one link in your About Me or About My Store page to your own website.

In early 2008, eBay reversed its position and prohibited sellers from putting *any* links to their website on their About Me or About My Store page. The outcry from the eBay selling community was so great that eBay reversed itself again and went back to permitting sellers one link to their website on their About Me or About My Store page. That is where things stand as this book goes to press.

You can find the current policy at pages.ebay.com/help/policies/listing-aboutme.html).

Note that eBay's policy does not allow you to link your About Me page to a site on Amazon, Yahoo!, or any other e-commerce platform—the one permitted link must be to your own business website.

The site really doesn't like sellers who build up solid reputations there only to leverage those reputations by directing traffic to other websites. This issue is likely to be a battleground between eBay and its selling community for years to come, and readers are advised to keep current on future changes in eBay's policy.

How to Learn More About eBay's Policies

It seems that every time eBay updates the Help section of its site to make it easier for sellers to learn more about eBay's policies, the policies become harder to find.

The best way to access them is to click on the Help tab in the upper right-hand corner of any page on the eBay site, and then click on the A–Z link (it's currently at the bottom of the Browse Help box). You will then see an alphabetical listing of all eBay rules and policies. (Pretty impressive, huh?)

Now do the following:

- Click on the letter "P" and scroll down to the word "Policy." You will see a listing of most relevant eBay policies.

- Click on the letter "S" and scroll down to the words "Selling Policy." You will see a listing of some eBay policies pertaining strictly to sellers (some of these are redundant with the Policy listings).

- For a comprehensive list of eBay's policies regarding what you can and cannot sell on the site, click on the letter "L" and scroll down to the words "Listing Policy."

- Finally, to make 100 percent sure you haven't missed anything, search in the alphabetical listing for the specific thing you want to do. For example, if you want to know whether eBay has any policies on what you can and cannot say in Reviews and Guides, click on the letter "R" and scroll down to the words "Reviews and Guides" (and, yep, there are several policies you need to know about).

For a more detailed discussion of the most important of eBay's selling rules and policies, readers are invited to check out Cliff Ennico's two other books about eBay: *The eBay Seller's Tax and Legal Answer Book* and *The eBay Business Answer Book*.

What People Look For When They Surf the Web

We've said it before, and we'll say it again: The key to success in marketing your eBay business, or indeed any other type of small business, is to keep the customers foremost in mind. Find out what they want and give it to them, whether you like it or not.

If you set up your eBay presence and your search engine marketing program the right way, it will be easy for your customers to find you. But in order to do that, you have to have some idea of what customers are looking for.

What exactly do people look for when they're surfing the Web? How can you anticipate the products, services, and information they will be looking for, so that it will be easy for them to find you?

The short answer is: We're not 100 percent sure. The Internet has been with us (well, as a mass medium, anyway) for only about twelve or thirteen years, and we're still learning things every day about what people do online and how they use the Internet. A number of companies, including eBay and Google, spend millions of dollars each year to learn what people actually do and how they behave online. We're presuming you don't have access to that in-depth knowledge and don't have the budget to duplicate it on your own.

Having said that, though, we do know something after more than twelve years on the Internet: There are four things people routinely look for when they go online, and your eBay business should feature as many of these as possible.

#1. People Look for Information

The Internet is the most amazing research tool ever invented—the biggest and greatest library that human history has ever known, available to anyone with a few clicks of a computer mouse. When people want to look up something quickly, they don't go to encyclopedias or libraries anymore, they go online. With a few mouse clicks, you usually can find the information you're looking for.

So, first off, your website needs to have more than just stuff to sell. It must have information that (1) people are looking for and (2) search engines will find easily. But not just any information. Because of a number of factors that we discussed previously, the information you put on the Web must be "cool" and "compelling."

It is not enough to put up merchandise for sale on eBay—you must also post information about that merchandise, or about the people who buy or collect it, that will strike a chord with your customers. Search engine spiders rarely point customers to an individual eBay auction listing, but they do pick up on an article, a blog posting, or an eBay Reviews and Guides page that talks about the merchandise you have listed. Customers can click on the search engine link to view that content, and if they like what they see (and they will if the content is cool and compelling), they will click on another link within the content that directs them to your eBay Store or Seller's Current Listings page.

If you have an eBay Store and are not taking advantage of the content pages an eBay Store offers, you are not realizing the full potential of the marketing tools eBay offers you. So write some articles, start a blog, or record a podcast on the stuff you sell, the types of people who buy your merchandise, your customers' passions, problems, hopes, and dreams (or just life in general)—and keep putting up new content every week so the search engines keep coming back and boost your search rankings.

#2. People Look for Stuff They Can't Find Locally

Ours is an age of instant gratification. If people can find the stuff you sell in their nearby Walmart or Costco, they won't be looking for it online. They won't want to wait a week for you to ship it to them, and they won't want to pay shipping and handling charges on top of a retail price.

Your best bet in selling online is to feature stuff that's difficult to find locally. People will buy from your website because they can get their hands on the stuff quickly, and they will pay a premium price, plus shipping charges, for that convenience.

If you are selling antiques, jewelry, or collectibles on eBay, this is easy—every item is unique by definition and hard to find in local stores. If, for example, you are a collector of antique mechanical banks from the 1800s, you may have to visit thirty different antiques stores before you find even one or two for sale—and you probably already have them, or they're not in the right condition. If you search on eBay for just a few minutes, you can find hundreds of listings of antique mechanical banks offered by dealers around the world in just about every price range.

One of the great contributions of eBay to the world of commerce is the commoditization of the antiques and collectibles business. That's a big word, but it really just means "making something easy to find that you used to have to search like crazy for." Once upon a time, an antiques dealer with a mechanical bank to sell could price it just about any way he wanted, because there was no way for buyers to comparison price shop with antiques dealers elsewhere who carried similar merchandise. Now, thanks to eBay, if an antiques buyer sees a mechanical bank in a dealer's booth that interests him, in less than five minutes he can find out in real time the exact market price of the exact same antique mechanical bank in similar condition, and he can know instantly whether the dealer is gouging his price. Ever see people at antiques shows carrying BlackBerries and Treos? What do you think they're looking at—the weather? Seriously, the next time you visit an antiques fair, look to see how many dealers post the notice that "a similar item sold last week on eBay for $500!" next to their $400 price tag.

Even if you're not selling antiques and collectibles, one of the best ways to make money on eBay is to corner the market in merchandise that isn't available in most places. Cliff Ennico uses an old Smith Corona typewriter to type envelopes and address labels. The company no longer makes typewriters or replacement parts. Where does Cliff go when he needs a new ribbon or Ko-Rec-Type reel for his typewriter? (Younger readers will have to look that up on Wikipedia.) He goes to eBay, of course! There are a handful of sellers who specialize in replacement parts for old typewriters—they ain't cheap, but where else on earth are you going to find them?

Here's a new phrase for you: *geographic arbitrage*. This means finding merchandise that is plentiful in some places (for example, homemade maple syrup in Vermont) but extremely difficult to find elsewhere (for example, Arizona), buying the merchandise cheaply in the place where it is common, putting it up for sale on eBay, and then targeting your marketing efforts to people living in the places where the merchandise is extremely difficult to find. It's quite time consuming but highly profitable if you can make it work.

#3. People Look for Great Deals on Stuff They Can Find Locally

But what if you are offering merchandise that can easily be found in local stores?

Last year Cliff's beloved thirty-year-old leather briefcase fell apart, and he needed a new one. Local stores had similar leather briefcases in the $200 to $250 range. Cliff went on eBay and found a slightly used one offered for sale from a guy in Texas who was cleaning out his spare closet. Cliff bid on it, and got it for $25 plus shipping. Enough said.

If you have a baby at home, you need diapers—lots of diapers. Go to your local supermarket, and you can pick up packages of ten diapers each. Go to your local warehouse store, such as Costco or BJ's Wholesale Club, and you can pick up packages of fifty each. Buying these packages from a warehouse club and putting them up on eBay will not give you much revenue, precisely because people *can* find these items locally. Given the choice between buying online, paying shipping and handling fees, and waiting a week for delivery (who in their right mind would wait a week for diapers?) on the one hand, and packing the kids in the SUV and driving to the nearest supermarket or warehouse club on the other hand, most sane people would clearly opt for the latter.

So if you are offering merchandise on eBay that is commonly available in brick-and-mortar stores (we don't recommend it, by the way), you must offer a deal that people can't get in their local stores. Maybe you know a source in China who will sell you diapers in hundred-unit packages, which you can then sell on eBay for a few bucks more than the fifty-unit packages at the local warehouse club sell for. That might actually work—there are people with large families, as well as some orphanages, hospital pediatric wards, day care centers, religious cults, and polygamous communities, who might want to buy diapers by the containerload, and you might find yourself a highly profitable market niche by discovering ways to satisfy that demand.

#4. People Look for Like-Minded People

People these days lament the decline of community spirit, but they're wrong. Communities are alive and well—they are just moving online. A lot of Web surfers are finding out they have more in common with someone halfway around the world than with their next-door neighbor.

Do what you can to create a community of people on your website who are talking to you, and to each other, about the passions your merchandise can arouse and/or the problems your merchandise can help solve. Because passions, problems, hopes, and dreams are the only things that motivate people to buy anything (see Chapter 1, "Step #2: Why Are These People Going to Buy from You?"), these are the things you want them talking about in your eBay blogs and other community-oriented parts of your eBay presence.

Three wonderful things will happen when you do this:

1. People will come back to your eBay Store or website over and over again to catch up with their online friends (and view your latest offerings).

2. People will view your eBay Store or website as a place where those with similar interests or problems hang out and will tell their friends about it.

3. You will get amazing free market research by watching their online postings, which will tell you what you're doing right with your eBay business; what you're not doing right; what stuff is selling; what stuff is not selling; what passions, problems, hopes, and dreams are moving your customers at this moment in time; and what new types of people (called *affinity groups* in marketing lingo) are out there who just might be interested in the merchandise you have to sell.

If your eBay Store, website, or other online marketing presence can offer all four things people look for when they surf the Web, that's terrific! But you don't have to offer all four. Try not to stretch to offer things through your Web presence that your customers really aren't looking for. For example, if you are selling auto parts on eBay Motors, your customers probably aren't looking for a social networking experience where they can discuss and celebrate their passion for serpentine belts. Just having the hard-to-find merchandise your customers are looking for is fine, thank you very much.

Marketing Tools Inside the eBay Store

Did you know that eBay provides store owners with a cornucopia of great stuff to market your business? Think of an eBay Store as a toolbox full of gear to promote your listings. If you navigate your way to the Manage My Store area and look on the left-hand side of the page, you'll see links under the Store Marketing section. Let's take a look at the various links and how they can help you build customer relations.

Customized E-Mails: Building Your Brand Recognition

With customized e-mails you can create continuity at every touch point with your customers. Within Selling Manager you can customize the end-of-auction e-mails, invoices, and follow-up e-mails. You can insert your logo into these follow-up e-mails to build brand recognition. Once it is added to the Picture Manager, you can use your logo over and over again.

Remember that Selling Manager/Selling Manager Pro (SMP) is one of the benefits of owning an eBay store. To include the logo in your e-mails, look for Selling Manager (or Selling Manager Pro) Automation Preferences in My eBay. Under Automated Emails for Buyers there is a link to customize e-mails. Click on the link and follow the instructions for inserting the logo. Once you have saved the settings, your customization goes into every e-mail eBay sends on your behalf.

You can add a custom message to the e-mail as well. To keep your Detailed Seller Ratings up, this is a great place to remind your customers about your five-star service—how your store strives to make every part of the customer's experience the best.

Your end-of-auction e-mail should have a statement similar to this:

> *Thanks for your purchase. We look forward to doing business with you. An e-mail with your total will be sent shortly.*
>
> *Remember, this item comes with my guarantee that you will be satisfied with your purchase. If you have any questions, please feel free to contact me at me@mystore.com.*
>
> *All items are shipped within 24 hours of payment, unless otherwise noted. We will provide UPS and FedEx tracking numbers when we use their service.*

An end-of-auction e-mail like the preceding sample tells your customers what to anticipate as they go through the purchasing process. It lets them know when they can expect a tracking or delivery confirmation number.

You can add a custom blurb on the invoices that are sent to your buyers as well. Repeating yourself is not bad. Buyers skim e-mails quickly and may miss information the first time. Restate what customers can expect during a transaction and how to contact you with questions. Your customers are looking for and reading these e-mails not only to find out how much they owe you but for guidance throughout the process as well.

With a subscription to a Premium or higher store (or with a subscription to Selling Manager Pro), you can automatically send an "item shipped" e-mail. This e-mail is triggered automatically as soon as you print a PayPal shipping label. If you use a different postage service, there is a one-button click to bulk-send "item shipped" notifications. This is a quick and easy way to let your customers know you've shipped their items. You can likewise customize this e-mail. This is a good place to remind customers of your five-star guarantee one more time and let them know how much you appreciate feedback. You can invite them to come

---

A SIMPLE WAY TO BUILD LOYAL CUSTOMERS AND KEEP YOUR SELLER RATINGS HIGH

By the way, even if your customers don't follow the items they have bought as they are shipped, they still like to receive the tracking number. They know they can check to see where the parcel is, instead of relying on you. This is a very big deal to most buyers. The extra step you take to make sure they receive the number will pay off. Send them "item shipped" e-mails with confirmation numbers, and they will keep your DSR rankings high.

back by offering an incentive for return purchases. Invite them to join your e-mail newsletter. Let your customers know that they are important to you.

Markdown Manager: Exciting Buyers with a Sale

Markdown Manager is another hidden gem inside the eBay store feature (see Figure 3.1). This marketing tool might be new to eBay, but the tactic has been used in retail marketing for ages. In the bricks-and-mortar world, stores have sales and advertise them heavily to bring buyers in. Sometimes these promotions are geared around a season; sometimes they are to clear out old inventory. Either way, shoppers love sales, and this is one way to entice them into buying or returning.

Before we talk about how to set up the markdown tool, let's talk a little about the different types of sales that store managers usually have.

- **Cross-selling:** The first type of sale, usually geared around a specific buying season, is used to lure customers into the store in the hopes of cross-selling products. The items on sale are referred to as *loss leaders*. As you can gather from the name, these items are usually money losers. Or are they? The store buyer purchases an abundance of product and tries to negotiate the best price. Often, even at the best price the store buyer can get, the item sells for less than the store paid for it. And what shopper can resist? An office supply store having a one-cent sale during the August/September back-to-school season gets those cash registers ringing. The amazing midnight sales advertised in newspapers for the day after Thanksgiving have people lined up hours early to get into the store. Do you think those shop-

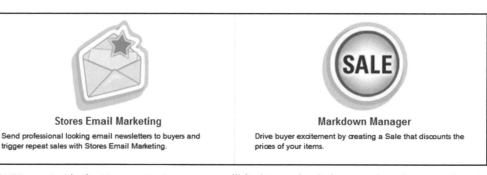

FIGURE 3.1   Inside the Manage My Store area you'll find icons that link to Email Marketing and Markdown Manager options.

pers buy only the items specifically on sale? The majority of shoppers buy other high-ticket items while in the store.

We are not advocating selling items for less than you paid for them. The lesson we can draw from using Markdown Manager to set up a sale is to *cross-promote* your merchandise as much as possible and offer combined shipping so that customers can purchase in quantity.

- **Inventory reduction:** The other common sale strategy is the inventory reduction sale. The store manager decides it's time to move out the seasonal inventory and fill the shelves with new products. To make these sales really appealing, the store owner usually marks these products below what the store paid for them. The purpose here is twofold: (1) Inventory that isn't selling costs the shopkeeper money because real estate costs money. (2) The inventory is tying up capital that could be used to purchase a better-selling item. If you use research tools like Terapeak.com to check sell-through rates before you buy stock, your inventory will be less at risk of lying fallow on your virtual shelf. But every eBay seller should periodically take some time to check out the cyber and storehouse shelf space. Clear out your shelves and remove that old, dusty stuff. Money in your pocket beats unsold inventory every time.

It doesn't really matter to customers why you are having a sale. They just want to get those items at a great price. The better the price reduction, the more excitement the sale will create. And, if you can add a little extra bundling to the deal— for example, combined shipping—shoppers will likely purchase more.

As an eBay Store owner, you can experiment and mix and match store promotion features to see what works best for moving your inventory. One seller of collectible art glass uses a combination of Markdown Manager and the Make Offer feature so that sale items draw attention to other products. He has a sale link in his listing frame that shows up on all his auction and fixed-priced listings. He changes out what's on sale every few weeks. Once customers enter the store to look at the sale items, they start browsing and may come across other pieces they like. If they see things that are not marked down, they can still make offers on nonsale items. This is a great way to make buyers feel like they can wheel and deal to get the best prices even on fixed-priced items.

Before you set up a sale using Markdown Manager, be sure to check your figures. Will you be able to make the appropriate margin on your product? If not, is it an item you can return to your supplier for a small restocking fee instead? Is it better to keep paying extra listing fees to eBay for the privilege of relisting the same items and wait until the items sell, or should you sell them below cost? You must make these tough business decisions. We are not suggesting that you sell items at less than you paid for them. We are suggesting that you carefully evaluate the costs of holding nonselling inventory over long periods. Every piece of merchandise requires its own analysis. In the end, you want to make the highest profit (or take the smallest loss) possible.

To use the eBay Markdown Manager feature, navigate to the Manage My Store area. You'll find Markdown Manager under the Sale icon. (Refer to Figure 3.1.) Click Create a New Sale to start. You have the ability to set up the size of the discount you wish to give or a specific markdown amount. You can even offer the ever-popular "free shipping" sale. You can choose the dates, which newsletter subscribers to send it to, and what, specifically, you wish to put on sale. Then eBay automatically sends out the e-mail at the start of the sale.

Testing is the best way to find out what works for your inventory mix. The one technique every successful shop owner uses is experimentation. Try different sales and reduction amounts to find the sweet spot that drives the most traffic and returns the best profit.

Joint Ventures: Tack onto Others' Efforts

You may have noticed a link under the Marketing Tools tab called Promoting to Other Sellers. When toggled on, this option shows your products on other seller's pages and end-of-auction e-mails. By toggling on the individual boxes, you can choose specifically which e-mails your products will show up on. The catch is that other sellers' items are shown on your outgoing e-mails.

Joint ventures in the Internet world are viable ways to get new buyers to see your products. Often these joint ventures are mutually beneficial and produce great results. Does the eBay feature work as well? Results vary. Our suggestion is to try it and see. Test and test and do some more testing, using eBay's tracking tools and your own common sense—this is the marketing mantra, and you should use it here as well.

Promotion Flyer

If you are not comfortable with designing your own toss-in, eBay provides you with an easily customizable flyer. Inside Manage My Store is a predesigned promotion flyer that you can print and toss into all your outgoing packages.

As soon as you feel comfortable, start creating your own toss-in. You can even use a simple, formatted letter typed out using Microsoft Word. It might not be as pretty, but sometimes the message means more than the format.

Customers really respond when you reach out to them. Contact them and remind them you're there. Provide them with content that's relevant to your relationship with them. They will respond to you by returning to your store and purchasing more.

Creating Buzz in the eBay Community

One of the most notable features of eBay has always been the feeling of community. Like-minded individuals talk to each other about their collectibles, the weather, eBay itself, or any of thousands of different topics. There are forums for talking to staff, town hall meetings for talking to management, and workshops that help sellers and buyers better understand eBay. This early adoption of community features helped skyrocket eBay to the number one place for buying and selling on the Internet (see Figure 3.2). The site continues to roll out new social features that help sellers promote their businesses and buyers find the products they are looking for. Let's take a look at these features and some of the ways you can use them to build a tribe of qualified buyers.

Neighborhoods

An eBay Neighborhood is a place for a small or tightly focused social network to share information or interact with other like-minded people. Each community is built around a theme. Any interested member can petition eBay to start a Neighborhood, but petitions must obtain approval because eBay doesn't want duplicate Neighborhoods with the same theme.

The Neighborhoods are designed to be friendly places to hang out and socialize. These groups are your chance to shine. Post as an expert. Don't be pushy; just answer questions that come up and offer information about your products. Whenever you post, eBay includes your user ID and a link to your feedback page. Interested buyers can click on this link to find out more about you. You are even allowed to link to items on eBay. Again, don't be overambitious, or you'll be ignored or yelled at. However, if you stay honest, become a contributing member, and continue to post, over time an occasional post about your new products will be well received.

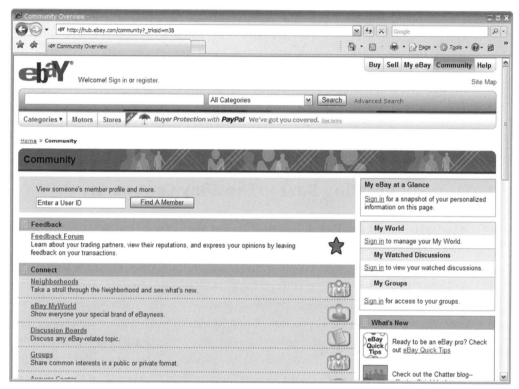

FIGURE 3.2   To find the Community section, click on the Community tab at the top of the eBay screen.

One of the most popular Neighborhoods is Coffee Lovers (see Figure 3.3), with over eight thousand members. If you sell coffee-related products, you can post and comment on the topics in this Neighborhood. This is an excellent way to get your store and product seen by a targeted group of potential buyers.

Each eBay Neighborhood is populated with products, Reviews and Guides, and eBay blogs related to the theme. This means that even if you are not a Neighborhood member but you just post on an eBay blog and it matches the theme of a Neighborhood, your post may show up on the page and a thumbnail photo of your listing may appear on the Neighborhood sidebar when a visitor clicks in.

Discussion Boards

When buyers or collectors are looking for specific information, they are more likely to turn to the eBay discussion boards, which are designed to help users

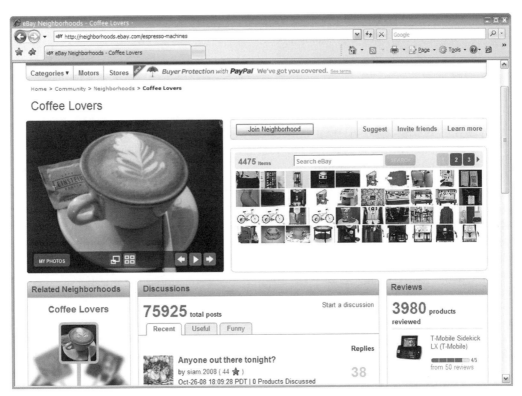

FIGURE 3.3   The most popular Neighborhood on eBay is Coffee Lovers.

find information about anything they might seek. Click on the Community tab on any eBay page, then click on Discussion Boards, and you will see a list of hundreds of topics that eBayers talk to each other about all the time. There are discussion boards for virtually all eBay product categories and for eBay sellers who live in certain countries, states, and cities, as well as an advice board for virtually all of eBay's seller tools.

The site sorts the discussion boards by type: Community Help Boards, eBay Tools, and Category Specific. Experts and eBay employees come together to help answer questions and assist each other. As with the Neighborhoods, this is your chance to participate, join in the conversation, ask questions, and help out when possible. You can find new buyers and burnish your company image by keeping your participation helpful and positive. Just be careful: If you continually ask lots of really dumb questions, you will find yourself the subject of quite a few, er, unfavorable postings—regulars on eBay are not known for holding in their feelings about things, and people, they don't like. Whenever the authors meet people we really do not like we hope that someday they will become the subject of a thread on one of the eBay discussion boards.

Groups

You can find a group on just about any topic, and if there isn't one already, you can start your own group. For example, if you are knowledgeable about collectible coins, you can help others in the coin collectors group. If a buyer has a question about a particular type of coin you specialize in, answering the question is a fantastic way to build trust with that buyer. When you post a reply, eBay includes your user ID and feedback score.

When you set up a group, you can make it public or private. From a marketer's perspective, think of getting the greatest number of qualified buyers you can, in which case you should keep the group public to maximize the number of potential subscribers. However, with the advent of the eBay Neighborhoods and the discussion boards, there may be no need to expend the extra effort on a public group. As a marketer, you already have that covered. Simply find the neighborhood or board best suited to your product and start leaving footprints.

CREATING YOUR OWN PRIVATE CLUB

Here's a little marketing secret: People love exclusive access. They pay extra to join private clubs, talk to mentors, and be the first in line for new gadgets. As an eBay seller, you can take advantage of that by offering your buyers exclusive access.

The formula: *Create an eBay group and make it private.* Then, as a value-added bonus, offer your customers access to your exclusive private group. The group can be about how to use a specific product or it can be a discussion group or a collector's group. Let's say you are the coin expert we talked about earlier. To reward buyers who purchase from you, offer them access to your private group, where you tell them about new items stocked in your store and mentor them on collecting.

Your job as group moderator is to allow membership access to the group, to monitor the posts, and to participate. What kind of group do your products lend themselves to? The sky is the limit!

You don't have to limit yourself to just the eBay Groups. There are lots of free places available on the Internet to carry out this strategy. Create a Yahoo! mailing list by invitation or a members-only section on a WordPress blog.

Reviews and Guides

Whenever you hear about these two, they are always mentioned together. In fact, Reviews and Guides are really two different features that have two different functions. You can find a link to the Reviews and Guides area under the Community tab, toward the bottom of the page, under More Community Programs. (See Figure 3.4.) Let's take a look at these two features.

Reviews

Reviews are designed as user-friendly ways to rate a product. Reviewers can write about how the product worked, whether they had any dislikes, and any specific information that might be of interest to other purchasers. This is a perfect example of how social marketing allows everyone a voice.

A reviewer writes the review, and others who are considering a purchase read

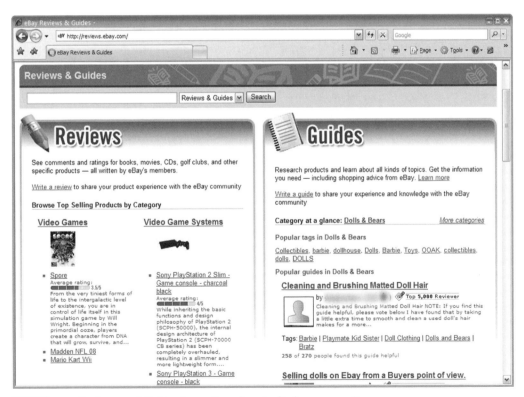

FIGURE 3.4   Reviews and Guides is another place to find a community.

the review. The reader can rate the author on how helpful the review was. This keeps the writers honest. They put their best efforts into reviews. Most reviewers take pride in what they write and want their rankings to stay high.

Each review page contains links to items that are similar to or the same as the product being reviewed. So a customer who is reading the review can click right to the listings on eBay. If you keep your DSR ratings high, your listing is more likely to appear here.

We do not condone "black-hat" marketing tactics, such as writing reviews of your own products. ("Black hat" tactics are used by bad people to "game the system" to get better search engine index rankings, or in this case higher ratings for their products, without generating real traffic. The term came from old cowboy movies, where you could always tell the bad guys because they wore black hats, while the good guys wore white hats.) However, this is a place where you can ask for a little help from satisfied customers. In your follow-up e-mail, ask your customers to review the product. If you can afford it, give samples of your product to known reviewers to use. You can ask them to review the product in exchange for keeping the item. If it's a more expensive item—a high-end camera, for example—loan it to a reviewer. Let the writer use it for a few weeks in exchange for a review. When you have the review, reuse the camera by asking a popular blogger to try it and review it on the blog, with a link to your eBay store.

Remember: Never demand a positive review—only an honest one.

Guides

Guides are designed to give readers more information about a subject. These can be item specific or on just about any topic. The eBay guides are very highly ranked by the search engines and are a simple way to build traffic to your store. Along the right-hand side of the guide is a link to your listings as well as other products that may match the subject you are writing about.

As with reviews, the community can participate in these guides and rank the authors by giving them stars. You might have noticed those Reviews and Guides writer icons after certain users' IDs. The icon you receive is based on the number of good reviews you get.

A guide is a very effective way to drive traffic to your listings. C.J. Jacinto, from XOXMAS, is a Trading Assistant. She was recently commissioned to sell antique carnival chalkware. One of her strategies was to write a short history of chalkware. It worked even better than she had hoped. To date, she's had thousands of visitors to that guide, where, with her listings on the page, the readers

FIGURE 3.5 C.J. Jacinto uses Reviews and Guides to promote special products in her store (http://stores.ebay.com/XOXmas-Vintage-Antique-COLLECTIBLES).

are just a click away from finding her offerings. It's impossible to overestimate how much this contributed to the success of the listings. (See Figure 3.5.)

Using the Community features on eBay helps buyers find your products. Participating in the eBay Neighborhoods, Community groups, and Reviews and Guides helps build a solid customer base. Start with these tools. Once you have established your presence, you can expand into the wide world of e-commerce outside of eBay to bring more buyers to your eBay Store, as discussed in Chapter 6.

Marketing by Doing Good

The eBay Giving Works program provides sellers with a powerful way to attract new customers as well as retain existing ones. It is run in conjunction with eBay's

MissionFish organization. Through this program, you, the seller, can donate all or a portion of your sales to a registered charity. The program is easy to use. You simply register with MissionFish and during the listing process choose which charity you'll donate to and how much of the final value to donate. As an extra incentive, eBay matches the percentage of your donation by offering that same percentage off the final value fees. More information about the program can be found at http://www.ebaygivingworks.com/ns/sell.html. Besides the feel-good value of helping a charity, there is strong evidence that being charitable actually builds your business, according to the 2007 Cone Cause Evolution Study (http://www.coneinc.com/files/2007ConeSurveyReport.pdf):

- Eighty-three percent of Americans say that companies have a responsibility to support causes.

- Ninety-two percent have a more positive image of a company that supports a cause they care about.

- Eighty-seven percent are likely to switch from one product to another (price and quality being equal) if the other product is associated with a good cause.

Using Giving Works, you can feed your soul and help your business financially. In an auction format, you can donate a portion of the sale to a strategically chosen charity. Research shows an average increase in selling price of 14 percent. One reason may be that the nonprofit's supporters add to your bidder base, which can increase your selling price. Even those who don't specifically support the charity may feel more predisposed toward bidding higher, knowing that the extra is supporting a worthy cause.

If you find what you thought was a rare gem while you were out buying one weekend and it turned out to be one of a dozen listed on eBay, one way to set yourself apart when selling it is to donate a portion of the proceeds to charity. Your listing will receive the little yellow ribbon icon on the search page, and a larger percentage of potential buyers will therefore be attracted to it. The listing will also be displayed on the MissionFish site, where buyers who specifically buy from charities are likely to shop.

Regularly donating to nonprofits helps build customer loyalty. If you are associated with a concern that your customers support, they are more likely to subscribe to your mailing list and watch your listings.

Here are some tips to maximize the potential when using this marketing strategy, both for the charity and for yourself:

- **Choose the right charity.** Pick one that matches your goals and inspires your customers. An animal shelter would be a great match for a pet supply store, or a children's charity for a baby stroller company.

- **Timing helps.** Watch eBay to see which charity the site is highlighting, and try to ride the coattail of publicity. Is there a national day or annual function created by the charity you are supporting? If so, plan your big sale around the same time.

- **Partner or engage in a joint venture** with others to promote your auctions.

- **Generally don't use the charity's name in your listing title.** This reduces the keyword capacity. However, there are rare cases where it may work such as the word(s) (Hurricane) *Katrina,* which saw an increase in searches right after the disaster.

Let your customers know that you are involved with a nonprofit. This is a great way to partner with your buyers to contribute. Send them newsletters and handouts, and write press releases. Send the press releases to local papers as well as submitting them to online press release companies.

To build interest, auction off a higher-value item with 100 percent of the proceeds going to the charity. To market this, send out a newsletter and press releases and contact the charity for additional publicity. If the cause is right, eBay might even highlight your auction on its eBay Chatter blog. Contact local agencies as well; they probably have printed a newsletter or flyers they can send to their contributors on your behalf. This one big splash could be repeated annually or semi-annually. Again, brag about the auction by creating a custom page about it.

Keys to Scoring That Online Sale

In Chapter 1 we discussed buyers' four main motivations for purchasing: passions, problems, hopes, and dreams. Any of these might drive customers to start the hunt for a product. In the end, what motivates a window-shopper to actually click that Buy Now button?

According to a recent marketing study called the Edelman Trust Barometer (http://www.edelman.com/TRUST/2008/TrustBarometer08_FINAL.pdf), conducted by StrategyOne, 88 percent of respondents reported they were more likely to buy from a company they "trust." It's really no secret: What buyers want from sellers is security and confidence. The Edelman Trust Barometer further states that "the most powerful drivers of trust are quality of products or services, customer service and a company's overall reputation." Building your brand around trust and safety is so important that it should be at the heart of everything you do, from creating a listing to sending follow-up e-mails. Once you've earned your customers' trust, they will return to your eBay store over and over again.

If you want buyers to keep coming back to your store—what marketers call a *sticky experience*—you must provide them with security and confidence. Don't mistake the topics we're covering in this section for the mechanics of selling on eBay. The way in which you present yourself and your store *is* marketing and branding your business.

Here are five ways to build trust and confidence.

1. Be Consistent

Your goal is to brand your store so buyers recognize it and feel comfortable as soon as they click into your listing. There is one uniform design throughout the eBay site. The layout inside a listing consists of a photo on the right, the bidding/buying price, time left, shipping costs, seller feedback, and so on. This above-the-fold view is consistent throughout the entire site. This is not an accident—eBay buyers depend on this consistency to help them navigate the buying process. Buyers need to be able to quickly locate the Buy Now button, especially if they are bidding at the last minute.

 You can take a lesson from the eBay website: Everything is designed to make bidding and buying easy. As buyers scroll down the page, they see your photos and descriptions. What will they notice? A bunch of misspellings, poorly exposed photographs, and capitalized words shouting "DON'TS" and "WON'TS"? Buyers size up a listing visually in seconds. If they have to wade through the listing or can't find what they want instantly, they'll move on.

Your branding, colors, and listing templates should be professional looking. Choose colors that complement your product line. If you don't know HTML or can't create a professional template, find a designer who can create a unique design for you for a modest price (see Chapter 2). There are also sites like Auctiva.com (www.auctiva.com) that offer free templates. Uniformity helps build your buyers' confidence in you.

2. Format Your Listing for Easy Reading and Put Things Where Your Buyers Want to See Them

Don't be afraid to stay slightly boring. You want your customers to easily recognize your store and know how to navigate your listings quickly. Use consistent formatting and color throughout the listing. There is nothing more distracting to customers than a listing that has a different-colored font in each paragraph or that has multiple fonts or sizes. Buyers don't know what to focus on because there is so much competing text popping out at them.

The easier your listing copy is to read, the longer prospective customers are likely to stay. When creating your listings, use an easy-to-read (sans serif) font such as Arial, Tahoma, or Verdana. This advice is exactly the opposite of book publishers' preference for readability; they use serif fonts like Garamond. What's the difference? A serif font has little extensions (the *serifs*) at the tips of each letter that help the eye move across the page. On a printed page using a serif font works well, but on a computer monitor with poor resolution those little extensions become fuzzy and are difficult for the eye to discern. Sans serif (meaning without the serifs) is clean looking on a computer screen and easier to read.

Use only one to three different font styles at the maximum; any more than that looks confusing. Younger audiences don't mind the smaller, eight-point fonts, so if they are your target, use them. However, remember that if you are targeting older readers, they really hate the extra work that it takes to read small letters. So if your average viewer is older, use a twelve-point font. Those do-it-yourselfers who are creating their own listing templates should try to keep the width of the template around 750 pixels, or table size to about 70 percent. This ensures that people with lower-resolution monitors do not have to scroll from side to side to read your text. As eBay transitions to the new listing template, those dimensions will continue to be adequate.

Text should be aligned left, not centered. Western readers are taught to read from left to right. Centered text, while nice looking, is harder to read. Do not justify the text on the right; allow it to break naturally. It's harder to read a uniform block of text.

Keep your paragraphs short, around three to five sentences. Give your viewers lots of white space to rest their eyes.

Use bold and italic type to draw attention to important words or features. Do not use bold or italics for a large section of words; it's hard to read. Large blocks of italic text dilute the emphases.

Use bullet points to highlight benefits and features so that busy shoppers can easily find them.

User studies done by eBay have concluded that buyers want to see a photograph next to the item description, not at the top or bottom of the listing. (See Figure 3.6.) Having a photograph alongside the text makes it easy to refer to while reading.

3. Use Clear Wording, Correct Spelling, and Proper Capitalization and Punctuation

Really, this isn't an English grammar tutorial; *it's about marketing.* It all goes back to convincing customers to click the Buy Now button. To get browsers to act, we

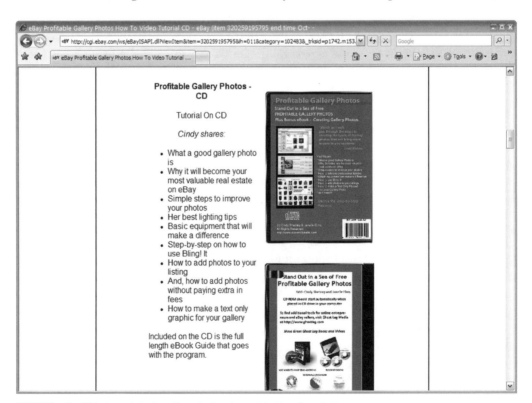

FIGURE 3.6   This template has the photo alongside the description.

go back to building security and confidence. People bring their prejudices to the marketplace, and many people judge your listings by the words, sentence structure, and grammar used in the listing.

Using rAndom caPitaLizatiOn or ALL CAPITAL LETTERS doesn't work to convince buyers they can trust you. Buyers might forgive a misspelling or two, but even that can be pushing it. Proofread your copy before hitting the List button. Use the spell-checker and the grammar checker, keep a dictionary close at hand, and if necessary take an English grammar refresher course from the local community college. You are selling to buyers in a written medium, and the extra time you invest to improve your writing skills will pay off.

4. Talk to Customers in Their Language

You need to know how to speak your customers' language. Understanding who buys your products and how to talk to them helps build a bond between you and your customers. It's a lot easier to sell the latest gadget to computer geeks if you know their slang or to sell a club to a golfer if you know the lingo. Familiarity with terminology and jargon, if not carried to extremes, demonstrates knowledge of the product and respect for the audience.

5. Include Gallery and Listing Photographs That Are Sharp and Clear

A professional-looking photo that accurately represents the product is very important. Your buyers can't examine the product, turn it over, or feel it. Your photo must provide all that information for them. If you purchase new items to resell, the manufacturer may offer product photos to you. In most cases, this is perfect. If you sell used items, it's up to you to provide professional photographs. If you are unfamiliar with techniques for producing great product photographs, there are several books on the subject, including *Easy Auction Photography: A Product Photography Guide for Everyone Who Sells on the Internet* by Cindy Shebley.

Generally, Internet retailers use a uniform, all-white background to display their items. Items stand out with no distractions, and the all-white background makes it easy to drop the image into any listing template.

These catalog-style images work in most circumstances. Once in a while, however, a good marketer needs to stand back and evaluate the industry standard to see whether it's best for the particular item. If you are selling in a highly

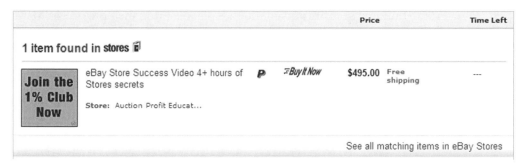

FIGURE 3.7   A catchy gallery image that's not a product photo.

competitive field with lots of similar merchandise, one way to stand out is to create a unique gallery image.

A standardized frame around all your gallery images (the thumbnail image that shows up outside the listing and at the top inside the listing) can brand your store. Your designer can create one to match your store, or if you have photo-editing software you can create one yourself.

If you have a product that is so standardized that buyers don't need to see it in a photo to know what it is—for instance, a DVD—you could replace the gallery photo with a placard to draw viewers' attention to your listing. Substituting an attention-grabbing few words such as *free shipping* or another catchy phrase (see Figure 3.7) instead of using a photograph is a trick that PowerSellers have found grabs viewers fast.

This section focused on ways to build security and confidence with your buyers. You may not have considered building credibility as a major part of your marketing campaign, but it is. The Internet takes away buyers' ability to look sellers in the eye and size them up. Buyers have heard Wild West stories about the scary Internet and are looking for a way to judge their trading partners. Once your buyers start to feel they can trust you, they are more willing to open their wallets and purchase from you.

Small Details That Build Loyalty

Everything from the label on the box to the filler inside is part of the branding and marketing experience. This can help achieve high DSR ratings and is one of the last chances you have to create repeat business.

Unboxing is a new term created recently by the blogosphere. Many computer geeks take videos and share them online when they unwrap a new item they've purchased, and with social networking the trend is growing. You may wonder who watches these videos. Believe it or not, some of these videos get thousands of hits. Is your item worthy of a five-star unboxing experience?

Needless to say, buyers want to open their purchases and be wowed. If you create an experience worth mentioning, fame on the Internet may find you. We hope it'll be good fame, because with Web 2.0 you are just as likely to be shown to thousands of others if you have wrapped the package poorly. That's marketing you really don't want.

How do you give your customers a little happiness when they open the box? Here are a few examples:

- A soap seller spends the extra time to package the product in nice tissue paper and adds a little fragrance, so when a buyer opens the box it is a complete sensual experience;

- An electronics seller makes sure the item is packaged well, using space economy within the box; or

- An organic store could make sure the wrapping used is made of 100 percent recycled material.

Let's take a look at the components that are important in creating an experience when customers receive an item purchased from your eBay Store.

Packaging

Your customer just spent seven long days fighting it out against another bidder and can hardly wait to receive the prized item. It is the crescendo of the eBay experience. Here's where you make or break the chance for repeat business. That art glass collector who just spent hundreds of dollars on the newest addition to his collection isn't going to be happy to see his prize arrive in a battered box. Your packaging says everything about your business, so don't take it lightly.

Labels

The label and stamp on the box are the first things your buyer sees. As a buyer, I always look to see where the package is from, and I feel a little let down if I don't recognize who sent it. If the seller is using the PayPal shipping label feature, it looks like it is from someone at PayPal. That's great for getting the word out about PayPal, but it does nothing for *your* business. A half-sheet shipping label has room for more than just a name and address. Services other than PayPal allow you to maximize your branding right on the label. Services such as Endicia and Stamps.com allow you to put your logo or slogan on the label. If you use a Dymo labeler, you can customize the label to let your buyer (and every postal employee who comes in contact with the package) know it's from your business.

Those sellers with larger budgets can brand the box. Have your logo printed on those boxes. Amazon.com does this very effectively. Have you ever considered how many times those Amazon boxes get used after the first shipment? That's the kind of branding that gets shown over and over again.

Toss-ins

Help your buyers remember you once they have unwrapped the packages. Toss in a flyer or postcard, a pen, or a refrigerator magnet. You can include a personalized letter thanking them for purchasing and letting them know how much you'd appreciate a five-star rating. You can create a document and print it on demand or use a service like VistaPrint.com for inexpensive but professional-looking postcards and flyers. The toss-in might be a coupon good for free shipping on the next order or a discount on the next purchase. Candy is a great bribe, too.

A BUYING STORY FROM CINDY SHEBLEY

This story tells you why you might decide to create your own toss-in.

The other day I decided to take matters into my own hands and clean the sensor on my digital camera. The manufacturers all warn that individuals should never do cleaning themselves; they should send the camera to a professional to clean. But that takes several weeks, and that's a long time without a camera.

So I bought a cleaning kit. When it arrived, I nervously opened the package. Right on top of the kit, was a three-page step-by-step guide that included pictures showing how to clean the sensor. What a relief! The seller wasn't the best author, there were a few misspellings, and the format wasn't pretty—*but* all the information I needed was there. I can't tell you how thankful I was for that. I'll be back to purchase more from that seller, who will be getting five stars from me!

A toss-in might include more information about the product. The user manual doesn't always tell it all. You can provide your customers with more information. This bonus will be received with open arms.

Marketing Doesn't Stop Once You Make the Sale

Want to know a marketing secret? Seventy percent of shoppers say a return policy is *very* important in a purchase decision. Companies like Amazon offer complete A-to-Z money-back guarantees because it's good for business. It is such an important part of today's Internet shopping world that eBay recently changed its listing policy. You are now required to include your return policy in every listing. Although you are not required by eBay to accept returns, it might be a good idea to start.

If you want customers to return to your store, it's important to consider your terms of service. How are you treating your customers? Do you act as if you treasure them, or do you act as if they are just in the way? Internet companies like Zappos have dominated their market because customers know they can talk to a live person no matter what time of day, for as long as they need. No rushed customer service representatives are being clocked and expected to get on to the next call. Buyers know they can return any purchases they don't feel comfortable with, no questions asked. Do they pay more for a pair of shoes than elsewhere online? You bet they do, but you'll find that consumers will pay more for the extra value Zappos offers with its policies.

Offering a money-back guarantee is an important way to gain your customers' trust and close the sale. Buyers need that security when they are purchasing from a stranger. They're putting out their hard-earned cash on that new widget. They want to get it at a good price, but they are willing to pay extra if they know it's going to work when they receive it.

Take a look at your policies and terms of service, review this guide, and see how you can build an army of return buyers.

Answer Buyer Questions Quickly and Professionally

The age of the Internet has brought instant communication. Buyers expect a quick follow-up to their questions. You may feel the need to sleep once in a while, but your customers don't think it should be while they're in the store.

ANSWER CUSTOMER E-MAILS QUICKLY USING eBAY'S RESPONSE SYSTEM

Want to make the sale? Answer your buyers' questions ASAP. Here's how to respond to buyer questions:

- Click on the Respond Now button in the e-mail to open the Respond to Questions page.

Or you can use My eBay:

- Go to My eBay; under Items I'm Selling, you will see Number of Questions Asked after the listing title. Click the number displayed, which takes you to the Respond to Questions page.

In case you don't have employees or can't be at your computer 24/7, eBay has created an easy-to-use solution for keeping in touch with your customers. You can set up a Frequently Asked Questions (FAQs) display for buyers. When they hit the Ask the Seller a Question button, the FAQs are displayed above the question box. Now your customers can quickly find the answers they seek. (See Figure 3.8.)

To create your own answers to frequently asked questions:

1. Collect the most frequently asked questions from your customers.

2. Go to My eBay Preferences.

3. Under the Ask Seller a Question section, click the Edit link.

4. Select the options you want to display on the Ask Seller a Question page.

5. Enter your questions and answers, and then preview your FAQs.

6. Click Submit when you are finished.

Follow-through

While we are on the subject of customer questions, let's talk a little about follow-through. Your customers want to know you received their orders, that you are processing them, and when you shipped them. They also want the security of knowing how the packages have been mailed. Most customers appreciate an

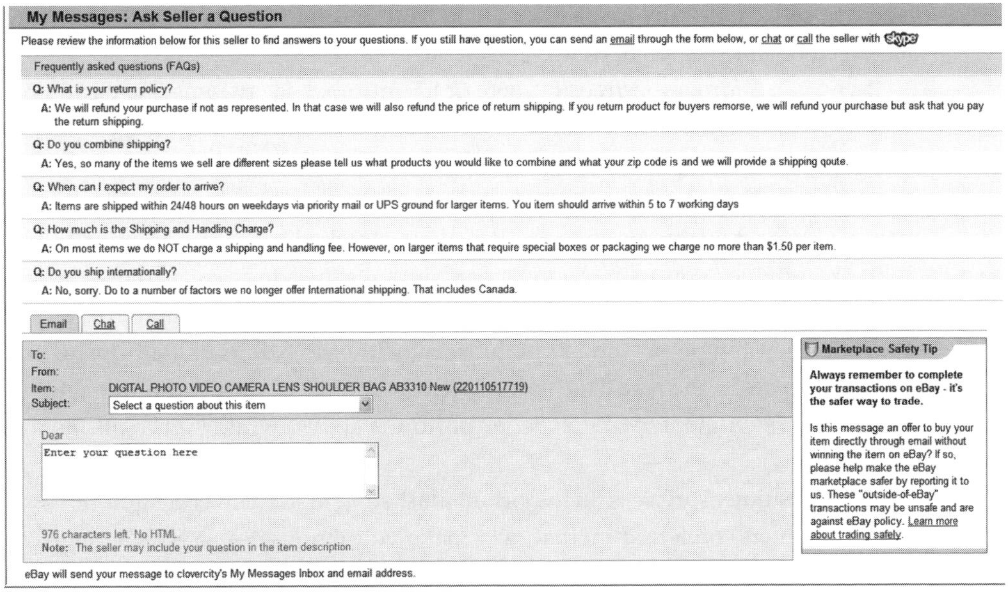

FIGURE 3.8   Sellers can create their own FAQs for buyers to access quickly.

"item shipped" e-mail. They want to know the shipping service you used and the tracking or delivery confirmation number.

If a customer has a problem, promptly attend to it. The sooner you take action, the happier your customer will be. A happy customer is going to tell others about the experience. The really scary part is that an unhappy customer is likely to tell *many more* people about a negative experience than the happy one did. An unhappy customer posting on a blog for hundreds or even thousands of readers to see is something you really don't want.

Use Skype to Keep in Touch with Buyers

Some people like talking on the phone, and some don't. Many Internet retailers choose selling on the Internet because they can avoid phone calls. However, to be successful you must live and sell where your customers live and buy. According to a May 2007 Harris Interactive Online Retail Report (http://www.rightnow .com/pdf/Online-Retail-Report.pdf), 48 percent of consumers want to chat live with a service agent when they have a question or need help during an online shopping experience. That means almost half of your customers prefer to talk to a sales or customer service person live rather than via e-mail. People who make a phone call are usually just a click away from hitting the Buy Now button and just need one or two small things clarified.

If you can afford a toll-free 800, 866, or 877 number so customers can call you, that's great. If not, another tool available to answer questions quickly is Skype (see Figure 3.9). Skype uses a technology referred to as Voice over Internet Protocol (VoIP). This simply means that it's like talking on the phone, only you are using a headset or microphone and speakers attached to your computer. Skype is an eBay-owned company, and eBay encourages the community to use the service. It's free to use Skype to call another Skype ID. You can set up a free Skype account, then toggle on the Skype button inside the Sell Your Item form, and eBay takes care of the rest. The Skype software monitors your computer activity. When you're online, the Skype Seller button is active; while you're offline, it's grayed out.

Good customer service is an important marketing tool. Answering questions via your customers' preferred method *will* make you more sales. It goes a long way toward building your buyers' trust and differentiates you from other sellers. Cus-

FIGURE 3.9 Skype is an easy way to chat with your customers.

tomers who know they can talk to you and ask questions are much more likely to return to your store. They are also much more likely to tell their friends about your outstanding customer service. And that's true word-of-mouth marketing!

High Detailed Seller Ratings

eBay is working with sellers to build buyer confidence, and the site encourages sellers by giving them incentives to keep their Detailed Seller Ratings (DSRs) high. In fact, if you can keep your score high, eBay elevates your listings in the site's new Best Match search results. The reason is simple: eBay knows that high positive feedback and DSR scores are the key to building credibility. Make it part of your marketing strategy to keep your DSR ratings high.

There are four criteria on which customers can rate you:

1. Item as described

2. Communication

3. Shipping time

4. Shipping and handling charges

Your customers can rate you by giving you one to five stars for each of these. The fewer the stars, the less satisfied buyers are with your performance in the category. These are subjective ratings, and they can tell you how buyers feel. Remember: It doesn't matter what you think, *it's what your customers think*.

Let's take a look at these scores and how to improve DSRs.

First Star

The first rating criterion is whether the item is as it was described, which seems pretty straightforward. Did you tell customers exactly what the item was and accurately describe its condition? A week later, when customers leave feedback, is your description what they remember? No, probably not. In our busy lives, extraordinary things stand out; the rest is a blur. Make sure your descriptions are easy to read and cleanly laid out. Make sure your tone is friendly and your terms easy to deal with. Then your customers are more likely to rate your listing as a five-star experience.

Second Star

The second rating star is for communication. Nothing boosts security and confidence faster than end-of-auction and "item shipped" e-mails. Let your buyers know what is happening every step of the way. When you receive payment, let them know. When the item is shipped, let them know. Provide tracking or delivery confirmation numbers. Send follow-up e-mails to make sure buyers are satisfied with the transaction. Buyers don't accept excuses for poor communication. If you have a Premium Store, eBay offers a subscription to Selling Manager Pro (SMP). If you don't have a store, you can subscribe to it as a stand-alone product. SMP will send out the e-mails automatically every step of the way. You can put in your own blurb to customize and personalize each e-mail. This is the perfect place to include information about the transaction and brand your business.

Third Star

The third rating star is for shipping time. All sellers believe they have no control over the speed of delivery once the item leaves their hands. But this rating really isn't as much about that as you might think. Customers do consider how long packages take to arrive, but they are usually reasonable as long as they know the sellers have done everything in their power to expedite shipping. Letting your buyers know their items have been posted and when to expect delivery gives them peace of mind, and they generally respond by rewarding the sellers with five stars.

Fourth Star

The fourth rating star is for shipping and handling (S&H) charges. A high rating here is the hardest to achieve. Many online retailers have found that offering free shipping is the best marketing move they've made. Buyers love free shipping. But does free shipping equal a five-star grade here? The bad news is that many sellers have found that even when they offer free shipping they might receive low ratings on S&H.

When customers choose how high to rank a seller, they tend to base their ratings on much more than just the shipping costs. Customers will pay extra to get a product from a trusted seller. Sellers who haven't gone to free shipping but are instead sending follow-up e-mails to their customers and providing tracking numbers are getting high marks. Of course, this isn't to say the sky is the limit when setting a shipping rate. Consumers are keenly aware of shipping costs and do not like to be overcharged. Set a fair rate and follow through, and your customers will treat you fairly as well.

One final note about DSR ratings: Let your customers know what kind of rating you want from them. Tell them in your listings that you provide five-star service. In a toss-in when you ship, remind them that you would appreciate a five-star rating.

A Question of Feedback: To Send a Reminder or Not?

Should you send e-mail reminders to your buyers if they have not left feedback? Generally, no. Buyers will feel like you are pressuring them and may consider it spam. If shoppers feel as though you are pestering them for feedback, they are more likely to give you a low rating. Sometimes it's better to leave well enough alone, even if you are just starting out and really need to build your feedback reputation.

Leaving Feedback

When you leave feedback, it should be friendly and thankful. You are grateful for those customers, right? No matter how pesky they are, you wouldn't have a job if you didn't have them. Leave it for your customers first, before they leave it for you. There is no reason to withhold feedback anymore. Provide feedback in good faith that your customers will reward you with good feedback as well. In your feedback to customers, let them know you think more of them than just A+++++ (which tells customers that you really couldn't think of anything special to say about them). Tell buyers that it was a great transaction and you hope they'll return. Then mention that five-star transaction, so that when they leave you feedback they'll know what to do. Finally, remind other shoppers who might be looking at the feedback what store the buyers purchased from. You might be thinking, "That's a lot to say in a very short form. How do I get it all in with only eighty characters?" Here are a few examples:

"Thank you for shopping at ABC Store! Our goal is five-star customer satisfaction."

"We appreciate you at ABC Store—and we aim to provide a five-gold-star experience!"

"ABC Store thanks you! Your complete satisfaction and five gold stars are our goals!"

These examples help brand your store and make it easier for your customers to find you later, when they return to eBay to shop again. Chapter 4 takes a look at other ways that encourage customers to return to your business over and over again.

4

Online Marketing Strategies and Tools

Two Fundamental Marketing Rules to Remember at All Times

When marketing your business on eBay, or indeed anywhere else online or offline, there are two fundamental rules you need to keep in mind at all times if you want to stay sane.

Rule #1: Market Only Where Your Customers Are, Not Where They Ain't

The Internet offers lots of new and challenging ways to market your business, and a lot of the new things you can do are really cool and fun.

But if they're not bringing customers to your eBay listings or eBay Store, they are a waste of your time—or, at best, a hobby you can pursue on your own time, when you're not generating revenue on eBay.

Earlier in this book we pointed out—and have emphasized in at least several instances—the importance of doing whatever your customers want you to do and being whatever your customers want you to be, regardless of whether it is something you want to do or think should be done. As in all aspects of marketing, "the customers are king." They will hang out wherever they want to hang out, not where you think they should hang out, and your mission is to hang out in the same places they hang out.

So, to use an obvious example, if your eBay business targets senior citizens, you are probably wasting your time taking out a profile page on MySpace or Facebook, because traffic data show that senior citizens do not hang out in droves on the social networking websites (although that may change over time, as generations that grew up with computers grow older). You would be much better advised to take out advertisements in magazines or other publications that target the senior community (such as *Prevention*), pointing the reader to your eBay Store or website.

If, however, you are targeting teens and young adults who are tech savvy and fond of video games, you should consider sponsoring a booth at the Digital Life trade show in New York City each year (www.digitallife.com), creating an avatar on the Second Life website (www.secondlife.com), and contacting game developers to negotiate product placement deals with their new products (where your merchandise appears within the game and players who want to buy it can click on a link to buy it online while the game is running—hey, this is really happening, folks).

Rule #2: Go Where Your Markets Are Today, Not Where They Will Be Five Years from Now

This rule has to do with the timing of your marketing efforts. Although, as a marketer, you should strive to be current with developments on the Web and elsewhere that will help you reach a broader market at low cost, sometimes you can be a little too far ahead of the curve, as we discuss later in this chapter.

It seems that every day we learn about something new that we can do on the Internet; there are entire trade shows and magazines devoted to the digital life, and more and more people are spending more and more of their time "living" online. We don't see that changing anytime soon, barring a major catastrophe or energy crisis that forces us to start using manual typewriters again.

You need to be sensitive to changes in your marketplace—if your customers are rushing somewhere online, you have to join the crowd and get there yourself.

Here's an example: When the social networking websites such as MySpace and Facebook started up a couple of years ago, a number of people complained that the site's users were heavily oriented toward two groups—teenagers and singles—and that there wasn't enough room for serious businesspeople to network in a professional manner on these sites.

So some brave soul set up a social networking site called LinkedIn, which today is the premier website for serious business networking (see Figure 4.1).

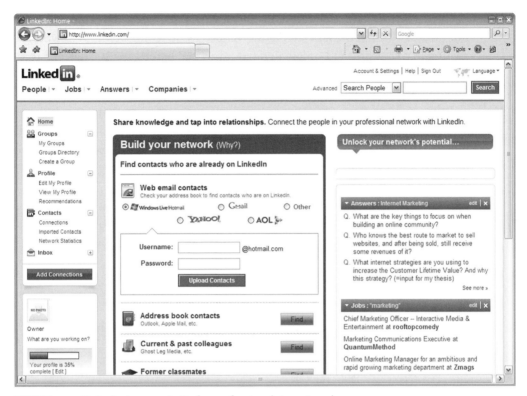

FIGURE 4.1   LinkedIn is a great site for professionals to network.

Soon after its launch, LinkedIn attracted tens of thousands of small businesses and professionals looking to network with each other. A lot of these folks have Facebook pages as well (it seems that every person who wants us to be their "friend" on Facebook contacts us two days later asking us to join their networking group on LinkedIn, but maybe that's just us). If your business targets small businesses or independent professionals, you would be overlooking many potential customers if you limited yourself to just one of the two sites.

But it's also possible to go overboard. It isn't worth spending more than a few hours each week on something that's attracting only a handful of new customers, even if they are "early adopters" who are always on the cutting edge of new Web developments. Many new marketing venues on the Web require a very steep learning curve, as the developers haven't worked out the bugs in their system and no easy-to-use handbooks have yet been published telling you how to get the most out of the site. You don't want to climb that learning curve unless the results, in the form of new traffic and increased sell-throughs on eBay, are worth the time and trouble.

Even eBay, which was launched in 1995, took a few years to become a household word. Many of the new marketing venues we're seeing on the Web won't be around in five years, and unless you have a crystal ball that is 100 percent accurate all the time (we don't), you shouldn't commit serious time to them until you know for sure they will be growing along with your business.

When looking at new technology or social media on the Web, it's often best to "let them grow up a little"—give the site's developers enough time to work out the bugs in their system, make their sites easier for people to use, figure out who their best customers are (if they aren't the same as your customers, forget about them), and perfect their marketing strategy.

Once everybody you know is registering on the site and talking about all the cool stuff they're doing there, it's time to jump in and let them know you're one of the club: "And, by the way, you should see some of the new merchandise I have in my eBay Store . . ."

What Internet Marketing Is (and Isn't) All About

It's no surprise that your main customer base will come from the eBay site. Therefore, it is of vital importance that you continue to produce keyword-rich titles and excellent ad copy to get buyers into your shop. However, it is also good business to reduce your dependence on eBay. With Web 2.0 social networks, you can attract buyers who are looking to buy your products.

The driving force behind the social media marketing is as old as business itself: word of mouth. Buyers have always shared advice with each other about purchasing decisions, and now sharing information with the world is as easy as a few mouse clicks. People find opinions on every product or purchase from trusted peers by using the Internet. The old push marketing tactics of yesterday are no longer effective. We consumers have grown up with TV commercials, billboard ads, celebrities, and athletes touting brands. In subway tunnels, advertisers shout at us via electronic billboards and ads smeared all over the trains. All this, we've learned to tune out. The same is true for those banner ads so many sites feature—it's just more advertising that people tune out.

Your customers are distrustful. They've been hyped and pitched all their lives. Everyone knows the sound volume on commercials is turned up. We learn to be cynical. People pay extra to tune advertisers out. We use Tivo so we can fast-forward through the commercials and choose what we want to see and when we want to see it.

We don't trust someone who is trying to sell us something. Rather, we listen to what our friends, coworkers, peers, and neighbors say about products, and we base buying decisions on these personal recommendations.

This crush of activity and information is why your customers don't heed old-style marketing and advertising. On-demand media are growing. There's a power shift happening on the Internet. Search engines (like Google) make it easy for like-minded people to share with each other via social media. Google loves conversation because it creates new information for indexing. Now anyone with a unique voice can build a tribe or group of people who share their thoughts, opinions, tastes, and so forth.

According to the 2008 Edelman Trust Barometer (http://www.edelman.com/TRUST/2008/TrustBarometer08_FINAL.pdf), people are more likely to trust "people like themselves." Social marketing (Web 2.0) is about *peer-to-peer* marketing. Your job as a social marketer is to show people who you are or who your company is. As we mentioned in Chapter 3, according to the Edelman Trust Barometer, people are "85% more likely to buy from a company they trust."

This section outlines today's major social media sites and shows you why and how you might use them to build your eBay business. Make no mistake, social marketing takes time to succeed. You must build relationships with potential clients and participate in their chosen venue. Think of it as online networking. When you network outside your business, whether in person or on the Web, it requires "face" time. You must be present. Let's be very clear on the etiquette as well. You will not find customers by dropping in with a post and a link and then disappearing again. Not only will no one click on the link, you'll be considered a spammer and may be removed permanently from the group.

Here are three steps that will maximize your qualified traffic and reduce the time spent away from your store:

1. **Leave footprints.** If you find a site that seems to be attracting your customers or others who can help you build your eBay business, participate as an expert. Monitor the site and answer questions. Help others out, and volunteer your time and information freely. Find blogs dedicated to your customers' interests; post comments on them with original content (not just something like "I agree"); leave your signature and store URL. By doing this, you are leaving links, or footprints, back to your store. The search engines build rankings by authority, and the more links you have on websites, blogs, or social networking profiles with high search engine rankings (known as *authority sites*), the more it will boost your SEO. You are also leaving bread crumbs for others to follow back to your store.

2. **Repurpose content.** On the Internet there is an expression that says, "Content is king." That includes written, spoken, and video content. People go on the Web to find information: how to do something, how to fix something, research about a product. Search engines serve up relevant answers to those queries. To make sure the researcher gets the best information, Google and others rank sites by content. The more relevant content you provide on your website or store page about your product or service, the higher you'll rank in the index. It's as simple as that. Where it gets complicated is that creating content—writing, blogging, videoing, or podcasting—takes an enormous amount of time. Whenever possible, reuse your content. Don't reuse it word for word. That's referred to as *duplicate content,* and the search engines consider it spam. You will be punished by lower rankings. Reuse your content, yes, but add to it or change it a little here and there. You should be safe if you follow Google's 20 percent rule: Each page should consist of 20 percent unique content. Here's an example: You write a newsletter article answering the most common questions buyers have about an item. To get more mileage out of it, you expand the article a little and offer it as a free e-book or you break it down into smaller pieces and post each piece as a daily tip on your blog.

3. **Go viral.** This one requires a little creativity or luck, but if you get it right, you'll hit a home run when it comes to getting traffic for your store. Viral marketing isn't normal marketing; it's about producing something so interesting or refreshing that people pass it along to each other. Here's a brief description of what *viral* means on the Internet, from Dany Byrne, of GhostLeg Media (www.ghostlegpress.com):

> A viral marketing campaign, as opposed to just marketing, means *everyone* is talking about it. A real viral campaign creates an emotional reaction in the viewers that not only engages them, but also turns them into evangelists. The customers spread the word and do the selling—not the marketers.

Viral Internet campaigns, planned or unplanned, can produce millions of hits in a couple of days from around the world. That's the kind of publicity we all dream of. Be creative, think outside the box, engage your audience, and entertain, and you might just find your product on the most viewed list.

VIRAL MARKETING CAMPAIGNS WE ALL KNOW

Will It Blend?

To show how powerful its blender is, Blendtec created a series of video clips called "Will It Blend?" Tom Dickson has blended a variety of items including Nike shoes, iPhones, a stun gun, and a video camera (http://www.willitblend.com).

Unleashing the Ideavirus, by Seth Godin

Seth gave the book away for free as a PDF file in prerelease of selling the hardback book. It is the number one downloaded e-book in history, and the paperback copy continues to sell well today (http://www.sethgodin.com/ideavirus/downloads/IdeaVirusReadandShare.pdf).

McKinney's Snow Globe Boy

McKinney ad agency put an employee into an inflatable snow globe for three days. Snow globe boy produced live 24-hour-a-day broadcasts from a webcam inside the globe, where he chatted with visitors and sent out "season's greetings"—a unique way to send an e-card. Using Facebook and YouTube videos, the site attracted over fifty thousand unique visits and press coverage.

TIPS FOR ONLINE NETWORKING

Before you get started:

1. Set your goals.

2. Find SEO keywords.

3. Find your community of buyers.

4. Lurk—read and learn the etiquette before posting.

5. Engage with others by submitting comments on blogs (be honest and authentic).

6. Test, start small, and build if a blog topic works great. If you're not seeing increased traffic in your store, you might want to try a different topic or social site (no big budget lost in the process of switching, just a little time).

There are so many avenues on the Web, and the opportunities continue to grow. With all the choices for social marketing, this section may seem a little overwhelming. Focus on finding out where your customers are, consider how the venue might improve your SEO, and factor in your time. Start slowly; set aside a daily or weekly allotment, and work on this a bit every day. If you have the budget, consider hiring help for some of the tasks. There are sites like Elance.com where you can hire blog writers, MySpace experts, and Web designers.

Search Engine Optimization

Your store is open for business, the Grand Opening or the Grand Reopening sign is out. But no one is coming into your store. The problem is, on eBay your store is just one of a few million. Getting shoppers into your listings can be a challenge. Marketing your business happens on many different levels, including building a store that is SEO friendly. Way back in Chapter 2, we talked about branding your business and making it people friendly. In this chapter we give you tips specifically designed to make your store spider friendly. Spiders are the robots that the search engines send out to crawl your store for information to help them index your site. Setting up your store is all about feeding the spiders with lots of great keywords placed in just the right spots.

The good news is that eBay does a heck of a lot to help sellers get traffic on Google and other search engines. If you've ever searched for something online and somebody's eBay store popped up on the first page of the search engine rankings, you know how powerful eBay's efforts can be. However, while eBay can offer suggestions, it cannot create your keywords or your store page content. The site relies on you to know your merchandise and customers—ultimately, that's the key to a successful SEO program.

Finding Good Keywords for Your Store

The secret to feeding the spiders is keyword-rich content. Building a good keyword-rich title helps buyers find your listings, and the words you use to describe your store, on your custom pages or in categories, help build your search index rankings. Once you have a list of the keywords that pertain to your store, you'll be able to employ them in a number of crucial locations.

So open up a spreadsheet and start listing words that describe the items you're selling. It's important to know what words your buyers use to search for the product you sell. If you can't come up with at least one hundred of them, you should get some help. Remember that you are not one of your buyers, and the keywords you select might be different from theirs. Luckily, there are several places on the Web to find the keywords they are using.

Use eBay's Pulse and Keywords Tool

There are several places on eBay where you can find keywords that are specific to your business.

The best of these is eBay Pulse, which you can find at http://pulse.ebay.com. Pulse tracks information about the hottest and most watched item in each category (see Figure 4.2). This information is valuable as a way to see what keywords

FIGURE 4.2   Find the most-searched-for keywords on eBay at Pulse.

successful sellers are using to drive traffic in. For example, when people search for antique mechanical banks on eBay, do they search for "mechanical banks," "antique mechanical banks," "penny banks," or "children's toy banks"? Pulse can help you answer that question by showing the keyword phrases that are most often used when users look for them on eBay

Another great keyword tool eBay makes available is simply called eBay Keywords. This list includes the top terms that people search for on eBay. You can find it at http://buy.ebay.com. It's designed for buyers, but it is also a fantastic tool for sellers to find out specifically how people are searching. This information can be used to add to your own keyword list and to place the most commonly used ones strategically.

The limitations of using the eBay site tools are that they show only the keywords that eBay members are using. On one hand, that's great because those are the buyers you are targeting. On the other hand, you don't want to put all your eggs into one basket. Your goal is to drive as much traffic to your eBay Store as possible, not just from eBay but from all over the Web.

There are a few other tools, some free and some subscription based, that can likewise help you find keywords.

Google Suggests and AdWords Suggestion Tool

Google Suggests is another free tool that helps you identify keywords or reality-check the keywords you are already using. If you want to know whether "antique mechanical banks" is a valid keyword combination, you can type it into Google Suggests, and the program, like Roget's Thesaurus, suggests other possible related keyword combinations, along with information about the number of Google searches for each one. You can use these suggestions to see how people are searching for your product.

Another free keyword tool from Google is the AdWords Suggestion tool, which many online merchants use when creating the pay-per-click ads they want to appear next to your search engine results. As with Google Suggests, you can type in a keyword or combination of keywords and get suggestions for other possible keywords and combinations. But what's really cool about this tool is that if you type in a reference to a specific page in your eBay Store, AdWords Suggestion looks at the content on that page in real time and offers keyword suggestions based on what it sees there. You can find AdWords Suggestion at https://adwords.google.com/select/KeywordToolExternal.

The main limitation of both of these Google tools is that you already have to have some idea of the correct keywords for your merchandise before you can use the tools effectively. If you're new to a particular type of merchandise or really don't know how to correctly describe the stuff you're selling on eBay (in which case, you really ought to reconsider whether you should be selling that merchandise at all), these tools won't give you the specific information you need to launch a successful SEO program.

Keyword Tracker

Keyword Tracker is a favorite among marketers looking for the terms buyers are typing into the search engines. Keyword Tracker offers simple searches for free at http://freekeywords.wordtracker.com. It does offer a paid subscription service that allows you to dig deeper for keywords. You can get a trial version of the full subscription for a few days to see whether it helps you.

If you typed the word *wreath* into Keyword Tracker, the search results would tell you what words or phrases people have used to search for a wreath in the last thirty days:

Number of Searches	Search Phrase
274	wreaths
153	wreath
103	balsam Christmas wreaths
92	decorative wreaths
86	door wreaths
73	dried wreaths
73	laurel wreath
73	twig wreaths
70	floral wreath
61	Christmas wreaths
57	seasonal wreaths
51	swags and wreaths
50	dried floral wreath
43	balsam wreaths

Looking at this list, you can quickly see that more people type in the plural *wreaths*. That's important to know if you used the singular form rather than the plural when listing the wreath(s). You can also see that *balsam, swags, decorative, door, dried,* and *floral* are all strong keywords to use if you are creating a store that specializes in wreaths.

Keyword Tracker not only displays the word but also shows long-tail phrases people are using. In this instance, *long-tail* refers to the whole phrase or words that the searcher is typing in. In the preceding example, you saw that people used longer phrases to narrow down exactly what they were looking for, such as those who searched "dried floral wreath."

Terapeak.com

Any successful seller should have a subscription to Terapeak. Although eBay offers a limited search of completed listings as part of its Advanced Search feature, it shows only those listings that closed within the previous fourteen days. Terapeak, which is independent from eBay, can give you longer-trending information: from thirty, sixty, or ninety days up to a year back.

Nothing is secret on the Internet. If it's happened, computers recorded it. That might make you feel a little paranoid as an individual, but it sure helps you as a seller. Terapeak serves up highly detailed information on what the best keywords are for your listing. But it does more than that—it also offers insight into the most effective selling practices of others. This can help sellers make up-to-date decisions about their listings.

Information offered by Terapeak includes:

- The average selling price

- The sell-through rate (how many times it had to be listed to sell)

- Best day to list

- Best listing duration

- Keywords that work the best

- Kind of listing to use (fixed-price, auction, etc.)

- Kind of listing promotion upgrades that were most successful

- Best price at which to start the listing

- Information about other sellers by ID

Optimizing Your Store

Now that you have selected your keywords, it is time to *optimize* your store. Basically, this means positioning your keywords in certain places within the store pages so that they are most likely to be viewed by the search engine spiders that determine your rankings in buyers' search results.

Store Header

The first step in optimizing your store is to set up the store description. This is the most important thing you can do to improve your SEO. Store designs are eye candy for people, but keyword-rich headers are food for the spiders.

If you wrote your store description a while ago, this might be a good time to review it. Review it even if your store design is layered over it. The SEO spiders are searching the description, and they are indexing it according to what's written there. It's important to make sure your title is full of highly searchable words and phrases. The spiders give this heading a lot of authority and index your store based on what you've written. (See Figure 4.3)

You have three hundred characters to describe your store. Make sure this area uses lots of keywords. Instead of describing your store as "the friendliest place on earth," write specifically about your products or services. Here's an example: "Plants Inc. carries organic garden tools and supplies including spades, forks, shovels, potting mixes, seeds, soil, fertilizer including popular brands like Sam & Paul, Little Gardner, Blue Willow, Country Wide, Flora & Fauna . . ." When in doubt, put in lots of nouns—search engine spiders love nouns—and keep adjectives and adverbs to a minimum.

When buyers type search words and phrases into their favorite search site, your store will be given a higher ranking if the header description is written properly. Another thing to note is how your store listing will show in the search results when the search happens, because your store header description is the "blurb" that is shown to potential buyers when they search for you on Google or via other indexing sites.

FIGURE 4.3   This store has a keyword-rich description, perfect for feeding the SEO spiders (http://stores.ebay.com/Drei-Katzen-Media).

Category Names

The eBay Store subscription gives you the opportunity to create your own navigation tools, including store categories and subcategories to help your buyers quickly locate the merchandise they're looking for. You are provided with up to three hundred separate product categories and subcategories that can be sorted by size, color, or brand. You can help customers by making these as user friendly as possible.

But don't forget the spiders. These categories also help the search engine spiders sort and index your site.

If your store categories are not clear or don't match your inventory, the spiders will not consider them relevant and your store will fall below others in the same niche. To prevent that, make sure your category titles are keyword rich. You have thirty characters to fill up; use as many as possible.

Here's an example:

Bad store category name: Multitools

Good store category name: Leatherman & Gerber Multitools

From doing keyword research, we've found that buyers search for specific names when looking for multitools. The two favorite searches are "Leatherman" and "Gerber." Of course, you must stock those brands to use them in your category title. If you carried only a generic multitool, you would not only be keyword spamming the spiders, you would run the risk of violating eBay's Verified Rights Owner (VeRO) Program, which protects product manufacturers and others against illegal use of their trademarks and copyrights.

As much as possible, avoid word duplication in the categories. You may need to repeat a word, but try to keep the number of instances of the word to a minimum. If the spiders see overduplication they consider it *keyword stuffing* and will rank you lower for trying to manipulate the system. The search engine algorithms are proprietary, and most of us don't know exactly how Google and the others rank sites. We do know that certain practices that worked well at the beginning of the Internet age are now like poison for getting good rankings. Overduplication of keywords is one of these practices.

Setting Up the Store Meta Tags

Meta Tags essentially consist of the keywords that pertain to your site. They help the search engine sort and index your eBay store. At one time, the Meta Tags were the main place the robots found information about your website. As the technology has progressed, Meta Tags are not as critical as they once were. However, the spiders read these words and then match them for relevance with the rest of your website.

By default, eBay sets up your Meta Tags behind the scenes for you by pulling them from your listing titles. This works for most categories, but you probably will find that you need to tweak the storefront page and your custom pages to maximize their chances of being indexed properly.

The first few keywords in the Meta Tags are used to describe your store, and they end up as the title when the information is displayed to searches on the indexing sites. Make sure those clearly state your store's objective. If you wonder

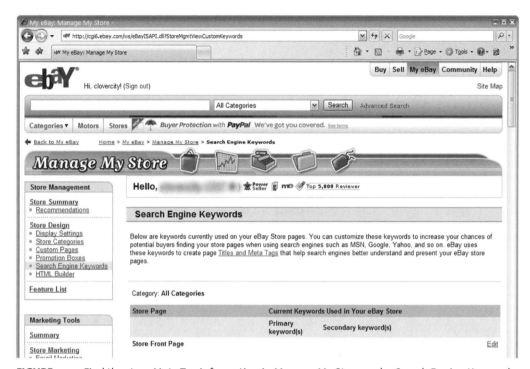

FIGURE 4.4   Find the store Meta Tag information in Manage My Store under Search Engine Keywords.

how they look, do a search for your store on Google or simply look up to the top navigation bar on your store's home page.

To change your Meta Tags, find them inside the Manage My Store area. On the left-hand navigation bar you'll find a link under Store Design called Search Engine Keywords (see Figure 4.4). You can update your Meta Tags there.

Keep in mind that overduplication of a keyword causes the index sites to rank you lower. Make use of that list of keywords to help improve your Meta Tags.

RSS Feeds

RSS feeds sound scary, right? We're sure you're asking, "What does that mean, and what does it have to do with marketing?" It's a computer geek term, but you don't need to worry. Just turn them on, and you'll never have to fret about them again.

For those who want to know, here's an explanation. "RSS" stands for *Real Simple Syndication.* RSS is a way for people to set up automatic feeds that send information directly to a place where they can read it. That feed can be sent to an RSS aggregator, such as iGoogle, or to one on their desktop applications that pops up to let readers know new information has arrived from that feed, or to their e-mail inbox, or even to their cell phone. For a marketer, this is a dream come true! If you have your RSS feed turned on, subscribers (store buyers) only have to click on a little orange button and then every time you list a new item they are sent an announcement.

To turn on the RSS feed, navigate to the Manage My Store area and look on the left-hand side for Listing Feeds under the Store Marketing area (see Figure 4.5). You'll be taken to a page that shows you whether you have opted in to the feeds or not. Change the radio button to Activate Your RSS Feeds. That's all there is to it. Once your store RSS feeds are activated, you'll see a little orange box at the bottom of your pages that subscribers can click on to gather your feed.

Extra tip: While you are still on the Listing Feeds page, turn on the feeds to the shopping comparison sites, such as Shopping.com and Googlebase. These sites try to help buyers find the best deals for certain types of merchandise. Buyers enter the merchandise they want, and the site spews out a list of vendors offering the best prices, warranty terms, and other variables so that shoppers can make

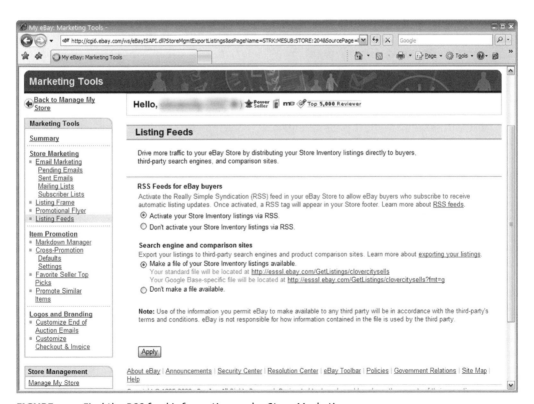

FIGURE 4.5   Find the RSS feed information under Store Marketing.

more intelligent buying choices. By turning on the shopping comparison site feeds, you create a file for shopping engines to gather data from your store and add it to the results they serve up to potential buyers. Shopping engines are growing in popularity every year.

E-Mail Newsletters

The newsletter is one of the most valuable features eBay Store owners have. The newsletter feature on eBay, while not as robust as some of the independent newsletter services, offers a great opportunity to keep in touch with your customers. It's worth repeating that *keeping* a customer is easier than making a new one. The eBay Store newsletter is simple to set up; eBay provides templates and even allows you to set up automatic e-mails, which you can turn on and forget about.

You might think your newsletter will be considered spam by its recipients. Everyone who has an e-mail account is bombarded with unwanted solicitations to purchase everything from get-rich-quick ventures to medicine that'll keep you and a loved one up all night. Your newsletter won't fall into that category for a simple reason: Your customers opted in to hear from you. They gave you specific permission to sell them more stuff. They want to hear from you! The May 2007 Harris Interactive Online Retail Report (http://www.rightnow.com/pdf/Online-Retail-Report.pdf) revealed that 68 percent of online shoppers feel compelled to browse an online retail website after receiving an e-mail from the store.

Another thing we frequently hear is that "I only have a few names on my list, so I'm going to wait until more people sign up." Now is the time to send out a newsletter, even if you have only one subscriber on the list. That one person has asked to hear from you and wants to buy more of your products. What are you waiting for?

Now that you've decided to send a newsletter, the next step is deciding what to say to your customers. One option is to send e-mails automatically (once you set it up), highlighting newly listed items. This is going to be very well received if you specialize in a niche. For example, let's say you sell everything about and related to soccer. You sell clothes, equipment, and limited-edition jerseys from the different teams. If your customers are collectors, you can bet they can hardly wait to hear when you have limited-edition jerseys in stock for their favorite teams.

When new merchandise arrives, your loyal soccer customers might like to be the first to know. Send them a special subscriber-only alert that lets them know when the jerseys have arrived. This gives them the chance to be the first to wear the new colors. These sorts of communications are hotly anticipated. An alternative is to set up an e-mail with listings for preordering the jerseys, so busy collectors don't have to worry about forgetting the arrival date (eBay allows sellers to list preorder items if the items will arrive within thirty days or less). That way, customers can purchase and have them shipped out as soon as you take delivery of the jerseys. Customers love to be treated specially and will respond by purchasing from you. (See Figure 4.6.)

Sales are another topic for your newsletter. Using Markdown Manager and the newsletter feature together delivers a surefire, one-two punch to pick up sales. Set up the sale to start in a couple of weeks. Send one newsletter to announce the dates, and seven days later send a second newsletter to announce the beginning of the sale. Note that when using this feature, you are not allowed to send a newsletter more than once a week. It's easier to build hype for a sale if you can

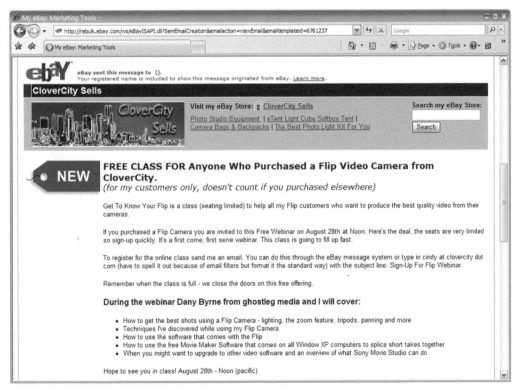

FIGURE 4.6 An eBay newsletter is a perfect way to bring buyers back to your store.

e-mail your customers more frequently, but think creatively within the boundaries of eBay's policies.

To build rapport with your customers, it's good to mix up your newsletter a little. Offer customers more than just information about sales. Make a habit of contacting your subscribers with tidbits about your company, product benefits, or information related to the product. One seller of relaxation CDs and self-help books uses his newsletter to send out inspirational quotes; his subscribers love them and forward them to friends. A fishing supply store might provide news and tips about the latest techniques, regulations, or hot spots for trying out that new fishing gear.

Creating and Formatting a Newsletter

To create a newsletter, navigate to the Manage My Store area. At the center of the page click on the link to Create An Email. The landing page summarizes all the e-mails you've sent (if any) and the number of e-mails you have remaining. The number of e-mails you can send varies according to your store subscription level.

Clicking on the Create An Email button starts the process. Here you can choose from five different predesigned templates. Notice that you can send out an automatic "welcome to my newsletter" e-mail when people subscribe. This is a point of contact where you can tell customers how much you appreciate their support. You might provide them with a secret word, which only subscribers can see, that they can use as a coupon for a discount or free shipping, with the stipulation that it be used to purchase within the next forty-eight hours. Don't forget: You want to give buyers a reason to act and start purchasing from you.

To build their confidence, in this first e-mail it's a good idea to let subscribers know that you won't share your e-mail list with anyone (eBay won't let you, but chances are that your customer doesn't know that), that you respect their busy schedules, and that you promise not to bombard them with junk e-mails.

The next automatic e-mail you can set up is for newly listed items. You select how often to send it to your clients and what day of the week. If you have a segmented list, you can choose specifically which group gets the e-mail. The eBay format already has some canned verbiage filled out. Customize it with your unique content. This automatic feature is terrific; you just set it and forget about it. However, there is a downside to this e-mail. The e-mail servers do not omit the e-mail if you have not listed any new items, which means that your subscribers could receive a blank e-mail from you. The servers are very literal and don't know to fill in blanks with other products instead. This shouldn't be a big deal if you list products regularly, but those sellers who list new items only occasionally should not set up the e-mail to send automatically.

There are other e-mail templates that you can use, depending on your preferences. You can choose which one works best for your store and tweak the format. There is a custom template as well that allows you to create your own style. Beware of a few pitfalls in designing your own template. If you use Microsoft Word or another word processing program to create the newsletter and copy/paste it into the text editor eBay provides, it may look fine on review. However, when the e-mail is sent, the formatting is often lost or changed. It's best to use a notepad and remove all Word formatting before you send the e-mail. The same is true for HTML. You can use basic HTML in the description, but the newsletter your recipients get is just as likely to look like HTML code rather than a formatted newsletter. Most commercial newsletter services allow you to send yourself a test copy before sending it to your clients. That test feature is not available from eBay at this time. There is a preview feature that you can look at before you send the e-mail, but the formatting it shows is not necessarily accurate. So for now, stick to plaintext, copy and paste it into the eBay word editor, and then format it using eBay's formatting tools.

Attracting Attention and Motivating Your Subscribers to Click Back to You

The title of your newsletter is essential in getting buyers to open it up. Make your title descriptive, and reach out and grab your customers by the throat. The difference between open rates for subject lines that *tell* versus those that *sell* can be huge. A number of marketing studies (for example, http://www.mailchimp .com/resources/subject-line-comparison.phtml) indicate open rates of 60 to 87 percent for informative, descriptive, or eye-catching subject lines versus 1 to 14 percent for "sales hype" subject lines. Keep in mind that you have only a fraction of a second to attract your customers' attention—the title needs to be compelling, and maybe even a little mysterious, to get people to stop and read further.

As an example, if you were scrolling through your e-mail inbox and hitting the delete key madly, which of the following two titles is more likely to make you stop and open the e-mail:

- New Strategies for Building a Successful e-Commerce Business

- Is Your Octopus Grabbing the Prey You Want? If Not, It's Sushi!

We guarantee the second title will reach more readers, if only out of curiosity to find out what the "octopus" reference means.

Marketers have found that a "traffic accident" title also works. You know the ones—they say something like "OPPS, I made a mistake" (*sic*—the typo is part of the pun) or "The Sky is Falling and the Stock Market Crashed." Yes, we all respond to fear and panic, but make sure your subject line fits the content of the newsletter. If it doesn't, expect customers to unsubscribe and report you as a spammer faster than you can say "Chicken Little."

Newsletters, like the text for listings, should always answer the question "What's in it for me" for your buyers. If you want to keep subscribers opening your e-mails, the content must be relevant to them, must have information they can benefit from, and must be easy to skim. Unless it's a very compelling topic, your newsletter readers will most likely just quickly skim the first few lines. Make it easy by stating the benefit of reading the newsletter as soon as they open it. Using bullet points makes it easy for them to digest the information in bite-size chunks.

Make sure your newsletter has a call to action. Give readers a reason to act— "limited to stock on hand" or "twenty-four hour sale," for example. Marketers have found that telling your customers what to do next helps; say "Click here to purchase" if that's what you want your buyers to do.

Segmenting your subscribers is important, especially if you sell different products from the same store. A buyer who is interested in your collectible Cabbage Patch dolls probably doesn't want to hear about the latest shipment of hunting knives. You can set up multiple lists by clicking on Create Mailing List on the Email Marketing Summary page.

Monitoring and Testing Your Newsletter Results

All professionals track results from their e-mail marketing campaigns. They want to know how successful the title was, how many people clicked links in the e-mail, what worked, and what didn't. Some basic eBay tracking features enable you to check your success rate. On the Email Marketing Summary page you can see how many e-mails were sent and how many e-mails were opened.

Creating a Newletter on a Platform Other Than eBay

There are four advantages to creating a newsletter outside of eBay:

1. eBay shields sellers from their subscribers and their e-mail addresses.

2. eBay newsletters have limited customization capability, including links. That's not a problem at first, but as your business grows you may find you want more freedom.

3. The eBay newsletter feature doesn't provide detailed tracking information.

4. eBay limits the number of e-mails you can send based on your store subscription level, as well as limiting how often you may send them.

While the eBay newsletter feature is perfect for those who are just getting started, it will eventually become too restrictive. Think of the eBay newsletter as version 101, and when you are ready to expand refer here for Newsletters 102. As soon as you start implementing marketing strategies outside of eBay—for example, a website or a blog—it's time to start collecting e-mail addresses.

A newsletter is such an important marketing tool that it is necessary to understand some of the more advanced newsletter marketing tactics, such as how to choose a provider, as well as a few things to watch out for when creating your own list.

Autoresponders

A mainstay of newsletters is the autoresponder. This marketing gem automates the process of sending e-mails without your having to manually send different e-mails to individual subscribers for varying purposes. Autoresponders can:

*   Be scheduled to send newsletters once a day, every few days, once a week, and so on

*   Be automated to welcome new subscribers

*   Be used to educate subscribers about your products

*   Provide follow-up to invite subscribers back to your website, blog, or eBay Store

An autoresponder is a powerful addition to an Internet marketer's toolbox. It can create a personal touch between you and your clients. When you set up the responder, it asks you to indicate a salutation and then draws from the database to address individual recipients by name. The names are taken from the information subscribers supplied when they signed up. Be sure to ask for first names as well as e-mail addresses. Not only do many marketers address recipients at the top of the e-mail with a greeting such as "Hi, Cliff," but somewhere midway through the e-mail text they'll use the reader's name again. People love seeing their name, and if they notice their name when skimming the e-mail, you can bet they'll stop and read.

You can use an autoresponder when asking buyers to sign up for your newsletter. Offer a free short class or other useful information if they join your mailing list. If you were selling crafts, your introductory e-mails could be a course sent out over a few days on how to create a wreath for the holidays. Or if you are selling antique car parts, a multipart course on how to restore the parts to their original condition would entice new subscribers. A coin collector could give a short course on grading coins.

Once subscribers enroll, the software sends out the prewritten e-mails at your scheduled released time. It doesn't matter when someone subscribes or how many others are already receiving the introductory e-mail, the software tracks every individual and sends the appropriate e-mail lesson in the sequence. Everyone starts at the beginning of your tutorial and goes through each lesson in the course.

When you set up the autoresponder, you will be prompted to schedule the length of time between e-mails. Generally, once a day or once every couple of days is most effective. Some marketers have found that once every four days is

---

USING AN AUTORESPONDER AS AN ETHICAL BRIBE

What's an ethical bribe? It's a phrase coined by Internet marketer Alex Mandossian: "An ethical bribe is offering someone something in return for access to their e-mail. An ethical bribe is just that, it's ethical and it's bribery. You're bribing them quid pro quo to take the next step."

Your ethical bribe should be something that doesn't cost you anything or something that you do not charge for. It can be an e-book that you created. It could be daily tips, links to information you've gathered, a short how-to course, or even your favorite photo. One of Cindy's favorite e-mail bribes is from a photography website that sends her a photo of the day.

often enough. In this time of e-mail overload, be sensitive to your readers. Your e-mails might be better received if they were sent out every few days.

One word of caution about autoresponders and the temptation to make each e-mail long: Don't! Even if you are offering an in-depth course, cut it into shorter chunks, something that can be quickly skimmed. Don't overdo the material or text; keep it short and in bite-size nuggets, with bullet points and short, snappy sentences. Don't talk about what your merchandise does or how it works—talk about the benefits your customers will reap from buying these wonderful things. If the e-mails are long and dry, people will tune them out, and before you know it, your e-mails will be tossed without being read.

It's important to offer your subscribers value in the short course. Your focus should not be to sell your customers through the course. Offer this course for free, to build rapport between you and your customers. That wreath-making course could include all the materials needed to construct the wreath, but it should focus on the creation process. At the bottom of the e-mail, you could include a link to your store for items you are selling, but keep it low-key. That might run counter to everything you've heard about marketing, but the purpose here is not selling, it's building a customer relationship. If buyers like you and decide you are an expert wreath crafter, then they will purchase from you. That's the true heart of Web 2.0 marketing: no more push. People don't want to be pushed; they want trusted sellers.

Remember that interacting with your customers and inviting their comments is important. You don't have to be pushy to sell people. Just be interested in them. Use a timed e-mail follow-up after you send out your short course. Set the autoresponder to send the final e-mail seven to ten days after the end of the course. In this e-mail you can ask your subscribers to take a survey, thank them for signing up, contact you with questions, or invite them to read your blog for more information.

Here's a sample:

> Hi, [*Customer's name*],
>
> I see you've finished our special wreath-building e-course. I enjoy teaching others how to create holiday wreaths that will bring joy for many seasons to come. I hope your wreath will hang in a place of honor.
>
> Don't forget, we have more guides and tutorials on our blog at www.wreathbuilder.com. While you are there, please leave a comment or join our community of wreath builders.

We carry a complete line of products for all of your wreath projects in our eBay Store at www.wreathbuildersstore.com.

If you have any questions, please feel free to contact us.

Thanks again,

Sally Smith

Using the personal touch can build a relationship with your clients. Tell them that you value their patronage. You are not trying to trick people into thinking you're sitting at your computer every second of the day sending e-mail, but sending a follow-up note specifically to new subscribers makes them feel welcome. The number of positive responses from this follow-up e-mail may surprise you.

Don't Leave Money Sitting on the Table

The purpose of your e-mail newsletter is to promote your products on eBay. For example, you might decide to send out regular e-mails about your weekly estate sale finds. When you attract buyers outside of eBay and direct them to your store, where they buy stuff, you are rewarded with a *referral credit*—basically, eBay deducts 75 percent of the final value fee it charges on each item you sell from your store this way.

To take advantage of the referral credit, be sure your link has the ?refid=store code at the end of the link to your listing, but be aware that this code doesn't work on auction items. So if you are promoting your latest auction items, use an affiliate link from the eBay Partner Network (EPN). This is eBay's *affiliate marketing* program for sellers; if a buyer clicks in from your listing and wins the bid, eBay shares the profit with you. For more information about the eBay Partner Network, go to https://ebaypartnernetwork.com/files/hub/en-US/howitWorks .html.

When you use the eBay Partner Network, you won't receive a payback bonus as big as the eBay Store 75 percent referral credit, but if your buyer bids and wins anything on eBay during that browser session, you'll get a credit. To sign up for an affiliate ID and create the code, visit https://www.ebaypartnernetwork.com.

One bit of fine print in the agreement with the Partner Network is that you must be approved if you want to use the code in your newsletters. Be sure to send EPN an e-mail and receive permission to use the code in your newsletter.

And speaking of permission . . .

Asking Permission

We cannot emphasize enough how important permission is. Official eBay policy does not allow you to capture names from information you glean during customers' purchases and automatically include them in your newsletter mailing lists. *You must ask your customers to sign up.* Policy aside, customers will put you on the spam list faster than a speeding bullet if you start sending them unsolicited e-mails. In this time-starved, overspammed society, people are selective about whom they are willing to receive e-mails from. Many have filters in place to block unwanted e-mails.

So be sure to ask your customers to join your mailing list. Include an invitation in the e-mail you send to follow up on a sale or print an invitation and toss it in each box you send. If a customer accepts your invitation to join the newsletter list, that's great. If some decide not to, leave them alone. Many newsletter service providers include a *double opt-in* feature whereby customers first sign up and then receive an e-mail asking them to confirm the sign-up by clicking on a link. It's a good idea to use this double opt-in feature. When the opt-in e-mail is sent, recipients are reminded that they subscribed. If that opt-in e-mail ends up in their spam folders and they never opt in, that's okay. If your subscribers want to receive the e-mails, they have to retrieve the opt-in offer from the spam filter and *whitelist* your e-mails. That way, when you send out your newsletters, they will go directly into their inboxes.

The reason this matters is that when Internet service providers (ISPs) see bulk e-mails that consistently go into spam folders, they block the sender. An ISP like AOL is very quick to block all your e-mails if even a few of them go directly to spam folders. If you have a large number of subscribers who are using the same ISP, all your e-mails will be blocked. So if a subscriber never finds the opt-in e-mail to subscribe, you may be better off losing that one subscriber than continuing to send e-mails that go directly to spam filters.

Not only is it the law, but it is also a good practice to provide your subscribers an easy way to unsubscribe. Make sure you include a link at the bottom of each e-mail you send out. Most e-mail service providers can be programmed to do this automatically.

Illogical as it seems, many people forget that they gave you permission to send these e-mails. To avoid quick rejection in those cases, most newsletter authors write a short blurb as an opening line in the e-mail reminding subscribers that they signed up.

Here's a sample blurb:

> You are receiving this because you subscribed to my newsletter. You may unsubscribe at any time by using the link at the bottom of this e-mail.

Sending Out Your Own Newsletter Versus Using a Provider

As you start out, you may find that keeping your customer list inside your e-mail software is the easiest thing to do. When you send the newsletter out, be sure that you put recipients' e-mail addresses in the blind copy (bcc) box to protect their privacy. Depending on the size of your list, administering it through your own software might become very time consuming. As your list starts growing, you may want to enlist a service to administer it. Also, many ISPs consider a large bcc field to be a sign of spamming.

There are several companies that will host your list, keep track of subscribers and unsubscribers, and give you tracking data and open rates. They will show you who opened the e-mail, which links they clicked on, and how effective your campaign was compared to others. Depending on the service you use, you may be able to set up autoresponders to send out prewritten e-mails on a schedule. Many newsletter services provide professional-looking templates. Some have easy-to-set-up PayPal buttons whereby you can offer subscribers exclusive e-mail-only deals. Selecting which newsletter service is right for your business requires a little planning and research. Let's look at some of the different features you should consider when choosing a newsletter service.

Formatting the Newsletter

Most businesses send out HTML newsletters with beautiful photos and nicely formatted text. These newsletter templates make you look professional. For the most part, it's great to present yourself as a professional. That's one of the benefits of using a newsletter service.

Whether or not these professional templates work is a hot topic of debate among Internet marketers. There are a few reasons why they believe the templates might not be as effective as most people think. First, many e-mail clients have the pictures feature turned off. That means that the photograph of a beautiful sweater you included in the e-mail might just appear as a big white space or, worse yet, one of those red X's. This can be a problem if you rely solely on photos to sell your products.

Some mail services block HTML e-mails instantly, and they go directly to spam folders without recipients ever seeing the e-mail.

Many services display the code in a jumble that doesn't come close to resembling the original e-mail. If you use a template provided by one of the big newsletter services, that shouldn't be a problem. Most services will provide a split list for HTML and plaintext subscribers. The only thing you'll need to do is create a copy in plaintext, then cut and paste it into the specified area. It's when you create your own HTML newsletter that you might run into a snag. You won't know which subscribers require plaintext and which don't.

As a result of these issues, many Internet marketers are going back to basics and sending plaintext newsletters. This provides the marketers with assured delivery of the e-mail. And, surprisingly, the very nature of the text document makes it seem more personal to recipients. Marketers are finding a much higher click-through rate when they use plaintext. However, some of the most useful tracking features are not available in plaintext, so many newsletters are now being created as HTML documents without the fancy formatting. They look like plaintext, but under the hood they still carry the code necessary to track open rates and so forth.

Other marketers are sending out—in plaintext—invitations to read their newsletters on a website. It's generally harder to get casual readers to click the links. If you choose this method, make sure to include the link to your website several times and fill the e-mail with benefit-rich reasons why your reader should click to read the newsletter immediately. Even with the best of intentions, once readers close your e-mail, they probably will never come back to it.

Things to Consider When Choosing a Newsletter Provider

Here is a list of things for sellers to keep in mind when deciding on a provider to send out your newsletter:

1. **Cost:** Some providers charge you a flat monthly rate; others charge per subscriber. Determine which would be the most cost-effective.

2. **Templates:** Many providers now offer HTML templates that are professional looking and easy to use. You can include your logo; simply type

your copy into a field. The service takes care of all the formatting to create a professional e-mail. If you don't know Web design, you'll find this feature a big bonus.

3. **Autoresponders:** These are a great way to keep a personal dialogue going with your customers with a minimum amount of effort. Not every service offers them, so check carefully if you want this feature.

4. **PayPal/shopping cart integration:** Again, you'll need to know what direction your business is going in. If you plan on a website with a shopping cart, make sure your newsletter service can provide integration. Most sellers are content with PayPal, and selecting a service with an easy way to include a PayPal Buy Now button will do.

5. **Surveys:** Involving your customers and getting feedback from them engages them and improves your business.

6. **Tracking information:** This is the most important feature you can have! The services can track how many e-mails were opened and by whom. They can provide information about who clicked on which link. Tracking gives you direct information about how successful the e-mail campaign was. This is the way you measure the effectiveness of your marketing. Without it, you are blind. So pay particular attention to the quality of the tracking features a potential newsletter service offers.

7. **List segmentation:** Segmenting your list allows you to drill down to specific areas your subscribers are interested in. With list segmentation you can offer your subscribers a choice of the specific topic(s) they would like to receive information about. Then you can send out topic-specific newsletters targeted to those subscribers. If you sold boots and equestrian supplies, for example, you could segment your list into two—one specifically for boot buyers and one for those who want to keep up to date with all your horse tack supplies.

8. **Split testing:** You can send out the same information in different formats or use different headlines sent to control groups. Then you can check the tracking information to see which newsletter received the most responses. Most services provide split testing; just check to see how many subscribers you need to start testing. Some require one hundred or more subscribers before you can use the feature.

9. **Ease of integration with websites or blogs:** Most services have cut–and-paste code for newsletter sign-up boxes that work easily with a website. You will find fewer that offer an easy way to integrate the sign-up box with blogging sites like WordPress. If you intend to have a newsletter sign-up on your blog, double-check.

10. **Customer support:** Use the Web and check out the service rating for customer support. Does the service offer an onsite link to a live operator? With all the complexity of getting e-mails to your clients, at one time or another you'll probably find yourself turning to the service for help. Make sure they get good rankings in this area.

Once you have selected your newsletter service, it is time to start considering other ways to market your business to bring traffic into your eBay listings. As we've mentioned, building your business's network takes time. The more ways you can automate and repurpose your written material, the more time you can spend running your shop. The next several sections take a look at a few other ways of marketing yourself online that can help you drive qualified traffic to your listings.

Blogs

At the time of this writing, there are over eight million blogs worldwide. That's a lot of people writing about lots of stuff! Whenever the subject of blogs comes up, a typical eBayer reaction is: "I don't have time to do one more thing, and, besides, what would I write about?" If you want to leave your competition in the dust, let those eBayers wonder while you start building a community of fans. Nothing is more important to your eBay Store than marketing. If you don't have time to market your store, you don't have your priorities straight. Blogs are great marketing tools precisely because the payback is so great compared to the small amount of time invested. If you could choose only one place outside of eBay to market your business, blogging would be it.

Blogs were created as a way to post bits of information quickly and regularly. Originally used by teenagers as online diaries, they were called *web logs*. The name was soon shortened to *blog*. As with many applications on the Web, blogs evolved and readership changed. They are quickly becoming the tool of choice for businesses as a way to communicate with customers.

The blog platform allows your users to choose the way they receive information. Busy readers can opt to browse your blog in their Google Reader, have it sent to them in e-mail, or aggregated with other favorite blogs to be read at once like a newspaper. This makes blogs extremely popular with overwhelmed readers who are bombarded with information. Allowing your readers the freedom to choose when and how they prefer to receive the information is valuable in this time-starved world.

Blogs are easy to set up, simple to edit, and, in many cases, free. A blog can look like a more traditional website but still include all the interactive functions that set blogs apart. There are designers who create templates, many of them free, that make for a professional-looking site requiring almost no technical expertise on the part of the blogger.

Components of a Successful Blog

A blog that is updated regularly is a magnet for the search engine spiders that prioritize websites for search results. The operative words here are "updated regularly." There is no sugarcoating this; a blog must have new material posted frequently, preferably every day. It doesn't work to create a blog, post once, and hope for traffic. The search engines will abandon it as quickly as you do. Visiting customers will think you are no longer in business when they come to a blog that hasn't been updated in months. At first it may seem like you are blogging into the wind. It may take a while, sometimes months and months, to build up content and readers. Don't give up. Keep posting new material. Write from the heart; stay authentic, consistent, and transparent; and eventually you will start building a following.

Your blog should have a focused purpose. Decide whom your blog is aimed at before you go forward. If you sell antique dolls, the purpose of your blog might be to talk about the collecting of antique dolls. If you sell golf equipment, you may decide to blog about the equipment or maybe the focus could be the best golf courses in the world. The blog should directly relate to what you are selling but doesn't necessarily have to be specifically about it.

Bryan and Nathan from Flightline Fabrications sell World War II reproduction stickers (see Figure 4.7). They created a blog that ties in to the theme and features regular interviews with World War II vets and Holocaust survivors, as well as historical tidbits. Of course, there are links to their eBay Store pages. The site uses

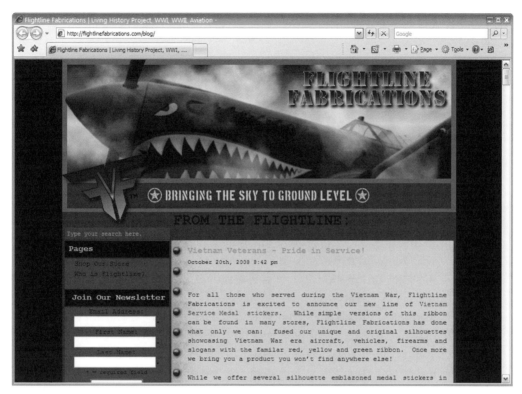

FIGURE 4.7   Brian and Nathan from Flightline Fabrications promote their eBay store by using consistent branding, interviews, and blog posts related to their products (http://flightlinefabrications .com/blog/).

the same look and feel as their eBay Store to keep branding consistent. They post regularly, have a specific theme in mind, and write in their own voices.

The Many Marketing Uses of a Blog

Blogs can be used the way websites have traditionally been used. Many websites are built on blogging software. Because search engines love changing content, they rank blogs high in the index, making it easier for bloggers to quickly build traffic. You can use a blog for many of the same purposes as a stand-alone website, and many Web merchants are migrating away from static websites in favor of the more interactive and lively blogs that can more easily be kept up to date (if not up to the minute).

Choosing a Platform

Which blogging platform should you use? Again, it depends on the focus of your business and how technical or computer savvy you or your team are.

eBay Blogs

To locate your eBay blog, go to Members Feedback and click on the View Members My World Page link. Have you ever stumbled upon the My World link and wondered what the heck it is? eBay rolled it out with much ado a few years ago. Some said it was going to replace the traditional feedback page, and others thought it would move eBay into the more social world of Web 2.0. Whatever it is or was intended to be, it hasn't become a very noteworthy eBay feature. Although all the information about the user is encapsulated onto the page, it is hard to find and nobody seems to use the page.

Nevertheless, this is there you will find the eBay blogs. The eBay blogs, provided for free, are good for posting short blurbs about your business. They are highly ranked on the search engines when updated regularly. Although they are easy to use and great for getting your feet wet in the blogosphere, they are not very customizable. In the past, eBay has made noises about allowing no links, and a blog without links makes an eBay blog like a race car with a flat tire.

That said, if this is where your customers are looking, then this is where you want to post. If not, you can still take advantage of the strong SEO rankings. If you have time (or have an employee who has time), repurpose content from other writings to post here. If you sent out a great newsletter and wish more people had the opportunity to read it—or you are planning a big sale—blog about it here. You can post items you've recently listed or use this as a way to update your customers about new finds.

Be sure to set up the *tags* on your blog. You'll find the link on the left-hand side of the page when you change templates for your blog. Use the keywords from your keyword list to fill them in. Tags are an important point for search engines to pick up relevant information about your posts. Spiders hunt for tags embedded in blog posts to return in search results. For example, if you write about the items you list, using search tags can set your blog apart from others with more general content. So if you wrote about bicycle shorts in your blog, use tags such as *bicycling, shorts,* and *touring* to increase your visibility in search results.

Yes, this free addition can help bump your eBay Store in the search engine, and eBay will populate your blog on a Neighborhood page if it matches a Neighborhood theme. But your blog will have no real commercial value when it comes to promoting outside of the eBay community. So if you're out to take on the world with your marketing strategy, you'll want an outside platform.

Other Platforms

Let's take a quick look at a few of the most popular platforms to use outside of eBay:

- **WordPress.com:** WordPress comes in two varieties. WordPress.com is a free, simple-to-use hosting service for your WordPress blog. There are many templates to choose from, and you can have a blog set up in minutes. Beware, though: WordPress.com has some very strict policies about using its platform for commercial gain. While this is a simple way to get started, it may not be the best choice for marketers, especially if you want to include affiliate links.

- **WordPress.org:** WordPress.org offers the WordPress software minus the hosting. It takes a little more effort to set up. You have to install software on your website. Some webhosts feature one-click installation from a service called Fantastico. If you are not familiar with installing software, you may have to hire a service to do it for you, but it's well worth it. Once the software has been installed, you have much more flexibility to commercialize and monetize the blog and add plug-ins and widgets to spruce it up. There is an amazing array of very professional looking templates available—some for free, and others for a small price. A big bonus of WordPress.org is the amazing SEO results you get from using it. For more information about WordPress blogs, we recommend that you read *Blogging with WordPress,* by Dany Byrne (http://www.ghostleg.com/blog-book.htm).

- **Blogger:** Google owns Blogger. It's easy to use, and you can set up a blog in minutes. There is limited customization on Blogger, but you can add links and a logo. Blogger is a great choice if you don't want to hire a webhosting company. It is a stand-alone application and doesn't require extra steps to install it. The downside is that Blogger is so simple to set up that it has become a magnet for spam blogs. Spam blogs are those blogs set up with no content, just an assortment of ads, so the unlucky person who stumbles on the blog will click them. Because there are so many of these spam blogs set up on Blogger, it has gotten a reputation as a seedy place to hang out. Google is taking aggressive steps to address this problem.

- **TypePad:** TypePad is aimed at business and professional users. TypePad was once the software of choice among pro bloggers, but it has lost popularity as WordPress has grown. It's a paid service, which means a couple of

---

TIP: USE PLUG-INS TO BUILD YOUR WORDPRESS BLOG INTO AN SEO POWERHOUSE

If you choose WordPress, you'll be able to add lots of extra features to your blog. These applications are installed using *plug-ins*—a techie term for features that are added to your site. You can find a complete list of plug-ins in the WordPress plug-in directory at http://wordpress.org/extend/plugins/.

Author Dany Byrne suggests a few important plug-ins for marketing your business using a blog:

- **Feedburner/Feedsmith:** A *feed* is the format that allows readers to customize the way they subscribe or get the blog information. This means that your readers can have your posts delivered via e-mail, they can receive a notification when you've updated the blog, or they can read the post in a preferred reader. This gives your customers control over how they want your content delivered.

- **Bookmarking plug-ins:** These include Share This and Add to Any plug-ins. These types of plug-ins allow users to "favorite" the posts in bookmarking sites such as Digg and Delicious.

- **Google Site Map Generator:** This is a plug-in that tells Google how to index your blog and quickly gets your new information indexed into Google search results.

- **Google Analytics:** This important plug-in gives you specific information about your visitors. You'll learn who, when, where, and why they came to your site. It's a must for marketing!

- **HeadSpace 2:** This is a plug-in that helps you optimize your tags, titles, and headlines for the search engines. This is another way to get top ranking on the search engines.

- **All In One SEO Pack:** This is yet another optimizer. We can't emphasize enough that readers—who will become buyers—often find you through search engines. Make sure your blog is set up to rank well on Google.

- **Contact form or plug-in:** This gives your customers a way to get in touch with you. Be sure to respond promptly to all requests and inquiries.

things. First, you won't have any unwanted advertisements on your blog. Many free services are advertiser sponsored, and you may end up with banner ads on your blog. Another benefit of TypePad is that you receive some really nice, professional-looking templates.

This is not a complete list—blogging is so popular that it is impossible to make a comprehensive list. This is a sampling of the main blog platforms that most marketers use. You should be able to build a blog from any of these services.

Writing Your Blog

Once you have the blog set up, it's time to focus on building traffic and promoting your business.

What do you write about? Well, here's what we write about:

- Stuff we know a lot about and want to share with the world at large

- Stuff that will help us make money—that is related in some way or other to the merchandise or services we sell

- Stuff that people *want* to know about and are looking for

- Stuff that isn't covered in a hundred million other blogs

Your blog should always be lively, cool, compelling, and—if you can pull it off—entertaining. People should *want* to look at your blog and eagerly await your latest postings. If your blog is dull, boring, pedantic, or basically just a clipping service of information the reader can easily find elsewhere on the Web, you won't get too many RSS subscriptions.

As we mentioned, it's important to post regularly. Set aside a little time each day or week to write your posts. Writing—even business writing—can be difficult to do on a schedule. Many bloggers find they have spurts of inspiration. During those times, they can write two or more posts at a time. To take advantage of those creative moments, software that allows you to schedule posts is built into most blogging programs. You can write several posts in one day and have them automatically scheduled to appear over a few days.

Mix up your content a bit, and keep your blog fresh by inviting guest bloggers to post. As you build your business, you'll have a chance to meet many experts in your field. Ask them to write about their products. If you offer a byline and a link to their website or blog, you'll both win. You'll have fresh content, and they'll be rewarded with new customers. Most blog writers will do it for free just to get their name out. By the same token, find blogs that might share the same audience as you and ask them whether you can write an article for them.

Should "Comments" Be Turned On or Off?

One question that comes up often when blogging is about the comments fields and whether you should allow them or moderate them. Blogging is as much about creating a dialogue as it is about selling your product. In fact, selling is distinctly secondary to your main purpose: engaging your readers. If you turn off the comments, you are cutting off your customers' ability to communicate with you. If possible, keep communication with your customers a two-way street. Ask for their comments when you post.

You may eventually get a negative or nasty remark. The Internet seems to encourage negative behavior, and many people post without thinking. But if it is a legitimate observation, wouldn't it be better to see it on your blog and respond to it than to find that unhappy person posting about the problem all over the Internet? Many companies have made the mistake of being inaccessible to their unhappy customers and found those customers' complaints getting top rankings on the search engines. Communicating with customers can be a messy process, but it's better to have that conversation on your blog, where you can respond and help relieve your buyers' dissatisfaction. In general, leave your comments fields open for anyone to post in them. If you have time, or can hire someone, moderate the comments. If you read and approve the comments before they are posted on the blog, you will be able to receive the feedback and decide whether to post it.

How to Squidoo

Launched in October 2005 by marketer Seth Godin, Squidoo is a unique site that makes it free and easy to post a webpage (which in Squidoo is called a *lens*) and attract the search engine spiders that rank your content in search results. A Squidoo page combines the best of several online tools. This hybrid between a blog and a website can help eBay store owners who can't post regularly on a blog and/or don't want a website. Using a Squidoo page, you can highlight the best of your blog writing and keep it front and center without the pressure of constantly updating it.

There is no limit to the number of lenses you can create—in fact, the more, the better. Publishing a lens is free, so you may create as many as possible and link them to your eBay store. You can use the lenses to highlight certain items or categories of goods or to give a brief tutorial about your product. And you can recycle your material as much as you want.

Stephanie Daugherty, eBay Store owner from Katiyana's Collectibles, builds lenses to promote her eBay store inventory (see Figure 4.8). Stephanie started lens building to promote her business in 2006, and by September 2007 she had found that Squidoo was the second-biggest traffic generator for her eBay Store. That's the first spot after eBay-generated traffic. She has created hundreds of lenses and

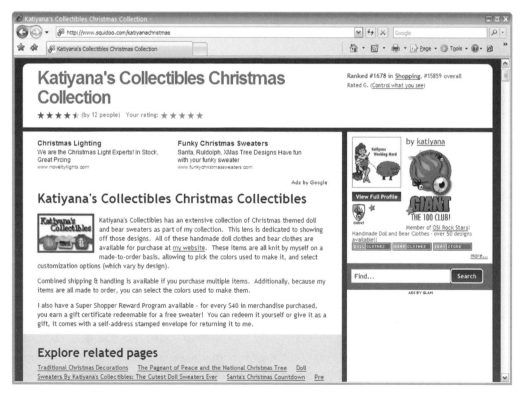

FIGURE 4.8 Stephanie Daugherty uses Squidoo to drive traffic to her eBay Store (http://www.squidoo.com/katiyanachristmas).

is now enjoying not only increased traffic to her store but monthly royalty payments into her PayPal account.

Increase Traffic Through SEO

Because Google loves content, Squidoo lenses make the most of search engine optimization. Getting to the top of the SEO ranks before Squidoo took weeks or even months. With a lens it takes less time because the search engine spiders troll Squidoo's content-laden pages constantly.

Squidoo is not only about creating blurbs on your topic. Like all good word-of-mouth marketing, it's about creating links. The more links you have pointing to your eBay Store, the higher it will be ranked by the search engines. This is especially true when the links are from a highly rated authority site. Because Squidoo receives lots of traffic and has lots of creators, it is considered an important authority site.

Earn Royalties

If a reader clicks on the link in the lens for your store and makes a purchase, Squidoo pays you a royalty. To be fair, the payout is not going to be as high as if you had used a website and the eBay Partner Network directly, but the upside is that you don't have to know anything about HTML or coding to use Squidoo. Those who do use the EPN directly can incorporate those links into their Squidoo lenses as well and keep 100 percent of the commissions for themselves.

Customizable eBay Module

Each lens you create allows you to link directly to your own eBay user ID. Squidoo has "modules" that allow you to customize your lens using feeds from various Internet sites. These modules are very easy to set up: Just click a button and choose the inventory that you'd like to showcase, and Squidoo populates your lens with the information. One of them, the eBay Module, shows readers a sample of your eBay listings and store merchandise. For more information about the eBay Module, go to http://www.squidoo.com/HowToSearchEbay.

Tips for Maximizing Your Efforts on Squidoo

Here's a quick list of ways to maximize Squidoo for marketing your eBay listings:

- Write a lens about your product or niche and include links to your store.

- Write how-to articles about using your products, with links to your store.

- Write about the history of your product or the story behind its creation.

- Do a best-of lens centered on a theme. If you are an eBay consignment seller, create a lens devoted to the best deals, the most interesting products, or the most unique gifts.

- Write a lens about the charity you support and donate all the lens royalties to the charity. Include a short blub about your store with links to products.

- Encourage your customers to write a lens around a theme related to your products and invite them to join your Squidoo group.

- Create a contest around your product, with the participants writing Squidoo lenses. Find judges, and award prizes. Make sure participants include your store inventory in a module with each entry.

- Create a lens and join a Squidoo group. Post and participate regularly in the group. Become a trusted expert, and buyers will purchase from you.

- Read other writers' lenses, rate them, and post comments. Make sure your signature line includes a link to your eBay Store.

- eBay Education Specialists should create lenses about themselves, including bios and links to their eBay Stores and their Education Specialist websites.

- Build lenses about other interests you have, such as books, movies, authors, and actors, and bring in products from Amazon and eBay to complement your topic. These lenses that aren't directly related to your own products bring more traffic to your lenses and provide opportunities to make affiliate sales commissions on products other than your own.

Podcasts

Although podcasting takes its name from Apple's popular iPod line of products, it isn't limited at all to iPod users and can indeed be an exciting and creative new way for you to promote your business. A *podcast* is a prerecorded audio program that is posted to a website and made available for download so people can listen to it on a personal computer or mobile device (including, yes, iPod products).

What distinguishes a podcast from other types of audio products on the Internet is that a podcaster can solicit subscriptions from listeners, so that when new podcasts are released they can automatically be delivered, or *fed,* to a subscriber's computer or mobile device. Usually, the podcast features an audio show with new episodes that are fed to your computer either sporadically or at planned intervals, such as daily or weekly. As with the old radio serials of the 1930s and 1940s, this encourages listeners to subscribe so they can find out what happens next.

You can effectively use podcasting as a way to position yourself as an expert in your field in marketing your eBay business. It doesn't matter whether your field is collecting presidential pinbacks, selling contractor equipment, or coaching eBay sellers.

Marlene Gavens, from The Savvy Seller (http://the-savvy-seller.com), has been podcasting for about a year. Her show, called *Tips From The Top,* is now in the top fifty of the eBay category on iTunes. Marlene finds that her show is "positioning her better in the eBay and online community." Not only does she interview experts in her field—eBay and online commerce generally—but she has also become a guest on other podcast shows. Marlene found that when she invites guests on her show, they in turn write to their followers about the appearance on their blogs, in their newsletters, and on Twitter. Thus, Marlene finds that she is reaching more and more listeners.

Once the podcast has been recorded, Marlene makes it viral by submitting the feed to various podcast directories, including the incredibly popular iTunes, where the broadcasts are available to potentially millions of listeners for later downloads.

Most podcasting hosts, including TalkShoe, have a simple widget that is easy to install on a blog or your website. Marlene finds that the more portable aspect of a podcast makes it easier for subscribers to consume the content. Thus, when subscribers see a podcast on the blog, they are much more likely to turn it on (or download it) and are likewise more likely to fully understand the content. (See Figure 4.9.)

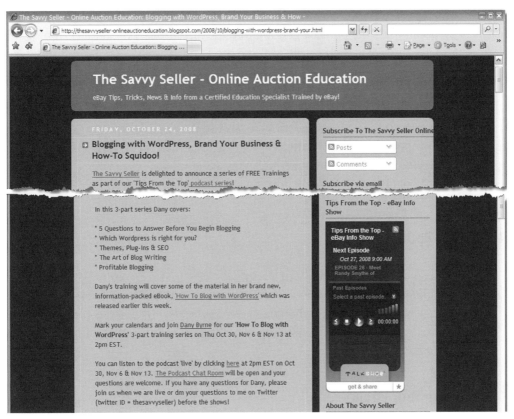

FIGURE 4.9   Marlene Gavens interviews her guests and then makes them available on her blog via an easy-to-install widget.

Marlene suggests that you keep your podcasts short. She focuses her interviews to keep them to about fifteen minutes. The shorter length is more convenient for the person who is asked to be interviewed, and she helps guests use the time efficiently by following a consistent format. She sends her guests the questions in advance. If you are a regular listener, you know what the agenda will be. She asks the same questions of each guest and, if time allows, takes questions from the audience via an instant message board offered as part of the TalkShoe platform.

Marlene finds that she prefers interviewing others to just talking to herself. "I find it easier to have a guest on. They in turn get the information out to their talkers (or sneezers). Having guests also helps fill in the gaps." However, there are other formats for podcasting. Many podcasters broadcast as individuals and build personal followings just like radio disk jockeys.

Because of the nature of podcasting, your broadcast can be immediate and contemporary. As soon as you hear breaking news in your industry, create a podcast about it. As the podcast gets fed into the directories, post it on your blog for those who listen on their computers and send out an e-mail. If you use Twitter, do that mavericky thing Twits do and post the link for your followers. This format can be used for breaking industry news or trips to industry-specific trade shows, and it can make you a trusted authority to your clients.

Once the podcast is recorded, you can use it in multiple ways. A free downloadable podcast is a great ethical bribe to get newsletter subscribers to sign up—or to entice viewers from your About Me page to click over to your website or for promotional handouts (if you burn them onto a CD).

Recording Podcasts

There are several ways to record a podcast. You can use an online service such as FreeConferencePro (www.freeconferencepro.com). With FreeConferencePro, you call in via your landline telephone, and the service records the call. There are many online services that work with Skype or VoIP software as well as with a telephone landline.

Using Your Phone

Services like TalkShoe (www.talkshoe.com) and BlogTalkRadio (www.blogtalkradio.com) allow you to simply dial in on a phone to create a recording. They record it and broadcast it to the podcast distributers (iTunes, etc.) with the click of a mouse. They make it very easy for the nontech person.

After researching her options, Marlene chose TalkShoe Radio as her podcasting service. This free service allows the host and a guest to use the telephone to record the podcasts. These phone conversations are broadcast live. Listeners have the ability to participate via a chat room, where they can type in questions.

Using Your Computer

Another way to create a podcast is to record it on your computer. You need a USB microphone and special podcast studio software to help you record and edit your podcasts. For Apple Macintosh computers, the software is called GarageBand and is part of the iLife software package (www.apple.com/ilife). The most popular podcast studio software for Windows computers is Audacity, available as a free download from http://audacity.sourceforge.net. The benefit of recording the podcast to your computer is that you have more control over the content and quality. You can edit the goofs and flubs. You also have more control over the distribution of the podcast. For example, you can record online broadcasts on your computer, edit them, and then burn (copy) them onto a CD. The CDs make great promotional handouts and upsells for products in your eBay Store.

Ensuring Good Sound Quality

Practice what you are going to say or prepare your script in advance to keep the editing time as short as possible. Using a service whereby you phone in the podcast has its disadvantages; if you pop your P's or breathe too heavily, it is all recorded and makes the recording hard for your listeners to follow. Most serious podcasters invest in a USB microphone and an inexpensive pop filter attachment to prevent those pops and breathing mistakes.

Many podcasting teams call each other on Skype and use software like Pamela to record the call. Each voice is recorded on its own audio track. Before the podcast is publically posted, the audio levels for each speaker can be evened out, resulting in a much better experience for the listeners.

Choosing a Host

Janelle Elms, from OSI Rock Stars (osirockstars.com), uses podcasting as a method to teach members how to sell effectively on eBay. Members pay to subscribe to her information, which they can download and listen to at their leisure. They access the information from her website, but the actual podcasts are housed on a remote computer/server. Podcasts use up a lot of bandwidth, and most webhosting services charge for the extra bandwidth you will use if hundreds of people are downloading your podcast feeds. Because she has so many listeners, Janelle has a server that is dedicated to hosting the podcasts. Many podcasters just starting out may not be ready for the expense. Also, if the server breaks down (which, as a mechanical object, it is inclined to do from time to time), you have to drop everything else you're doing and get it fixed, or else you're "off the air." This is one of the big advantages of using a host service like TalkShoe or BlogTalkRadio, because they host the large files and distribute them for free in exchange for advertising.

Posting Content on a Website

Once your podcast is recorded, you have to post it to a website, either by pushing a button or by uploading it via a service (depending on how you recorded it). Many podcasters post them on their websites and blogs and on iTunes, which so far has the largest podcast inventory available anywhere on the Web.

Podcasting is an exciting new medium that allows your customers a way to build a relationship with you and your company. With emerging technology on the Web such as TalkShoe, BlogTalkRadio, and even Skype, broadcasting is an easy way to dialogue with your customers.

Videocasts

There's no doubt the eBay marketplace is getting more and more congested. It's hard to stand out from the crowd. As broadband Internet access continues to grow, Internet video has come of age. Yet a study done by hosting site Vzaar.com found that less than 1 percent of eBay sellers are using videos in their listings. With so few sellers using video, it means smart marketers have a wide-open field to take advantage of this marketing bonanza. To make the most of video as a marketing tool, your videos need to do double duty. They should both sell among eBay shoppers and drive traffic to you from outside the site.

Gain your customers' trust as well as increase sales and profits by using video. Providing a video of the product you are selling can:

- Bring qualified buyers to your listings from YouTube

- Create a sense of personal connection between you and your customer

- Explain the features and benefits of ownership

- Demonstrate the movement, sound, or purpose of the item

- Show customers how a product is used

- Offer an orientation for your About Me or store landing page

- Showcase customer testimonials

Hosting

There are several eBay-approved sites where you can host the video for free and then embed it into your listings. To do this, eBay requires that the video be in flash format from an approved provider. A list of eBay-approved video providers can be found at http://pages.ebay.com/help/policies/listing-links.html. One site, Vzaar.com, has a one-button insert. It's easy—you don't have to do anything more than upload the video to the Vzaar site just as you would a photo. For high-quality results, use either Vzaar or one of the services targeted at eBay users.

Heavily trafficked sites like YouTube, MySpace, Google Video, and MSN allow you to upload your video, grab the code, and put it into your listings. It's an extra step, but the payoff is worth it. Google ranks YouTube videos in top spots very rapidly. If you use keyword-rich titles and tags, buyers who are looking for your product are likely to stumble upon the videos quickly. In fact, it's a great SEO strategy to list your video on all the sites you can, because with video there is no Google duplicate content penalty.

Shooting Your Video

You don't need a fancy video camera to make a movie. Most point-and-shoot digital cameras have the capability to make short clips with sound. Even your cell phone might record movies. Or you can purchase an inexpensive webcam or a video camera such as a Flip. Video editing software is already installed on your computer with programs like Windows Movie Maker and Apple's iMovie. These free programs allow you to edit video clips into a movie. Producing a commercial about your item is very much within your capabilities.

Let's talk about a few basic principles to help you create the best-looking and most effective video to sell your product.

Sloppy Success

If you wait until you have the perfect movie or prop or stage or lighting, you'll probably never accomplish the task. Don't expect to be the next Steven Spielberg when creating your video. Do the best you can, yes, but don't try for fancy special effects. Keep it simple, and allow it to be less than perfect. It's better to get the word out in your own voice than to hope for a Hollywood box office hit. The movie isn't about special effects; it's about your product. Rough authenticity is still a good marketing strategy.

Equipment

Camera. As we mentioned earlier, you don't need a professional movie camera to produce the video. If your digital camera doesn't have the capabilities to produce videos, you could purchase a camcorder. The number of videos you intend to produce dictates what you need in terms of equipment. If your plan is to produce one or two short takes occasionally, then a Flip video camera will do nicely. If you plan on making how-to DVDs as part of your marketing campaign, then a more expensive camcorder purchase would be in order.

Lights. Shoppers will not watch a poorly lit video for more than a few seconds. You don't necessarily need expensive studio equipment—a few shop lights will work—but understanding the principles of lighting helps. Just as in still photography, check that your subject is well lit. Try to soften the shadows by diffusing or bouncing the light. We suggest you spend a little time researching how to produce a well-lit studio subject.

Microphone. If you are going to be a spokesperson, you might find that your camera's onboard microphone picks up too much ambient noise. One of the first things you may want to purchase as you produce more clips is a *lavaliere* microphone (one that clips onto your lapel) to keep your voice clear.

Keep It Short. You may not believe this, but keeping your videos short is the hardest part. It's also a key ingredient in success. If you spend anytime watching TV, you know an advertiser can convey a lot of information about a product in fifteen seconds. When you try it yourself, it'll take minutes. The problem is, your audience wants short, quick blurbs, not minutes of monologue. List the benefits quickly, and let them read about the features when they go to your eBay listing. Try to keep your video under three minutes.

Storyboard

To help keep your clips short, write or draw the scenes out beforehand. Professionals do this. It helps you to shoot the whole project quickly. Once you have it out on a storyboard, you can review it and look for places you can cut before you ever start shooting. If you've never written a storyboard or are not sure what it is, you can find a sample at www.ghostleg.com/storyboard.

What to Shoot and What to Say

Benefits over features! Don't waste buyers' time dwelling on every feature. Always tell your audience what's in it for them. Your videos should always be entertaining and fun, but they must also be focused on the results you want to achieve—selling your merchandise! A lot of great, memorable advertisements did nothing to move the product they advertised. When in doubt, go for substance rather than glitz. You could, for example:

- Demonstrate the item.

- Gather testimonials from users and create a montage.

- Tell people why they should purchase from you.

Don't Forget Your URL

Before you render or do the final save on your video, don't forget your URL. It's important to help your viewers find their way into your store. Be sure to include your website address in your video: Either speak it a few times or show it as a title card at the end of the video. Here's where having that short, memorable store URL helps get you traffic and the 75 percent referral credit with eBay. If you have included a link to your store within the video, visitors will be tracked as being brought in by you and eBay *will pay you* the referral credit when these new buyers purchase.

Janelle Elms takes links on YouTube one step further and has reported great success. She includes a final title card in her videos with an arrow pointing off-screen to the right, where YouTube shows information about the video (see Figure 4.10). Instead of a video title, she uses a sign-up-now invitation. It's an effective call to action because the arrow points to the one clickable link on the YouTube page that's hers. She's reporting daily sign-ups from the use of just a few videos. To do this yourself, make sure to put your entire eBay Store URL, including the http:// part, in your YouTube video description box.

FIGURE 4.10 Give your buyers a call to action at the end of the video: "Click here to . . ."

Where to Post

For the highest-quality output, using a site like Vzaar is your best bet. Having high-quality output is especially important when you offer rapidly changing auction items on eBay, because your buyers will be most concerned about a clear picture. If your video is intended to achieve a longer-term goal—for example, if it's an infomercial offering general information about your eBay Store content (what marketers call *name recognition* marketing)—a better choice might be a social site like YouTube, where you are likely to find communities of like-minded people who share an interest in your merchandise. Of course, there is no restriction on the number of places you can put the video, and it's best from a marketing perspective to use as many as possible.

In fact, as a marketer, you really should consider putting your video on *all* the video-sharing sites you can. The more it's out there, the more potential buyers will see it. The problem is that video files are big and there are a lot of video-sharing sites out there. It takes a great deal of time to upload them to each site. The good news is that there is a free broadcasting service called TubeMogul

(tubemogul.com) that automatically transfers your video to as many sites as you choose after you upload the video. TubeMogul also offers performance statistics, a must for successful marketing campaigns.

We can't emphasize strongly enough how quickly you can rank high in the search engines by using videos. Cindy created a video for one of her products, a photographer's gray card. She listed the video on several video-sharing sites as well as within the eBay listing. When you search for gray cards on Google there are literally millions of hits listed, but because Cindy shot a video and uploaded it to several spots, her gray card dominates the first page of Google Video. A year later she continues to get steady traffic to her listing from this video.

Effectively marketing your brand or product using video requires very little upfront expense. You can start on a small budget. With free hosting sites, free built-in software, and inexpensive technology, there's no reason not to start producing and profiting from videos.

Social Networking

One of the more recent developments in the evolution of the Web and e-commerce is the social networking website, often referred to by the shorthand *Web 2.0.*

Basically, *Web 2.0* refers to a website, or webpage, that is interactive: People don't just look at content there, they actually interact with the content—responding to it, adding to it, (sometimes) editing, and making changes to it online. Here are some examples of Web 2.0 sites you probably have seen:

- **Wikis** such as Wikipedia.org, where online users collaborate to create articles and other Web content

- **Social networking** platforms such as MySpace and Facebook, where users create *profile pages* (essentially, mini-websites) about themselves and invite people to join online communities based on the content that appears on the profile page

- **Blogs** (discussed previously), or interactive diaries

Because Web 2.0 sites are so new, we are still learning a lot about them and what they can do for folks. For people with large families that are geographically scattered, social networking sites are a godsend for staying in touch. Last year, Cliff Ennico received over a hundred holiday newsletters in the mail from people he hadn't seen in a while. This year, a lot of those people simply included in their holiday cards an invitation to "view my page on Facebook," where Cliff could read the newsletter, see photos of the family's vacation and pets, and send a response, without having to write a card or put a stamp on an envelope.

Also, people looking to create fan clubs find the whole social networking phenomenon very attractive. No sooner does a rock-and-roll band launch their first CD than they set up a MySpace page where their fans can comment on the CD, rave about the lyrics or the bands' tattoos, and so forth.

There is one question that haunts all of the currently existing Web 2.0 products, though: How do we make money from these sites? We have heard differing reports from eBay sellers about the effectiveness of participating in social networking websites (other than blogs, which seem to work quite well), so in many ways the jury is still out on these.

Still, if you have the time and patience to keep track of your online profiles, by joining or starting the right community you can find and interact with a whole group of people who are interested in your products. Social networking sites are an ideal way to join in the conversation.

There are so many different social networking sites that choosing the right one might seem overwhelming. This section covers a few of the major sites on the Internet, discusses the types of people you might find there, and explains how this can benefit your business.

Before we get started, here are a few guidelines for success.

Don't Spread Yourself Too Thin.
Don't blanket the social networks; don't spread yourself all over the Web. Find out where *your* community or group of talkers is. You might think you need to have thousands of friends to succeed. It's not true. Furthermore, if you randomly cultivate friends with no interest in you or your product, then it's not going to help your business. Start small. If you have ten people, you have a great network. Don't go for quantity; go for quality. Do not focus your networking on the sandwich-eating masses.

Don't Hit and Run.
We're going to show you how to leave footprints and reach your talkers via bulletin boards and posting. Don't post and go. That won't help you build a relationship; you'll just be viewed as another social website spammer.

Don't Talk to Strangers. Generally, don't invite people you don't know into your network of friends. Collecting thousands of names won't help you. You are going to be judged by the company you keep. Try to keep your social group to like-minded people. A vintage car collector wants to find other car collectors, not a bunch of rock climbers. If you enjoy both, perhaps two separate IDs are better. It's also a great idea to keep your business ID and your personal ID separate. Your friends and family may want to know a step-by-step account of your gall bladder operation. Most business associates would prefer just to send you a get-well card.

Don't Talk About What You Had for Lunch. Unless, of course, it was with someone really interesting and he or she paid the bill. If you want to have your friends unsubscribe from your feed fast, start Twittering every few minutes about your breakfast, walking the dogs, and cleaning the cat boxes.

This is a business tool. The best marketing is about your audience, not you. Keep your comments focused on things that benefit your buyers.

Remember that to have friends, you sometimes have to be a friend. Social networking profile pages are not banner ads. They are interactive, which means that information and commentary go both ways. If you want your friends on Facebook to buy your latest book, that may give them the right (at least occasionally) to ask you to buy *their* latest book or contribute to their favorite charity, and so on.

Make sure your online friends are people you really want to hang out with—people you care about, who share your values, and whom you are proud to be associated with. Remember that basic rule of social interaction your grandmother told you: People judge you by the company you keep. If we look at your Facebook page and think that all of your friends are idiots, we are likely to think (unfairly, of course) that you are an idiot as well. To avoid being considered an idiot on a Web 2.0 site, don't hang out with idiots.

Manage Your Brands and Products as Proactively as Possible. The wonderful thing about social networks is their open architecture. Users create a community or content easily around a subject or topic of common interest. This gives everyone the freedom to post rants and raves about anything. And once you post something, it will be forever recorded by the indexing sites. This means that a complaint or kudos about your product can show up quickly in the top ranking on Google, Yahoo!, MSN, or any search engine. Although the post may linger, it's how you handle it that will keep you in the green.

Set up a Google alert so you are notified every time your name or product is mentioned on the Web. As soon as you receive the e-mail, respond to the comment. If it's a complaint, respond in a positive way. You are in a very public medium; the way in which you handle these communications will make or break your company. Never respond negatively to a disgruntled customer. Never denigrate a competitor. Always keep your focus on the great, quiet mass of people who are reading and judging your response. If an unhappy buyer acts like a jerk and you respond with kindness and concern, *you win*.

Now that we've talked about the biggest social mistakes to avoid, let's take a look at a few of the different sites.

MySpace

Ranked number three on the list of the most-visited sites on the Internet, My-Space started in 1996. It began as a site for musicians to post their gigs and fans to keep up with them. Music is MySpace's territory. They host millions of artist and band pages. One of the first things any new band does is create a MySpace page. Some artists have millions of friends, and the bio pages allow for a great deal of freedom, including streaming music and artist control over the look and feel of the site.

If you have a product that is geared to the music industry, it's easy to see that you should be on MySpace. Comedians, actors, political candidates, and many other public figures also have MySpace pages. However, not just artists use My-Space to socialize. A younger group visits MySpace, and if your target is the twenty- to thirty-year-olds, here is where you want to be.

On your MySpace profile page you can post widgets (small bites of code) that showcase your eBay inventory, set up slideshows, or show videos of your products. Lee and Rhonda Walmsley, from Fastbackstack, have set up an outstanding MySpace page to drive targeted traffic to their eBay Store, where they sell vintage Ford Mustangs. Their MySpace page features the latest items they have listed on eBay, slideshows of restored Mustangs, music (of course—this is MySpace), and links to friends who are mainly other eBay sellers and Mustang collectors. (See Figure 4.11.)

FIGURE 4.11 Lee and Rhonda Walmsley use their MySpace page to drive traffic into their eBay Store (www.myspace.com/fastbackstack).

Bulletin Board

On MySpace your profile is public, and people communicate with each other by becoming *friends*. Friends can post your blurbs on the bulletin board. The bulletin board posts are part of each member's landing page. When you post on the bulletin board, it is broadcast to the bulletin space of every one of your friends. This makes it a great place to highlight new happenings in your store or with your business. Having a special sale? Post it here.

Blogs

MySpace also provides you with a blog. If you don't want to use one of the other blogging services we discussed, you can use the MySpace blog. Your updates will be spidered, and snippets of the content will be featured on your

MySpace page. As with any other blog, encourage comments and keep the page updated regularly.

Comments

Another important, although somewhat time-consuming, feature is the ability to post comments on your friends' MySpace pages. If you have lots of friends on MySpace, hire someone to do this for you. Post help-wanted classified ads on Elance or Craigslist. Remember that, as a small business owner, your time is valuable.

At the time of this writing, you are still allowed to include a link in the comments on MySpace. The comments have become colorful little greetings, and there is a whole bunch of greetings that flash, blink, and are attention getters. This is a wonderful place to leave a link. Post a greeting on your friends' pages, and leave a link to your eBay Store. Because it is so easy to link to your store or website, many people become friends with thousands of people. The comments are now somewhat spammy, and MySpace is starting to change some of its links policies. It won't be long before the search engines ignore them as well, so don't invest weeks of effort in this area.

Facebook

Now ranking number five on the Web, with over ninety million users, this site originally started for college students. Facebook allowed any student who had a university e-mail extension to join. Recently, Facebook opened its doors to everyone. Users communicate with each other via groups and applications like the Wall.

Unlike MySpace, Facebook is designed more to keep you in contact with people you actually know. You must ask to be a friend, and the recipient must approve. Because of this more private feeling, the site has seen tremendous growth among the lucrative twenty-five- to fifty-four-year-old group. These individuals are the perfect demographic for marketers: postcollege education, high discretionary income, early adopters, and so on.

As an eBay marketer, you can use the Facebook site in a number of ways. The eBay To Go application is easy to set up and automatically posts listing updates. Invite your buyers to become your friends, or set up a group on Facebook where like-minded individuals can find you. This is especially valuable for collectors and hobbyists.

There are a number of applications or APIs that allow you to synchronize your blog updates, Twitter updates, Vimeo videos, and more. Because Facebook makes it easy for anyone to create an application, you'll find that just about every company you work with has a Facebook widget to put on your page.

Users send each other drinks, nudge each other, write on the Wall, and socialize. Groups are a main feature of Facebook, and you can create one specifically around your niche. You can upload pictures, and others can comment on them. If your business focus is garage sale finds, this would be a fantastic place to start posting pictures of interesting or unusual stuff you have sold on eBay. Others can look at the photos and comment on them. Encourage participation. Make your group about the members.

Another less-well-known but extremely powerful feature of the Facebook application is called Pages (see Figure 4.12). Click on the Advertising link to find the

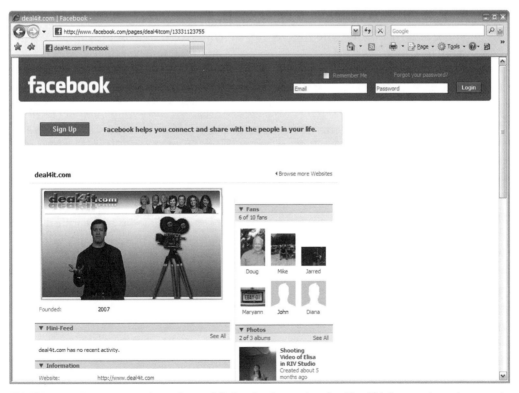

FIGURE 4.12   Anyone can set up a free public Facebook page to advertise. This is a great way to promote your business and create authority links to your site (http://www.facebook.com/pages/deal4itcom/13331123755).

Facebook Pages. Here you can set up a free individual page about your product or service—you can post photos, link to your eBay Store, brand it with a store logo, and more. Other users can become fans of your page to help make it viral. If you don't have a website, here is a place to hang your shingle without having to do any Web design. Because Facebook is such a high-ranking site, any links from this page are going to get the authority mark from the search engines and help with your SEO.

LinkedIn

With twenty-seven million members and growing, this site is gaining notice. Billed not as a social network but as a *professional network,* LinkedIn has a more exclusive air about it. It attracts a more business-oriented user compared to other social networking sites, and you might say that LinkedIn is more dialed down. This is a business site specifically geared to making contacts. People are much more selective about who friends are. Given the option to approve each contact added to your network, you can pick and choose whom you wish to keep company with.

Members network to find new clients and job opportunities, check references, and get advice from mentors. There are groups you can join or create to promote a topic. The average annual household income of the typical LinkedIn user is $109,000, and the average age is forty-one. Because this site focuses on professionals, it is an excellent place for eBay Education Specialists and Trading Assistants to find clients. The demographics make it a prime place to find higher-end items. Although many executives and professionals might want to sell their items on eBay, they often have neither the time for nor the interest in doing it themselves. An eBay seller who takes consignments (such as an eBay Trading Assistant) and networks here is sure to come into contact with those executives looking for someone to help them sell those items.

Twitter

A new kid on the social networking scene, Twitter started just a couple of years ago and is growing quickly. It is referred to as a *microblogging* platform because posts are limited to 140 characters. These short blurbs can be broadcast directly to users via the Twitter website, instant messaging, SMS (short message service), RSS, or e-mail, or through an application such as Twitterrific or Facebook.

As with the other social sites, you become friends and subscribe to other users' Twitter feeds. To find conversations or your targeted group of users, you can use www.search.twitter.com. Of course, you can also invite users to join you on Twitter. This is where the real beauty of Twitter lies for an eBay seller.

Let's say you are a book picker (someone who goes looking for rare and collectible books), and you have built up a base of users who want to be the first to know about your finds. Finding the books takes a great deal of time. You may have a newsletter to keep in touch with customers that talks about how to restore old books. But you can never really send it out quickly or often enough to let customers know of your recent discoveries. However, you carry your cell phone with you wherever you go because you never know when you'll want to check on the value of a book you come across. Keep that cell phone handy, and once you've scored a rare book, text your Twitter feed and let your customers know you've just found it. Buyers will flock to your store, creating competition and driving up bids. To encourage your newsletter subscribers to join Twitter, put an invitation in your e-mail. Don't forget the ethical bribe (or tell them what's in it for them). In this case it would be an invite to be the very first to know when you score that rare J.R.R. Tolkien book.

You can use a plug-in that will automatically post the first few sentences of your blog posts on Twitter, with a link to your blog, to entice readers to take a look. There is a widget that quickly updates your latest Tweet on your Facebook page as well. If you have a group on Facebook, this is a way to keep them up to date.

The effort required to follow all of the steps outlined in this chapter may seem overwhelming to you. If you start small and target your online marketing to where your group of clients is, you will maximize your return. You don't need to worry about the sandwich-eating public (unless, of course, you are a chef selling delicious recipes). Don't try to do everything at once. Stay focused. Keep the benefits to your audience at the heart of your actions.

A little trial and error will help you find your ideal venue. Budget time for yourself each day to participate in the social media. Sitting at home all day, alone and in front of a computer, once sounded romantic, but now you might find yourself a little lonely. Who knows, you might find that you enjoy the social networking. Try some of the different sites, and if they don't fit, move on. The wonderful thing about the places we've mentioned is that they are either free or cost very little.

Making the Most of Web 2.0

When people talk about Web 2.0, the social networking sites such as MySpace and Facebook generate most of the publicity. But Web 2.0 covers a lot more ground than that. Here are some other Web 2.0 applications that you should consider when building an online marketing program.

Wikipedia and Other Wikis

Wikipedia is the biggest multilingual free-content encyclopedia on the Internet. It includes more than seven million articles in over two hundred languages, and it is still growing.

Users build this free encyclopedia collaboratively using Wiki software. A user can post an article, and another member can add to the article, challenge the writing, or edit it. Because of the ever-changing content and user base, this site ranks high in the search engines.

According to the Edelman Trust Barometer, people rank Wikipedia number two among the most credible sources for information. This is powerful! If you can post information about your products, they can rank high. This is great news if you are trying to get information out about a little-known or new product on the market.

Knol

Google has introduced a new platform that is a mix of Wikipedia and Squidoo. Users create one-page posts around a topic or service. As with Wikipedia, you can show your expertise here. Readers are allowed to comment on your Knol and rate it. Knol allows you to post pictures, text articles, and links, and it even allows you to have adwords automatically placed on your sidebar. If you have a popular Knol page, you'll not only drive traffic to your site, you'll have the opportunity to make a little in affiliate income.

Because it is a Google application, this is surely a great place to build SEO and drive traffic into your eBay Store. This can be a great site for eBay Education Specialists and Trading Assistants (consignment sellers) to post their bios or business information.

Bookmarking Sites

Whenever you come across a website you like and want to find again on short notice, you can *bookmark* it on your Web browser. By clicking on the Bookmarks link on your Web browser, you can see at a glance all the sites you have bookmarked. A bookmarking site is very similar, except that it lives online, and other people can view your list of bookmarks. For example, if I am a fan of the rock star Bruce Springsteen, I can create a bookmarking page with lists of articles and blog postings about "The Boss" that I agree with. Other people can look at these and rank them depending on how much they agree or disagree that I have a deeper understanding of Bruce Springsteen than anyone else on the planet.

Those readers who are familiar with the lists feature on Amazon.com—where, for example, users can make up lists of "The Ten Greatest 1980s Heavy Metal Bands of All Time" that will pop up next to searches for Def Leppard or AC/DC—will have a fairly good idea of what a bookmarking site does.

Bookmarking sites include Digg, Del.icio.us, StumbleUpon, Reddit, Yahoo! Bookmarks, BlinkList, Google Bookmarks, Furl, and many more. There are even smaller, topic-specific bookmarking sites. A bookmarking site allows users to keep track of their favorite websites, blogs, social networking profiles, and other Internet locations by making detailed lists, which are then either made public to all users of the site or restricted so that only your "friends and family" can see them. The more advanced bookmarking sites allow users to not only see your bookmarks, but rate and comment on them as well.

Many people use bookmarking sites as a way to keep track of their favorite websites, while others use them to socialize and recommend articles to others. One of the most powerful sites for this purpose is Digg.com. Here users *digg* a blog post or new article they've read, and others rate it. This is where viral marketing takes off. A popular article can skyrocket to the top of Digg quickly and create server-crashing traffic to a site in a matter of minutes.

While some articles arrive at the top by pure luck and good content, many are skyrocketed to the top because of the *Digger*. Popular Diggers have followers who watch what they digg and quickly rate it.

How can you use a bookmarking site to build your traffic? Chances are, just joining Digg and bookmarking your blog posts won't do it. To become a popular Digger takes time and requires that you submit quality content regularly, Most popular Diggers bookmark different articles they've read several times a day. Focusing on a niche builds your audience faster.

It might be easier and less time consuming to focus your energy on creating quality content on your blog and then making sure you have a very easy, one-button submittal to Digg.com for those popular diggers out there patrolling for their next bookmark.

Online Forums

Online forums and bulletin boards are very similar to the eBay discussion boards in terms of their value to marketers. The advantage of using the boards outside eBay is the larger audience.

These typically unmoderated or loosely moderated boards are gathering grounds for like-minded individuals. People who post can ask questions, discuss topics of the day, and talk about their latest interests.

Your job is to learn your way around the board and, once you are familiar with the social etiquette of the forum, participate. If there's a member with a question that you can answer, jump in. If your product offers a solution, let the person know. Be transparent about it—don't try to be clever and hide the fact that your recommendation is anything but biased. You'll get a lot more respect that way. If the question doesn't call for a plug for your product, don't offer it. Simply post the answer. Build your credibility by being a helpful expert rather than a sales-person.

Every time you post something on the forum or group, include your signature line. Make sure you have a quick statement about yourself and the URL to your store. In time, people will wonder about you and click over to your store.

E-Zines

Bloggers and reporters are always on the prowl for new articles. They might not have time to post, or they might just be out of ideas. When that happens, they start looking for content. One place they go to is the e-zine article sites. Writers post articles with the goal of being republished throughout the Web and in print media in exchange for a byline with a link.

Because of the ever-changing content, these sites get ranked highly by the search engines, so links from the sites are given authority points. Often when you've written an article you'll find it top-ranked on Google within days. This cuts both ways. Your best article might point to an e-zine site rather than your store. Be sure to post strategically, and always include links to and information about your eBay business in every article.

These sites allow you to post short articles of around five hundred words about a topic of your choice. As a business owner, you know lots of stuff about your products. Here's one place to take advantage of that knowledge to become an expert and get valuable links to your eBay Store or blog.

Here's a quick list a few of the most popular e-zine sites:

http://ezinearticles.com

http://www.articlealley.com

http://www.articlestop.com

http://articleavenue.com

http://zinos.com

Online Press Releases

Submitting a press release to an online source can drive traffic to your site. There are many services that will submit your press release to various publications for you. This might be okay for a politician, but not necessarily the best for your business. If you are going to spend time writing a press release, then spend a little extra time finding the publication that writes for your market segment.

In addition to the tips and techniques for writing press releases that are covered in Chapter 5 of this book, there are a few specific considerations for writing online. Write the press release with the intention that it can be "borrowed." Keep it fairly short so that it will fit into a blog post neatly. Bloggers are always looking for events and interesting stuff to post about. If your press release can simply be cut and pasted, it's much more likely to be spread.

When writing press releases, keep in mind that you are writing for readers and bloggers *and* for the search engine spiders. Stay aware of keyword density while you are writing. Include your keyword phrases in three places:

1. In the title

2. About midway through the body of the press release

3. At the end of your press release

Positioning keywords in these three spots reinforces the legitimacy and relevance of the article to the search engines when they index the article.

Marketing in a Virtual World

One of the hottest new developments on the Internet is the virtual reality sites, the most prominent of which is Second Life (www.secondlife.com).

Second Life is a parallel reality world—an artificial online universe that mimics our own. You can create your own *avatar*—a duplicate "you." Your avatar doesn't have to look like you. You can create an avatar that's better looking than you or one that looks like a robot or a character from Tolkien's *Lord of the Rings*. If you are male, your avatar can be female; if you're straight, your avatar can be gay; and so forth. You then send your avatar off on its own adventures in Second Life, where it interacts with other avatars, and, well, anything can happen. This includes building businesses, buying real estate, and interacting with other businesses on Second Life, using the site's own virtual currency called Linden Dollars. There are people on eBay who will sell you Linden Dollars so you can buy your own island or rent out their penthouse condo in one of Second Life's several virtual metropolises (search eBay for "second life" and see what pops up).

Should your business have a virtual store on Second Life? It depends on whether you find your target market there. Want to know more? Here's a book that will help you make the decision: *The Unofficial Guide to Building Your Business in the Second Life Virtual World,* by Sue Martin Mahar and Jay Mahar.

But be forewarned: Once you get hooked on Second Life, you may never, ever want to live or sell in the real world again.

Should You Be on the Cutting Edge of Web Commerce?

It seems that just about every week there's something new to do on the Internet—a new social networking site, a new way to create affiliate programs, a new offering from Google or Yahoo!—all designed to create more opportunities for people to market their businesses online.

Does it make sense to take advantage of these opportunities when they become available? The short answer, at least as we see it, is . . ."maybe."

For example, Internet radio is one of the fastest-growing online media today, as we discuss later in this book. But in 1998, Internet radio was in its infancy. Cliff Ennico was contacted by a magazine that was launching one of the first-ever Internet radio networks and wanted someone to host a weekly small business radio show. At the time, Cliff was the host of *Money Hunt,* a popular PBS television show for entrepreneurs, and the Internet broadcaster thought that Cliff's name would help build traffic for the network.

The price was right, so Cliff said yes.

Four times a year, Cliff flew from his home in Connecticut to the Los Angeles area, stopped off at the broadcaster's studios, and spent the next three days recording about a dozen Internet radio shows featuring prominent guests from the world of entrepreneurship as well as Cliff's off-the-cuff (and frequently off-the-wall) comments on the state of small business in America. According to the ratings services available at that time, Cliff's show was the most popular Internet radio show in North America.

How many people listened to Cliff's show? Three hundred fifty. You got it—350 people all over North America tuned in to Cliff's show to listen to what he had to say. Why such a small number? Back in 1998, very few people had invested in broadband connections to access the Internet. The vast majority of people surfing the Internet in 1998 were still using dial-up connections, and you need a broadband connection to listen to Internet radio.

The moral of Cliff's story is that sometimes you can be so far ahead of the curve that you disappear from view.

Pioneers Pay a Price

Whenever new technologies, media, or resources appear on the Internet horizon, it's tempting to want to jump in feet first and become one of the pioneers in that field.

However, when you're trying to build a successful business presence on eBay or elsewhere on the Internet, you have to weigh the costs against the benefits. Those costs are likely to be large, for a number of reasons:

- The new technology or medium probably hasn't been tested yet. There will probably be defects and bugs to work out, and you will be the beta tester, or guinea pig, who will find them before anyone else.

- Even if the new technology or medium is relatively defect free, there are no guidebooks or Web support sites for the new technology or medium. You will have to figure out everything yourself, and you probably will be the one to write the guidebook once the technology or medium takes off.

- Most important, there is no assurance that the technology or medium will become dominant. Someone brighter and more clever may come up with something that's even cooler, and the technology or medium you've invested countless hours and dollars in will be left in the dust.

Your Most Important Asset

When you're in business for yourself, your most valuable asset—more valuable even than money or your reputation—is your time.

There are only twenty-four hours in a day, and seven days in a week. Nobody gives you any more than that. Your job is to spend those hours wisely and reap the best return on your investment of time that you possible can. Spending countless hours trying to master a new technology or medium that might not even be around in three years may not be the wisest way for you to market, build, and grow your online business.

If a new technology or medium is attracting lots of young tech-heads and generating tons of buzz in that community, and your business targets young tech-heads and has an image of being ahead of the curve on all things Internet, then it's an investment you may have to make. But for the vast majority of eBay sellers, it probably isn't.

When evaluating new technologies and media on the Internet, it's best to take a wait-and-see attitude—by all means, keep an eye on it and maybe try to learn a little bit about it, but don't jump in until you see that your customers are signing up for the new technology or media in sufficient numbers that it makes sense for your business to have an online presence there. Once that happens, you should certainly jump in . . . with both feet.

Track What's Working and What Isn't

Now that you have a website and blog set up and are the social butterfly of the Internet, you may be wondering how effective all this social hopping is. You know it's important to focus your attention on what works and not waste valuable time on those things that aren't working. How do you monitor results? This chapter covers how to track incoming customer traffic and gauge effectiveness. We recommend using eBay's Traffic Reports for your eBay Store and Google Analytics to track activity on your other websites.

As an eBay Store owner, you can monitor incoming traffic by using eBay's Traffic Reports. The amount of data you'll see depends on your store subscription level. Even the basic store gives you sufficient information to monitor trends. You will find the link to your store reports under the Manage My Store area. The first time you click in, you'll have to agree to let the tracking company add cookies to your store. Once agreed, Omniture will start monitoring your site.

Omniture tracks your traffic over time and provides visitor profiles and month-to-month and year-over-year reports. You'll find information about the most popular listings, referring sites, and search engine terms. This information is invaluable in running your business from both a merchant's and a marketer's perspective. Of course, as a merchant, you need to watch to make sure your traffic is converting and your sales are growing. You must know what the most popular items are and how many return customers you have. As a marketer, you can also monitor how successful your campaigns are, what customers are looking for, and how they arrived at your listings. The following section focuses on analytics from a marketer's perspective.

Things You Can Find Out in the Traffic Reports

Return Frequency

The first place to check is the Return Frequency report. This shows you the days between repeat visits. It can help you identify the number of return visitors, how *sticky* your store is (the average length of time people stay on your site before clicking off it), and how compelling your newsletter and other promotions are in prompting return visits.

Finding Methods

To learn how your customers are finding you in the first place, use the Finding Methods report. This tells you how many visits came from which sites. Expect eBay to always top the list, then Google. Your goal for driving traffic into your store is to make your website or blog show up high on the list. The more traffic from your site, the better. When you bring buyers in through your referring ID, you'll receive eBay's referral credit of 75 percent of the final value fee eBay charges on the purchase price of each item.

One great thing about the Finding Method report is discovering the other sites that might be referring to you. If you notice traffic coming from a discussion board or a particular website, check it out! If it's a discussion board, you now have another place to participate and leave more footprints. A referral from a website could mean a marketing opportunity or a link exchange. If you have considered pay-per-click advertising, you might be able to target those specific websites in your Google AdWords campaigns, or you may want to approach the owners directly about placing banners on their sites. An incoming link from a blog post means you should comment on the post. You might also ask the blog creator if he or she would like you to write a guest article about the particular product under discussion. These are the sorts of marketing opportunities you can't buy. Do not pass them up.

Store Keyword Search

The Store Keyword Search report is full of useful information about how your visitors found you through the search engines. When you set up your store, you relied heavily on eBay's keyword suggestions. You found others by watching successful auctions. Those tools gave you keywords that were used in the past. Using the Store Keyword Search report, you get contemporary trending information. You'll know exactly what your potential customers are typing in to find your products. Keep track of these words and phrases, and update your store and listing keywords regularly. Be sure that buyers who are already searching for items you sell are able to find your store.

The Store Keyword Search report is a gold mine of ideas. If you learn that your customers are finding their way into your store because they are looking for the answer to a question, write a guide, custom page, or blog post about it. Link it to your store for added SEO, and your customers will be one click closer to purchasing when they land on your information page. Don't forget your call to action. It will be subtler than a "click to buy" button, but be sure to encourage readers to visit your store.

Most Popular Pages

You can track the results of your newly minted custom page by checking Most Popular Pages under custom reports. This one ranks which pages are getting the most traffic. This can give you insight about how to tweak your pages for maximum traffic. For example, if you find that your About Me page is outranking your storefront page, make sure your store Meta Tags are current. If you have a higher ranking in the search engines for your About Me page, make sure non-eBay browsers can find their way into the store by placing a prominent link to the store above the fold of the About Me page.

Most Popular Listings

The Most Popular Listings report seems almost redundant. This report can tell you which products are drawing the most hits, a way to double-check the keywords in your titles. But it also has a hidden benefit. It's designed to help you do split testing and check results. Doing an A/B test with a title, you can see which listing is getting the most visits.

Store Search Terms

The Store Search Terms report is valuable beyond gold, not only for the enterprising seller who wonders what to stock in inventory but for the marketer as well. Here you can see specifically what people search for once they are inside the store. Are they asking questions? Do they seem to be able to navigate through the categories? Do your customers respond to your branding? You can tell right away by the store search terms. If you find that people are searching for completely unrelated products, it indicates that the browsers believe they are still on the main eBay site, not inside your unique store. A customer search for "citrus" when you sell truck accessories might mean you missed the mark with your keywords. Unless, of course, the customer is searching for citrus-scented car air freshener. In that case, give your customers what they want and start stocking the new item.

Tracking on Sites Outside eBay

These eBay Traffic Reports can tell you specifically how successful you are at finding and targeting your market group. They can tell you how well the funnel from outside source to eBay is working. But how about those blogs and websites you've set up to drive traffic into eBay? Are they effective in their job of finding the searchers and bringing them to this middle ground? To find out more about your target group, turn to the giant of searches: Google Analytics (http://www.google .com/analytics). Google Analytics is a powerful tool for insightful information about your traffic.

Google Analytics requires a simple-to-install bit of code that goes into your website or blog. Google Analytics can give marketers extremely useful information. Analytics can track incoming traffic with more depth and detail than you get from the eBay Traffic Reports. Unfortunately, you cannot install it in your eBay Store.

These reports are geared specifically to outside websites and blogs. We mention them here because it's so important to have a blog or website to build your traffic into eBay. Google Analytics tells you how visitors found your site and how they interact with it. You can compare the behavior and profitability of visitors who were referred from each of your ads, keywords, search engines, and e-mails, and you can gain valuable insight into how to improve your site's content and design. However large or small your site—and however you drive traffic to it, whether it's via unpaid search, partner sites, AdWords, or other cost-per-click programs—Google Analytics tracks it, from click to conversion.

For AdWords users in particular, Google Analytics provides the actionable information that you can use to increase your return on investment (ROI) by tracking cost data for all your campaigns and combining that data with conversion information on a page-by-page basis. Google Analytics automatically imports AdWords cost data so that you can track the effectiveness of your AdWords campaigns, and it automatically tags your AdWords destination URLs to track keyword and campaign conversion rates with no effort on your part. To find out more about AdWords, go to the AdWords home page at https://adwords.google.com or read Greg Holden's excellent book *Go Google: 20 Ways to Reach More Customers and Build Revenue with Google Business Tools.*

5

Offline Marketing Strategies and Tools

When the Best Way to Market an
Online Business Is Offline

"Why use offline strategies at all?" you might ask. "After all, people are going to be looking online for an Internet-based business, aren't they?"

Well, maybe . . .

Fifteen years ago, when the Internet burst into the public consciousness, there weren't too many effective ways to find websites and other Internet content online. Journalists surfed the Internet, found cool and interesting content, and then wrote articles for print magazines and newspapers featuring the URLs they discovered online. People reading the articles would make a note of the URLs and look them up the next time they were online.

It's fifteen years later, of course, and we have massive search engines that can comb every square inch of the Internet looking for stuff that other people might have missed. But one of the dirtiest little secrets of the online world is that even today, fifteen years after the Internet first became popular with the public, most people still find out about new websites and content by offline means.

If you doubt this, ask yourself this question: When was the last time you first learned of a new website by one of the following means?

- A newspaper or magazine article

- A book like this one

- A friend or family member

- An office colleague

- Someone in one of the associations or networking groups you belong to

If you said anything longer than a week ago, we would be very surprised.

While you should, of course, do everything you can to market your eBay business online, you should not neglect offline marketing techniques that can often be highly successful in attracting new customers to your eBay listings or eBay Store.

All Business—Well, a Lot of Business—Is Local

We can almost hear some of you saying, "But gee, guys, traditional offline marketing is for businesses that are targeting a primarily local or regional market. Isn't the whole beauty of eBay, and the Internet in general, the fact that I can put up a website or eBay Store and people from all over the world can look at it and buy stuff from me?"

Certainly when you put up a website or eBay Store, the whole world *might* be watching, but that doesn't mean they actually *are,* according to Randye Spina, founder and chief solutions officer of Affordable Marketing Solutions LLC in Bridgeport, Connecticut (www.myaffordablemarketing.com). "It's true that everybody on the Internet can see anything that's happening on the Internet all the time, but first they have to find you, and it's tough to get on their radar screens when you're first getting off the ground," says Spina. She explains that "what we're seeing with online businesses, just like traditional 'brick and mortar' small businesses, is that most of them get started by building a strong local following, then move regionally, then nationally. Once they start growing rapidly and building a brand or following outside of their home base, the odds of favorable search engine placement and nationwide and international sales increase geometrically."

Japanese samurai of the sixteenth century carried two swords with them at all times—a long sword or broadsword for open field combat and a short sword or dagger for close encounters and tight situations. The samurai master Miyamoto Musashi, in his classic treatise on military strategy, *A Book of Five Rings*, wrote about the need for a successful samurai to learn how to use both his long sword and his short sword—being the master of only one was not sufficient. When you're selling online, your Internet marketing strategy is your "long sword," but you should also master the "short sword" that will reach customers who aren't online twenty-four hours a day, seven days a week, looking for new and interesting information—which, when you come to think about it, is most of the people on earth.

Now That We're Back in 3-D, It's Time to Push

Throughout this book we have emphasized that selling on the Internet is about *pulling* your customers to your Web presence. *Push* marketing techniques—rubbing your marketing message in people's faces—simply don't work well on the Internet.

Well, we're not on the Web anymore, baby—we're back in the physical world, and it's okay to use push marketing techniques. In fact, when it comes to local or regional marketing offline, push strategies tend to be as effective as, if not sometimes more effective than, pull strategies.

The sections that follow give you an overview of offline marketing strategies and tactics that you should at least consider when building a business on eBay or, indeed, anywhere else on the Internet.

Press Releases

While your eBay business is busy selling things every day, it is also doing things that might actually be newsworthy. For example, you may be launching a major charity initiative on eBay using eBay Giving Works to raise money to help a local child fight a life-threatening illness. If you are doing things that would make a great news story, then you are missing out on an excellent marketing opportunity by not shouting it from the rooftops and letting the local news media know about it. Press releases can be a great way to generate publicity in local, industry, and other publications about your online business and create buzz in your target markets that leads to both website traffic and future sales. However, press releases need to be handled in a very specific way—there is definitely an art to doing them right.

Reporters and journalists receive about a dozen press releases a day from local organizations and businesses hoping to get mentioned in their articles and weekly columns. Most of them are promptly deposited in the trash basket. Editors and journalists are extremely busy people—they are *always* on deadline, and anything that interrupts their flow is considered a distraction at best and a nuisance at worst. To get their attention, you have to hit them over the head with a baseball bat (figuratively speaking, of course) and let them know that what you're talking about in your press release is more important and urgent than whatever they are working on at the moment.

Most eBay businesses are too small to hire an outside publicity or public relations professional to do their releases for them. You have to do them yourself. The good news is that once you get the hang of writing them, you can follow the same format over and over again (kind of like putting up eBay listings, when you think about it).

Here's some advice on how to write press releases that will work most of the time.

What Do You Write About?

The biggest mistake—by far—that people make when writing press releases is talking too much about themselves or their businesses. Most press releases follow the same dull, boring format: "Here's a company. It made money. It has a new product or service that will help its customers do X. It is also donating _____ dollars to a local charity. Whoopee." Well intentioned, of course, but similar to at least a hundred releases that are being sent out at the same time, and destined for the wastepaper basket or shredder.

Every book and article you read about press releases begins by saying that the release should be "newsworthy"—that it should grab the reporter's or editor's attention and talk about a timely topic or issue he or she is researching right at that moment in time. Editors and journalists are always looking for local people who are doing things that tie in to national or international events—for example, someone who has found a way to run a motorcycle on vegetable oil. By announcing that you are such a person and are available to be interviewed, you have just saved the editor or reporter countless hours of research, and he or she will be grateful to you for "volunteering."

Before sitting down to write a press release, you should reread Chapter 1 of this book, especially the section on why people will buy your merchandise on eBay. You are not writing a press release to tell the world what a great human being you are. You are writing the release to promote your business and generate sales. Your press release needs to clearly identify a passion, hope, or dream that your customers are feeling or a problem they have, and what your business is doing to either gratify that passion, hope, or dream or solve that problem. Stories like that always generate responses.

Here are some common events that can justify your issuing a press release:

- When you launch a new website or e-commerce platform, such as an eBay Store

- When you add new products to your merchandise mix

- When you arrange events such as public speaking engagements, open houses, seminars, or fairs

- If your company creates new partnerships or alliances with other companies

- When you run contests on your website

- If you are arranging fund-raisers and donations

- If your company or merchandise gets a major award or accomplishment (such as being nominated for the eBay Seller's Hall of Fame or achieving Platinum PowerSeller status)

The focus of this press release, as you can see, is on a local event the eBay seller is sponsoring. But even a casual reading of the release makes it clear (1) that Cliff's Antiques has a strong inventory of U.S. political memorabilia, (2) that Cliff's presentation is likely to be a fun and lively one given the topic, and (3) that Cliff's Antiques has a website where people can buy political memorabilia.

Tips on Writing a Press Release

Although journalists strive to be objective and dispassionate when writing news stories, they are human beings just like everyone else and can be "sold" if a proper appeal is made to their passions, problems, hopes, and dreams—in this case, the passion for a highly entertaining and amusing story tied to a presidential election that everyone is talking about (which at the same time alleviates the reporter's fear of losing his or her job). If you can get a cynical editor and reporter—don't forget, these people have heard it all—to say, "Wow, this is cool!," you will get favorable publicity for your business. It's that simple.

SAMPLE PRESS RELEASE
LOCAL DEALER PUTS MUDSLINGING POLITICAL ADS IN PERSPECTIVE

FOR IMMEDIATE RELEASE

HORSEHEADS, NEW YORK, April 1, 2008—Upset by the negative tone of the radio and TV ads you are hearing during this hotly contested presidential election year?

There's nothing new about it.

Once upon a time, there was a candidate for president who was called "a one-eyed lying jackal," "a bearded jackass," "a warmongering scoundrel," and much worse, by the news media of his day.

His name was Abraham Lincoln.

"Negative political attack ads are nothing new," says local antiques dealer Cliff Ennico, of Cliff's Antiques in Horseheads, New York. "With the exception perhaps of George Washington, just about every candidate for president has been called terrible names by their opponents at just about every stage of their career."

Ennico will be hosting an illustrated talk entitled "Vote for Our Candidate Because Even Though He's a Jerk the Other Candidate is a Bigger Jerk" at the Horseheads Public Library, Tuesday, April 1, at 8:00 p.m. The talk will feature a slide presentation of cartoons, posters and broadsides, and other political memorabilia from every presidential election from 1800 to 2000 that was designed to cast the opposing candidate in the most negative light possible. Some of the slides can be viewed in advance on the Cliff's Antiques website at www.cliffsfunkypoliticalcollectibles.com. Admission is free, and attendees will be invited to show off any "negative political memorabilia" from their private collections.

###

Your press release should contain all of the following:

- **An angle** that ties in to other stories the press is writing about

- **An eye-catching headline** that "grabs the reader by the throat and doesn't let go"

- **A direct and immediate appeal to a passion, problem, hope, or dream** that a large number of people are experiencing at the present moment (in our example, a passion—anger at some of the excessively abusive charges made in negative political advertising)

- **A humorous, entertaining style** (remember our discussion of marketainment from Chapter 2?)

Read lots of news stories, and try to write the release in exactly the way you would like it to appear in print. Buy a book on the Associated Press style—this is the way most reporters are taught to write their news stories—and follow that format closely when writing your release. Remember that reporters are often under tight time deadlines and will love you if you do a lot of the writing work for them.

Ingredients of a Press Release

Focus on what journalists call the "five W's and the H"—the who, what, when, where, why, and how. Here's a sample outline of a typical press release:

- The headline

- The summary or introduction of the news

- The event or achievement

- The product

- The people (always use interviews and quotes)

- The concluding summary, again

- The company

- Your contact information, so the reporter can call you if he or she has questions or wants to blow up your release into a bigger article

Create an Eye-Catching Headline

Many journalists and columnists use the Preview pane in Microsoft Outlook, so that when a new e-mail comes up in their inbox they can read the first few words of the message without actually having to open it. When looking at their incoming messages they probably hit the delete key at least twice a second. That's how long they're looking at each message before deciding whether or not to save it—a fraction of a second. That's how long you, as a marketer, have to grab the attention of your press release's intended reader.

The headline is by far the most important part of any press release. You should spend at least twice the amount of time crafting your headline as you do writing the actual body of the press release.

There is no such thing as a headline that screams too loudly. You've got to get your readers' attention before you can ever hope to sell them on the story you describe in the body of the press release. If you are selling plush toy animals featuring a variety of insects, the headline KILLER BEES COMING TO SKANEATELES is bound to make even the most jaded reporter stop hitting the delete key and open your message.

"Just the Facts, Ma'am"

Remember that you are writing a factual story about something that is happening in your world. While you are trying to sell the editor or reporter on your story (by appealing to his or her passions, problems, hopes, and dreams, as in any sales pitch), you are not selling merchandise. A too-blatant sales pitch in a press release is an instant turnoff for any editor or reporter. Although many journalists are extremely likable people, always remember that their job is not to help you build your business but to build *their* business by writing consistently entertaining and relevant news stories that grow and retain their circulation.

Write in Third-Person Form

Unlike an e-mail newsletter or blog that is written in a personal voice, a press release must be presented objectively, from a third-person point of view. Every journalist has a duty to provide readers with impartial facts and figures, and he or she must not be seen as endorsing your products or business. When drafting a press release, be sure to do the following:

- Refrain from using any sales pitch–type language.

- Remove *you, I, we,* and *us* and replace them with *he* or *she* and *they.*

- Provide references for any statistics, facts, and figures cited in the press release.

- Refrain from expressing personal opinions, unless they are put within quotation marks.

- Draw conclusions from facts and statistics only, not from general opinion.

The Beginning and the End: Some Style Points

Take a look at the sample press release earlier in this chapter that described Cliff's library talk on political memorabilia, and focus on the beginning and end of the release.

Always begin your release with the headline.

Next add the words "For Immediate Release." This tells the publication that your story is meant to be published now, not sometime in the future.

Follow by listing the city and state from which the release is emanating and the date of release.

At the end of the release, insert three # symbols (like so: ###), centered directly underneath the last line of the release. This is a journalistic standard to signify the end of an article.

How Long Should Each Press Release Be?

You should set up your press release as follows:

- Make it one page in lengthy ideally, two at the most.

- Make it 400 to 500 words in total length (including your contact information).

- Print it on one side of the page only.

- Double-space it.

To Whom Do You Send Your Press Releases?

Once you have perfected your press release for impact, search for suitable media outlets to broadcast your message. Local and/or small media are most likely to be interested in your story, and it's the perfect way to hone your release-writing skills. Try local newspapers, trade journals, industry-specific magazines, websites, radio shows, and television shows. So, for example, if you have an eBay Store that specializes in antique mechanical banks and other toys from the 1800s, a copy of your press release should be sent to *The Mechanical Banker,* a quarterly publication of the Mechanical Bank Collectors of America (www.mbca.com). To find collectors' organizations with regular newsletters and periodicals, consult the *Encyclopedia of Associations* in the reference section of your local library—just about every club, trade group, and industry association in the United States is listed there.

Where do you find local media? Your local library is probably the best place to learn about them, because they generally subscribe to everything that's published in your area. Gebbie Press (www.gebbieinc.com) has created a comprehensive website with professional news contacts, which guides you through the process of assembling your own press list.

You can also consult with Web companies that send your release out for you. There are a number of sites that require payment, such as PR Newswire (www .prnewswire.com). However, there are a few good free websites as well. Some of these are www.free-press-release.com and www.usanews.net. Don't forget to search on popular search engines for websites in your industry that might be interested in running your story. MediaPost (www.mediapost.com), which is an extensive directory for U.S. media, may be a good place to submit press releases.

Always remember to get specific contact information for your press release. A release address to a particular person will receive a lot more attention than a general release sent to the media outlet.

How Do You Send Your Press Release?

Most businesses send their press releases first-class via the U.S. Postal Service ("snail mail"). This is a mistake.

The good news is that most editors and reporters open their "snail mail," because, hey, you never know, "there might actually be a good story idea in one of these things."

When you have identified the reporters and editors at your local newspaper or a relevant trade publication who might be interested in the story you have to tell, you should get the message across in a way that is guaranteed to get their attention and make them open your submission before anyone else's.

UPS Ground is a fairly effective way to do this—it's relatively inexpensive and sends the message that the contents are urgent. Also, when you send messages by UPS Ground, you get a tracking number, so you can confirm when and by whom the package was received; then you can follow up with a timely telephone call or e-mail asking politely whether the release was received.

For local media, study each individual editor's and reporter's work, and find out the method by which he or she prefers to receive press releases. Don't automatically send them by e-mail, because some will prefer mail or fax. Find out their deadlines, especially for monthly or quarterly publications, because if you miss these, your story will become stale in a hurry (since monthlies and quarterlies have to wait another month or quarter before releasing it, they would be more inclined to toss out a late release than would a daily or weekly publication).

Just about every local newspaper and trade journal has posted information, either in the publication itself or on the publication's website, telling people how to submit a press release. Find this information, and follow their guidelines closely.

If you are sending your release by e-mail, never send an attachment. Copy and paste your release into the body of the e-mail. Never send bulk e-mail; address e-mails individually.

Following Up on Press Releases

One of the big mistakes businesses make when sending out press releases is forgetting about them once they've been mailed. A successful media strategy depends on following up on your releases and developing long-term relationships with the editors and journalists who are most interested in the stories you have to tell. That doesn't happen when you send junk mail.

In researching local and trade publications, start collecting the e-mail addresses of relevant journalists and reporters. Once you know the release has been received, follow up with a short e-mail in which you do three things:

1. Ask for confirmation that the release was received.

2. Offer some additional content to show that the release is relevant and timely (for example, "since mailing our release, sales of Halloween-themed items have jumped 300 percent, surpassing all of our expectations and showing that Halloween is indeed bigger than Christmas nowadays"). Keep the additional content short and sweet—no more than a paragraph

3. Ask the editor or journalist to contact you and let you know if the release you sent wasn't relevant. Most won't respond (they're simply too busy meeting deadlines), but a few will, and they will give you insight into how you can make your releases more effective.

Newspaper, Magazine, and Print Advertising

Print advertising is one of the oldest means of sending an advertising message to the general public. While many people today believe the Internet will supersede print publications in the next couple of decades, traditional print advertising may be useful in promoting your eBay presence, especially to a targeted niche audience.

Newspaper Classified Ads

It's accepted wisdom that most eBay sellers do not drive much traffic to their websites or eBay Stores by taking out ads in local newspapers. There is, however, one major exception to that rule: eBay sellers who take consignments.

You do not have to declare yourself an eBay consignment shop, or purchase one of several available eBay consignment shop franchises, in order to take consignments of inventory from people in your area. There is no license required. All you have to do is advertise your willingness and ability to take consignments from people, and you're in business!

Of course, people wanting to consign merchandise won't be knocking on your door unless they know you're there. And local advertising is one of the best ways to reach these people, as most customers will not consign goods to an eBay seller who is located more than thirty or forty miles from their home. When people look for a local eBay seller, they are likely to look in one of two pages: the local Yellow Pages of the telephone directory (see the discussion of Yellow Pages advertising later in this chapter) or the classified ad pages of their local newspaper or supermarket *PennySaver*.

Consider taking out a simple classified ad in your local newspaper or *PennySaver* like this one:

> Want to clean out your attic, garage, or basement? Want to sell that stuff on eBay but don't know how? We take consignments! No lot too large or small. Affordable rates. Call Cliff's Antiques at 1–800-ILUVJNK.

To make your ad stand out, consider adding a photo of yourself, a photo of a beloved pet, or a hand-drawn cartoon; classified ad pages tend to be long, unbroken columns of gray type, and a photo or other illustration pops out from the page more than it would in, say, a display ad.

Magazine Ads

No, we're not talking about full-page spreads in *Vogue* or *Mademoiselle* (or even *Antiques*). Nevertheless, magazine advertising can be very useful for certain eBay selling businesses that specialize in handicrafts, decorative items, and other custom or difficult-to-find merchandise.

Pick up a copy of *The New Yorker* or *Atlantic Monthly*, and turn to the back half of the magazine. See all the little ads along one side of each page? Many, if not most, of these are for smaller businesses, mostly craftspeople and designers, who specialize in a limited line of merchandise: crystal jewelry, trilby hats, custom-built kayaks, and so forth. If you are an artist or craftsperson and have one-of-a-kind merchandise that would appeal to upper-crust customers (or, possibly, to interior designers and other centers of influence, as discussed later in this chapter), an ad in *The New Yorker* might be a terrific way to reach these folks. People are obviously reading these ads, or else sellers wouldn't take them out—we've seen several companies that have run their ads in *The New Yorker* for years, so they must be getting results.

Of course, the best magazines for eBay sellers to advertise in are newsletters and journals that target collectors. The circulations of these publications are often quite small, but (1) the readership consists mostly of tightly targeted consumers, virtually all of whom will be interested in your marketing message, and (2) the advertising rates are usually quite inexpensive (sometimes they are even free). So, for example, if you have an eBay Store specializing in antique mechanical banks and other antique toys from the 1800s, an ad in *Antique Toy World* magazine (www.antiquetoyworld.com) or *The Mechanical Banker,* a quarterly publication put out by the Mechanical Bank Collectors of America (www.mbca.com) will be much more effective and less costly than a quarter-page ad in *The New York Times.*

When dealing with any specialized magazine, newsletter, or journal, ask if they could also post a mention of your company on their website. Many smaller publications have not thoroughly integrated their websites with their print publications, and they may be willing to offer you a free banner ad on their website home pages as an inducement to your taking out a print ad, as long as your Web designer assists them in putting up the banner ad.

Advertising in a collectors' magazine also enhances your credibility in that field of collecting, as collectors want to deal with sellers who know and specialize in the merchandise they love and whom they perceive as "members of the club." A collector of antique mechanical banks is likely to feel squeamish about an eBay seller who says he specializes in antique toys but does not advertise regularly in *The Mechanical Banker* or *Antique Toy World*. Sometimes, to be taken seriously by serious collectors, an ad in the right publication is the ticket that has to be punched before you are admitted to the inner sanctum.

Radio, Television, and Billboards

We can hear some of you laughing out loud: *"Are you guys crazy?* I'm barely scratching out a living on eBay, and you want me to advertise on television?!"

Hear us out for a minute, okay? Obviously, television and radio advertising is extremely expensive, and regular ads on network television, or a sixty-second spot during the Super Bowl, are within the reach of only a handful of eBay's top sellers (okay, maybe even eBay itself wouldn't advertise on the Super Bowl).

However, one of your missions as an eBay seller is to build a brand for your business and your merchandise, getting customers to realize that you are *the* go-to seller if they are looking to buy, say, an antique mechanical bank or typewriter supplies on eBay. Branding on eBay—or anywhere else on the Internet, for that matter—is getting the word out that you are an expert in your field of merchandise. To paraphrase 1970s disco queen Donna Summer, you can "say it really loud, when you say it on the air, on the radio."

Radio Talk Shows

There are many talk radio shows, and an increasing number of them are focusing on small business and e-commerce issues. They are always—and we mean *always*—looking out for good guests.

Where to Find Business Talk Radio Shows

There is no comprehensive directory of radio talk shows available in print or on the Internet. Back in the 1990s, Annie Brewer published *Talk Shows and Hosts on Radio: A Directory Including Show Titles and Formats, Biographical Information on Hosts, and Topic/Subject Index*, but it's long been out of print. Still, if you can find a used copy online (they go for about $5), it's a worthwhile investment and a good place to start, as a lot of talk shows that were around then are still around today.

A couple of books you should invest in if you're serious about becoming a talk radio personality are *How to Get on Radio Talk Shows All Across America without Leaving Your Home or Office,* by Joe Sabah (Pacesetter Publications, 1999), and *Ready, Set, Talk! A Guide to Getting Your Message Heard by Millions on Talk Radio, Talk Television, and Talk Internet,* by Ellen Ratner and Kathie Scarrah (Chelsea

Green Publications, 2006), both of which have a partial list of the leading radio talk shows in each major format.

Your best bet for finding business talk radio shows is to look online. By typing "talk radio [*name of state*]," you should get at least a partial list of radio stations in that state specializing in the talk radio format. From there, you will have to look at each station's website to find out whether it has a business talk show. If so, there is usually an e-mail link to the show's producer, where you can send a press release or a brief description of what you would talk about on the show.

When looking for talk radio shows, don't be afraid to be a bit creative. Political talk radio shows generally attract a much broader and bigger listenership than business talk radio shows do. If your business is involved in any way in the political process, or if you sell politics-related merchandise, an appearance on one of these shows might help you reach a sizable audience of political junkies who will stop at your eBay Store or website to see the great stuff you've got.

You stand a better chance of finding shows when it comes to Internet talk radio—one of the fastest-growing media in the United States today. The DMOZ Open Directory Project offers a wiki-style directory of Internet radio stations at www.dmoz.org/Arts/Radio/Internet. The last time we looked, there were several dozen entries from Internet radio stations around the United States, organized by format (political, sports, business, Christian, and so forth).

The problem with Internet radio is that it's currently highly fragmented—there are lots of Internet radio stations out there, but no industry leaders that are garnering a wide listenership. The stations are extremely niche-oriented and reach only a handful of regular listeners. The good news is that Internet radio programs are usually preserved as podcasts on the station, so your interview will be available for replay and downloading weeks or months after it takes place, unlike terrestrial radio, where it's gone the minute it's over. Do a good interview on an Internet radio station, and not only will they post the podcast on their website, where it can be found by the search engine spiders, but they will usually give you a copy you can upload to your own website.

Speaking of Internet radio, did we mention that both eBay and PayPal have their own radio programs on the Internet? Jim "Griff" Griffith, the "Dean of eBay Education" and unofficial godfather of the eBay community, hosts a weekly show at eBay Radio, while Jason Miner, PayPal's Community Education Specialist, hosts the PayPal show. Both are available at www.wsradio.com. Send an e-mail with an interesting idea to Griff at griff@ebay.com or to Jason at jminer@paypal.com, and you stand a good chance of being invited to appear on one of their programs, which reach thousands of other eBayers nationwide.

Booking Appearances on Radio

The trick to booking appearances on talk radio shows is the same as getting publicity in local newspapers: Send them a press release! Then follow up your press release with a telephone call to the show's producer—you probably will get a voice-mail message, but in our experience most talk show producers actually listen to their recorded messages for at least a few seconds, so you have a chance of attracting the producer's attention if you prepare your call in advance and get your story message across in the first few seconds of your message.

Rules for Appearing on the Radio

When appearing on talk radio, whether on the air or on the Internet, there are two very important rules:

1. Keep it lively and entertaining.

2. Be concise.

Radio shows can be quite intense. The producers are always afraid that if someone gets on the air who is very dull and boring, people will change channels in a heartbeat. This is why most radio segments are extremely short (five to eight minutes is a typical segment length). When you're on the air, you have to be *on* in every sense of that word. When he's a guest on a talk radio show, Cliff Ennico can actually "feel his hair growing" when he's speaking. You have to make sure that everything you say is lively, dynamic, informative, and entertaining, and keep your audience awake at all costs. Stumble over your words or forget your script for even a few seconds, and the producer might cut you off in midsentence to avoid every radio producer's dread—more than one second of silence, or what radio people refer to as "dead air."

You must also keep your comments short, crisp, and concise—this is one place you *cannot* be long-winded. Your goal is to prepare a handful of sound bites about your topic, get them on the air quickly, and make sure you mention your website URL or eBay Store address before the producer cuts you off at the end of the segment. Sometimes the show hosts help you by mentioning your website in their closing comments at the end of your segment, but sometimes they won't. If you sense that you're down to the last minute of your segment, finish your current thought and blurt out, "I've got a lot more information on this topic on my website at www.[*insert your website name*].com" before saying anything else.

Television

Advertising your eBay business on local television probably won't attract many buyers. However, if you take consignments as part of your eBay business, it's something you should consider.

Back in the 1990s, an estate auctioneer in southern Connecticut built a huge following by taking out five-second advertising spots on the local cable television news and weather programs. That's right, five seconds! The ads were simplicity itself: A handheld camera focused tightly on the auctioneer's face in front of a bookcase as he intoned in a New England drawl, "So-and-so Auctioneers in Stamford, Connecticut. We buy, we sell, we take consignments!" while his toll-free telephone number and Web address appeared just below his chin. Say it out loud—it's exactly five seconds long.

Your local cable television station might be interested in such an ad, as frequently their segments fall short of their allotted time and a brief ad is needed as filler to get back on schedule. A five-second ad might actually run more times than a much longer ad for this reason. Give it some thought.

If you want to build a brand around the merchandise you sell, why not consider hosting a television show about it on your local public interest cable television channel? Every local cable station has a channel for public interest programming, and they *must*—by federal law—make it available to you if you ask. You may have to pay a fee to have one of the station's employees produce your show (we recommend that you do that, because they're familiar with the equipment and the station's personnel who will be running your show), but there is usually no fee for the airtime itself.

Most public interest cable shows are extremely basic—a coffee table or card table with a black backdrop. You invite a guest to the studio, treat the person to dinner, and spend a half hour with him or her talking about whatever it is you sell on eBay or any other topic you think might be of interest to your customers, while a camera rolls. You can even insert "commercials" for your website or eBay business as long as they're not too blatantly recognizable as sales pitches. Not only will your show air frequently on your local public interest cable channel (because programming is sparse on most such channels, your program will probably air several times a day in most markets), but you will get a DVD of the program, which you can excerpt and post on your website or on YouTube.

There are several Internet television stations, most notably www.blip.tv and www.ustream.tv, where you can create your own Internet television show in the same way as on public interest cable channels. However, Internet television is really in its infancy as this book is being written, and few people are watching these sites. If you do create a show for one of these channels, you are doing it with the primary intent of creating an infomercial you can post on your website or on YouTube.

Billboards

If you're driving down an interstate highway in the United States, and a giant billboard looms on the horizon saying www.renegadelawyers.com and nothing more (or perhaps it is prefaced by a short, cryptic question such as "Afraid of Lawyers?")—let's face it, you're a little curious, aren't you? You might just check out this website the next time you're online.

Billboards can be an effective and relatively cheap way to impress your Web address or eBay Store name on thousands of people in your area—if it's easy to remember and will arouse curiosity in the people who view it. Remember: Drivers have only a few seconds to read the message, and they won't have a pen or pencil handy to write down the information; it will have to stick in their memories until they get to their computers, hours or even days later.

To find a local billboard company in your area, go to your favorite search engine and type "billboard advertising [*your city and state*]" in the search box. You will most likely find a directory of local advertisers. Or you can check out a nationwide directory on the following websites:

- Outdoor Advertising Association of America, Inc. (www.oaaa.org)

- Billboard Connection (www.thebillboardconnection.com)

Call your local billboard companies and let them know you want to rent a board for only a couple of months. Most billboard advertisers rent space for six or twelve months at a time, and there are frequent in-between periods during which the board will not have a subscribing advertiser. Most billboard companies fill these in-between periods by putting up public service announcements, but if they can make a few bucks putting your board up for two months, they probably will cut you a deal.

The Marketing Power of Adult Education

Teaching others can be one of the most rewarding moves that you can make, both monetarily and emotionally. Teaching others how to master a skill that improves their lives—or simply helps them get more out of a tool they already have—is truly heartwarming.

There's another aspect to teaching that you may have never considered. When you help others learn how to use your products, you build a bond with them. Book authors know this; it is one of the reasons they tour the country when they release a new best seller. People love to meet them face-to-face and hear them read a chapter or two. You may not be a celebrity author, but you can certainly become a celebrity teacher and use that fame to sell more of your widgets.

This offline strategy can build your business. It sets you apart and makes you the area expert. Your class does not have to be—in fact, should not be—a two-hour-long sales pitch about your product to convince consumers to spend at your store. Your job as marketer/teacher is to show people how to get the best value from the product or to validate what they already know. Adults don't really learn the same way children do. Adults learn by confirmation of an idea they already have. If you can help your students enjoy their hobby more, teach them how to eat a healthier diet (if you sell health foods), or just show them a new technique, you'll surely win their confidence in you and, ultimately, in your product.

If you live in an urban area, your local community center likely has thousands of names and addresses of potential clients. If you work with them, the center may agree to send out an invitation to your class to the people on their mailing list. Interested readers enroll and are funneled into your class. How wonderful is that? This is an inexpensive, or maybe even free, way to get the word out about your business. You'll probably get paid to teach the class to a presorted and highly targeted group of motivated buyers! Because most classes are planned in advance, there is plenty of time for you to send out a general press release to the local paper. Most newspapers publish "for free" announcements about community events, and your class will be included for thousands more to see. Local reporters write about current area events, and if your press release catches their eye you might find yourself being interviewed about the class or your specialty.

Adult education programs, whether through colleges, community centers, civic groups, or even clubs, are always on the lookout for new classes. For the kind of teaching we are talking about here, you don't need years of university training—although some might be useful. To train adults, you mostly need to have an understanding or passion about a subject area and the desire to teach others. If you sell vintage radios, there are clubs that would love to hear you speak about your specialized knowledge. A sewing supply store might offer a chance to teach others quilting or crafting.

Once they get over the fear of public speaking, one of the biggest concerns new educators have is that they don't know everything. Although it is a good idea to know your subject inside and out, no one can know the answer to every question students might have. If you find you don't know the answer to a question, be honest—don't try to make something up. Say something like this: "That's a great question; I don't know the answer to that, but I'll see if I can find out for you and answer you next session" or "I don't know, but I can tell you where you might be able to find the answer . . ."

Don't make stuff up. Students know when you are trying to pull something over on them, so honesty is always the best policy. Paradoxically, it also goes a long way toward boosting your credibility to admit that you don't know an answer. Your students see that you are honest, and they will transfer this view to your products. That is, they will be less cynical about your sales pitch (so don't overhype your products).

To become a workshop leader at a community center or adult education class, determine what you plan on teaching. If you are an eBay Education Specialist, then you already know what you want to teach. But this opportunity is not open only to eBay Education Specialists. Your products may not have anything to do with eBay itself, other than being sold there. This section is about teaching others as a way to build a relationship and trust with your customers.

Equipment

Let's take a look at some of the equipment you'll need to get the maximum number of engagements. Of course, if you want to start small, you don't need everything, but investing in a projector and a laptop computer opens up more venues for you to teach in.

For a PowerPoint presentation, you'll need a computer and a projector if you are teaching more than one or two students. If you are doing a less formal, hands-on training session, you probably don't need to do a PowerPoint presentation, but PowerPoint is considered standard fare in public speaking.

Most colleges and universities have a computer, projector, and PowerPoint software installed and available for you to use. But once you start booking your own venues and renting meeting rooms, you may find that they do not have audiovisual equipment available.

Each subject is a little different in terms of the needs of the presenter and the student. You might simply need to show up and talk, no extras necessary, or you might need everything from a projector and screen to a cart for your laptop. You might also need the individual parts to put together the project that you are demonstrating. Make a list before the class, and check off the items as you get ready to go. Here's a general list of items most teachers pack:

- Projector

- Remote clicker

- Laptop computer

- USB key with presentation, with PowerPoint saved via Pack and Go in case the host's computer doesn't have PowerPoint (some school computers no longer have CD access drawers)

- Extension cord(s)

- Dry-erase pen

- Bottle of water

- Handouts and workbooks (with the presenter's URL all over them!)

- Newsletter sign-up sheet (remember the ethical bribe?—it works here, too)

This is one of those places where having a URL redirect to your eBay store comes in very handy. It's a lot easier for students to find your online store if you treat it like a unique destination with its own URL. So instead of handing out leaflets with the clunky-looking eBay store URL, create a unique domain name for your store. Then link from the URL home page to your eBay Store (for example, by a button that says Check Out My eBay Store!). It's a lot easier for students to type in *www.wreathcrafts.com*, then click on your eBay Store link, than it is for students to remember the eBay URL that directs them to eBay, then to your store, and looks something like http://stores.ebay.com/wreath-craft. For more information about this, refer to "Your eBay User ID and Store ID" in Chapter 2.

Venues

Let's take a look at some of the many options you have for teaching venues. If you are teaching to promote your business, your main focus is to find a targeted audience. There are lots of choices. Community colleges and centers are great for finding general audiences; clubs and professional organizations provide niche-targeted opportunities.

Community Centers

If you live in an urban area, contact the local community center. Most of these centers host classes and are always looking for instructors. Community centers are more casual than colleges. Most have mailing lists that they send to regularly. In the area in which Cindy Shebley teaches, one local community center's list tops forty thousand names. This is one of the most economical ways to advertise a class. The community center takes care of the registration, sets aside the room, advertises, and generally gives the speaker between 40 and 75 percent of the student tuition. It's a great opportunity to get yourself known and establish yourself as the local expert in your field.

Many centers ask you whether the students need to purchase additional supplies (from you) and how much the additional costs will be. This is the perfect opportunity to sell products as part of the class material. For instance, imagine you are teaching a wreath-making class. Creating a wreath requires lots of supplies—wire, the base, flowers or leaves, ribbons, bows, and more. Instead of sending the students a list of items to purchase and have them bring the stuff to the class, you order the items wholesale and provide them during the class at retail price. You need to let the recreation director know what the price of the materials will be so that this information can be included in their course mailing.

You might find that contacting the recreation director requires persistence. Many community centers are experiencing budget cutbacks, and the employees often work part-time. It might take several phone calls. Don't expect someone to return your call, and don't rely on e-mail—keep calling until you speak to the contact.

Continuing Education

The continuing education department at your local community college is, naturally, another place to offer classes. If you don't know how to find yours, or you need to find the address and phone number of your contact, look for a link to the U.S. government Web database of all community colleges in the country at http://nces.ed.gov/globallocator/.

Community colleges are a little more formal than community centers; thus, it requires more preparation on your part to get accepted. Many colleges actually hire you as a part-time employee when you teach through their programs, so they expect more from you. To propose a class, expect to fill out several documents, including a class syllabus, a series of definable goals for your students, a short blurb of one hundred to two hundred words about the class for the student catalog, and a biography of yourself as a teacher. The college may also ask for references from places you have already taught.

Community colleges usually have a number of different programs you can participate in. Your community college may have a continued learning segment for students fifty and older, which is funded separately from the regular continuing education program; a section funded by the Small Business Administration; and the regular adult education curriculum.

There are lots of opportunities at community colleges. Don't forget that there are a number of private colleges as well. In the Northwest there is a local Indian College with satellite campuses all over the area. If you lived there and were hired, you would have the opportunity to travel throughout the region teaching classes.

One thing to note: Classes at the community centers and colleges tend to be planned months in advance. Long before the first class is taught in the fall, plans are already under way for the winter quarter. So expect that when you contract with them it'll be months before the actual date of the first class you'll teach.

Many universities have adult education classes as well. The University of Washington has an Experimental College where teachers create their own curricula, book classrooms at the university, and collect the specified fees on the day of the class(es). The university supports the teachers with enrollment and facilities details. Teaching at a university campus naturally bumps your authority rankings. You can't overestimate the importance of your authority ranking when it comes to building security and confidence with buyers.

You don't have to limit yourself to community centers and colleges. There are lots of other ways to get yourself out there. Look around your community—senior centers and senior communities are always on the lookout for new classes and recreation activities to offer. When contacting a senior community, ask to speak to the recreation director.

Civic Groups

The local chamber of commerce may be on the lookout for presentations it can offer on business-related topics. You may find clubs or other smaller groups that are looking for speakers. Don't be shy!

Churches, Synagogues, and Other Houses of Worship

Churches, synagogues, and other houses of worship often host speakers. Some are even willing to pay a small fee to have you come and teach them your craft.

Libraries

Another overlooked venue is the local library, although teaching for profit can be a bit tricky. Many libraries will not let you use their rooms or promote you or your classes if you charge a fee. Teaching for free may not be an issue if your main goal is to get the word out about your products. Keep in mind your marketing strategy and budget. Is it worth a few hours of your time and a tank of gas to talk to prospective customers? If so, how many is the minimum number of students you'll do it for? What are goodwill and reputation worth in your community?

In the eBay world, there are several eBay Education Specialists who teach classes right in their own homes—so don't rule out the possibility. However, do check on the zoning laws in your city. Some have strict restrictions on what you can and can't do when you run a business in your home. Most of the rules and restrictions concern the number of people who are allowed in your residence at a time and for how long. Parking is likewise usually an issue. It may be a good idea to warn neighbors before you host a gathering.

Another Education Specialist found a storage unit with power and heat and teaches regular classes of about five students from this storage locker. Doing this not only pays for the storage locker space, but you'll have inventory to show and sell as you teach!

You may have never considered teaching as a way to market your store. However, marketers have found it to be very effective. Many information marketers have found public speaking so powerful in growing their tribe of buyers that they'll travel thousands of miles and speak with no fee (all at the marketer's expense). They know the power of in-person contact and how important it is, especially in this Internet age. You may not have the budget to fly across the country, but there might be a local community center full of potential customers waiting to hear from you. And when they get home from your class, you never know where their e-mails about the class may go.

Guerrilla Marketing

The term *guerrilla marketing* has a number of different meanings, depending on the person you're talking to.

Back in the 1980s, a marketing guru named Jay Conrad Levinson coined the term *guerrilla marketing* to describe a number of low-tech, cost-effective strategies that entrepreneurs and small business owners could use to compete head-on with larger companies and their huge advertising budgets. Type Levinson's name into any of the major search engines, and you will see a list of over a dozen books and audio and video products, all of which are useful tools for anybody building a small business, whether on eBay or elsewhere.

However, the term *guerrilla marketing* has taken on a life of its own in the marketing world, and it's a lot like the famous U.S. Supreme Court definition of *pornography*: You can't define it precisely, but you certainly know it when you see it.

Loosely defined, *guerrilla marketing* refers to any marketing strategy or tactic that gets your business's name in front of the public in a low-cost way and in such a creative manner that people gasp in amazement at your sheer audacity, saying, "Wow! That is really an in-your-face way of getting your message out—good for you!"

A Great Guerrilla Marketing Story

Probably the best example of guerrilla marketing we have seen took place several years ago at a major industry trade show in the Midwest. A giant corporate sponsor of the trade show had invited its suppliers and key customers to exhibit their wares at the show, and a couple dozen of them rented booth space at the exhibition hall on the main trade show floor.

Two weeks before the trade show was to begin, the giant corporate sponsor decided to terminate one of its suppliers and do business with one of the supplier's competitors instead—which it proceeded to do in a very public manner. As part of its dismissal, the corporate sponsor "disinvited" the supplier from participating in the trade show and awarded the supplier's coveted booth space to its competitor, with which the sponsor was now doing business.

The terminated supplier, seething with rage, decided not to get mad . . . but to get even.

Having looked over the convention center where the trade show was to be held, the supplier noted that there were no parking areas within the convention center itself. People who wanted to attend the trade show would have to park in one of four nearby municipal parking lots and then walk several blocks to reach the main entrance of the convention floor. This triggered an idea for a guerrilla marketing campaign the trade show's corporate sponsor would never forget.

The terminated supplier had ten thousand shopping bags printed up with its company name and logo in big, bright, shocking pink letters—the kind of shopping bag you could see from outer space. The supplier then flew the shopping bags, along with several of its junior employees, to the city where the trade show was being held and put them up in a hotel on the other side of town from the convention center—a hotel where they wouldn't be noticed by the trade show's sponsor or any of the trade show attendees.

On the first morning of the trade show, and on each morning thereafter, these junior employees stationed themselves in the four municipal parking areas surrounding the convention center. As trade show attendees parked their cars and exited the parking area to walk over to the convention center, they were greeted by a smiling young person in a crisp company uniform, who said, "Welcome to the show!" and handed them shocking pink shopping bags to carry their goodies in while they attended the trade show. Of course, these people assumed that the company was one of the trade show exhibitors, and they carried the shocking pink shopping bags into the convention center and onto the trade show floor.

Picture, if you will, a trade show with thousands of attendees—human billboards, all—carrying identical shocking pink shopping bags bearing the name of a company that did not have a booth on the trade show floor! Can you imagine the reaction of the other exhibitors, to say nothing of the corporate sponsor of the trade show that had very publicly terminated its relationship with this company?

And yet, because the shopping bag guerrillas were on public property, there was nothing the corporate sponsor could do about it—this was guerrilla marketing at its best!

Another Great Guerrilla Marketing Story

Janelle Elms is a former eBay University instructor as well as an author and head rocker chick at OSI Rock Stars (www.osirockstars.com), a membership site specifically focused on training Internet entrepreneurs. She knew her core market would be attending eBay Live!, the national convention for eBay buyers and sellers, which is held (usually) every year or two in a major metropolitan city somewhere in the United States.

Janelle believed that if eBay sellers who attended the gathering learned about her site, they would jump at the opportunity to join. Her mission: to grab their attention. Janelle knew that she could join the crowd of vendors in the trade show exhibition hall (called the "Solutions Floor") giving out tchotchkes. But she also knew her service would be just another face in the crowd if she used the traditional method.

Janelle was sure that if others saw and heard from her band of already successful members they would definitely sign up. Being proud of them, Janelle was more than happy to show them off. And that became the seed of her plan to promote her business, guerrilla marketing style.

Janelle started by letting her members know that "something big" was happening at eBay Live! that would help promote their businesses. She posted a video message to her members that, in itself, was fun and somewhat viral. It soon became the site's big joke. For several weeks, members guessed at what the big eBay Live! event would be by trading posts and videos on the site. By the time eBay Live! rolled around, the members could hardly wait to see what Janelle had planned for them.

She hired actors to pass out flyers with the OSI Rock Star members' names and photos. These actors, dressed as paparazzi (those in-your-face photographers who are always stalking celebrities), enlisted the help of eBay attendees as they searched high and low for Rock Stars. And when they found one, flashes went off, cameras rolled, fans squealed in delight, and the reporters questioned the OSI Rock Star about their "key to success." Nothing grabs people's attention faster than a swarm of press swarming a celebrity! (See Figure 5.1.)

Janelle's favorite moment came just before Seth Godin, legendary marketer, founder of Squidoo.com, and author of *Purple Cow,* among many other books, came onstage to give his talk at eBay Live! Janelle's "paparazzi" swarmed the hall looking for Rock Stars and handing out flyers. Of course, being "paparazzi," they caused a ruckus and were eventually asked to leave, but not before drawing

FIGURE 5.1 *Paparazzi grab eBay Live! attendees to promote the OSI Rock Stars website.*

the attention of all the conference attendees and Seth himself—who was truly impressed at Janelle's marketing genius.

Looking for More Information So You Can "Go Guerrilla"?

For creative ideas on guerrilla marketing strategies that might work for your business, we refer you to any of Jay Conrad Levinson's books, which are highly recommended.

There are only three limits to guerrilla marketing:

1. Your own imagination

2. The boundaries of good taste (as perceived by your customers, not your competitors)

3. The law

When planning a guerrilla marketing strategy, especially one (like the previous trade show story) in which you will be marketing in the face of your competitors and stealing their thunder, consult with a lawyer first to make sure you are not breaking any legal rules. The negative publicity of an unfair trade practice lawsuit—or a guerrilla marketing campaign that ticks off or grosses out your customers—will far exceed any positive publicity the guerrilla marketing strategy will generate for your business.

Everything Your Customer Sees Is a Marketing Opportunity

Every moment you are out in public is a potential opportunity to market your business, and every contact you make in life is a potential customer or referral source (somebody who may or may not be a customer him- or herself but knows people who might be interested in what you have to offer).

Direct marketing is a catchall phrase used to describe any marketing strategy or tactic whereby sellers communicate their message directly to prospective buyers or customers using a tangible, physical medium. Anytime you send a letter, flyer, or postcard to someone, anytime you hand someone your business card, anytime you paint "Joe's Garage" on your pickup truck, you are "direct marketing."

Direct marketing will not help you reach millions of buyers worldwide, but if done right it can help you build a strong local following of people who will refer you to their friends, who in turn will refer you to *their* friends, and so forth.

Are You in Acquisition Mode or Retention Mode?

"Most successful small businesses, even online businesses, start by building a strong local following," says Randye Spina, founder and chief solutions officer of Affordable Marketing Solutions LLC, a marketing consulting firm based in Bridgeport, Connecticut, that specializes in direct-marketing strategies for small businesses (www.myaffordablemarketing.com). (By the way, note Randye's website URL—it's not her company name, but a mini-advertisement assuring customers they can afford her services.)

According to Randye, every online business goes through two phases: the *acquisition* phase and the *retention* phase. "When you first open your website or eBay Store, nobody knows you exist, so you have to tell everyone, buy mailing lists, send out flyers or postcards, and generate as many customers as you can," says Randye, referring to this as being in acquisition mode. Once a small business has built a following and a database of customers who have ordered at least once from the firm, it then moves into retention mode. Randye explains: "The goal now is to keep your customers and get them to buy more stuff from you and refer you to the people they know; you don't have to buy mailing lists anymore at this stage because you have a 'House List' and the trick now is to grow that 'House List.' "

Here are some strategies Randye recommends for her online business clients that can be used effectively at both the acquisition phase and the retention phase of your business.

Your Business Cards

Randye's Rules

Randye has three rules about business cards:

1. Carry them wherever you go.

2. Put them everywhere you can without getting arrested.

3. Give them to everyone you meet.

What *Should* Be on Your Business Card

Your business card should, of course, have your name, your regular mailing address, and your e-mail address. It should also have your website URL (people always expect that you have a website), your eBay user ID, and your eBay Store name. Randye advises that you "make sure your website URL is printed on the business card along with the rest of your contact information. Don't take a ballpoint pen and write your Web address on each card because you're too cheap to order new cards—that really makes you look like an amateur."

A word about addresses: When designing business cards, flyers, and other communications your customers will see, always put "USA" at the end of your mailing address—that gives the impression you are selling internationally and

---

USING VISTAPRINT.COM AS A LOW-COST PRINTER

Like the word *free*? So do many online retailers—especially when the *free* offer is something of value! For the price of postage, VistaPrint.com offers free full-color business cards, postcards, flyers, door magnets, and other print advertising for your business. Cindy Shebley uses their services to print up multiple business cards, shipping toss-ins, and refrigerator magnets. To find out how to get in on their free offering, go to www.vistaprint.com and sign up for their mailing list.

---

operating a business that is worldwide in scope. Which, of course, you eventually will ☺.

What *Should Not* Be on Your Business Card

The eBay logo should not appear on your business card. This is a registered trademark of eBay Inc., and you are not allowed to use it *in any way* without eBay's permission. You can, however, use the word *ebay* in plain black letters that are all the same size (in other words, don't make the "Y" bigger than the other letters, the way eBay does in its logo).

Who Should Get Your Cards

Everyone, everyone, and everyone. Randye advises that you drive around town and look for places where people have to wait in line for something—for example, banks, car washes, UPS Stores, and restaurants (especially pizzerias and Chinese takeout places). Many of these places have bulletin boards in or near the waiting area where people can post notices of upcoming events. Tack up a business card at every location.

Of course, if you're selling antique pocket watches, this won't help you much. However, sellers who take consignments of merchandise for sale on eBay will almost certainly pick up some business this way. Keep your expenses down by taking advantage of VistaPrint.com's free business cards (see box).

If any of your friends or neighbors are holding a tag sale or participating in a flea market, give them a bunch of your cards to put on their tables so people can pick them up.

Don't be afraid to be creative. We know of a used book dealer who goes to every library book sale in his area with a stack of business cards. He places a business card in every book that he thinks people will buy and then leaves without buying anything. People picking up the books see his cards and assume he was the anonymous donor.

There are limits, however. For a blatant example, see the first few minutes of the movie *The Verdict.* The late Paul Newman, playing a down-at-the-heels trial lawyer, makes a practice of visiting funeral parlors, pretending to be a relative or friend of the deceased, and leaving his business cards—well, you get the idea. If people are likely to be offended when they find your business card someplace that business cards should never be, it can only hurt your business and your reputation.

Designing Your Business Card

How crazy should you get when designing your business card? Randye says to use common sense, and consider your target market. "If you're running a business where design is important, your card needs to be well designed; if you are selling female-friendly 'girly girl' merchandise, your card should not be too masculine—go crazy with a more feminine design and colors."

Randye advises that you spend some time choosing the right fonts and typefaces for your business card: "I once had a client who ran an elder care business, and when he gave me his card the print was so small I had to use a magnifying glass to read it. And I'm a heckuva lot younger than most of his customers!"

What if you're just starting out and haven't identified your target markets yet? (However, as we have advised, you should have done that already.) "Be as neutral as you can with your colors—black and white is still highly acceptable, and you can't make any mistakes there," says Randye. "And watch your typeface—'script' fonts don't appeal to men, and Gothic script—like *The New York Times* masthead—will brand you as an old fogey, or perhaps a vampire."

The Biggest Mistake People Make with Their Business Cards

The biggest mistake people make is "not using the back of the business card, without a doubt," says Randye. For a few extra dollars, most printing companies will put something on the back of your business card, and that something can do wonders to help you build business. See the example in Figure 5.2.

Here are some of the things Randye has advised clients to put on the backs of their cards:

Your E-Mail Address

Your e-mail address is one of the most important pieces of information that should appear on your business cards, flyers, handouts, business stationery, and everywhere else. But as Randye Spina points out, "Your e-mail address can also send your customers the wrong message."

If you have a website, your e-mail address should be tied to that URL. Do not use an America Online, Hotmail, Gmail, or local cable company address, because it sends the signal that you're really an amateur. If you're creating the image of an online store, on eBay or anywhere else, an e-mail address of pat@aol.com just doesn't cut it. You should be pat@myonlinewebsite.com, because it ties you to your business and reinforces your name in people's minds."

Just be careful not to use the word *ebay* as part of your e-mail address, unless eBay has specifically given you permission to do so.

Your Voice-Mail Message

Your voice-mail message is another essential offline marketing tool. According to Randye, your recorded message must be professional and appropriate for your business—no background noises like a vacuum cleaner or a crying child. Use it to enforce a short branding message, such as "Thank you for calling XYZ Organization, the company that [*fill in the blank*]."

You should do this even if you use your home phone line as your business phone. It is imperative that when consumers call, they know they dialed the right number and will be dealing with a real business.

Also, do not hesitate to use your voice-mail message to advertise your business or announce new developments. In his voice-mail message, Cliff announces himself as follows: "Hi, you've reached Cliff Ennico, attorney-at-law and author of several books on small business management and e-commerce, most recently *The eBay Marketing Bible . . .*"

Flyers and Handouts

Most eBay sellers will not spend the time or money to create a gorgeous, four-color marketing brochure, nor do they really need one. But Randye says a basic one-page flyer or handout can do wonders to build your business.

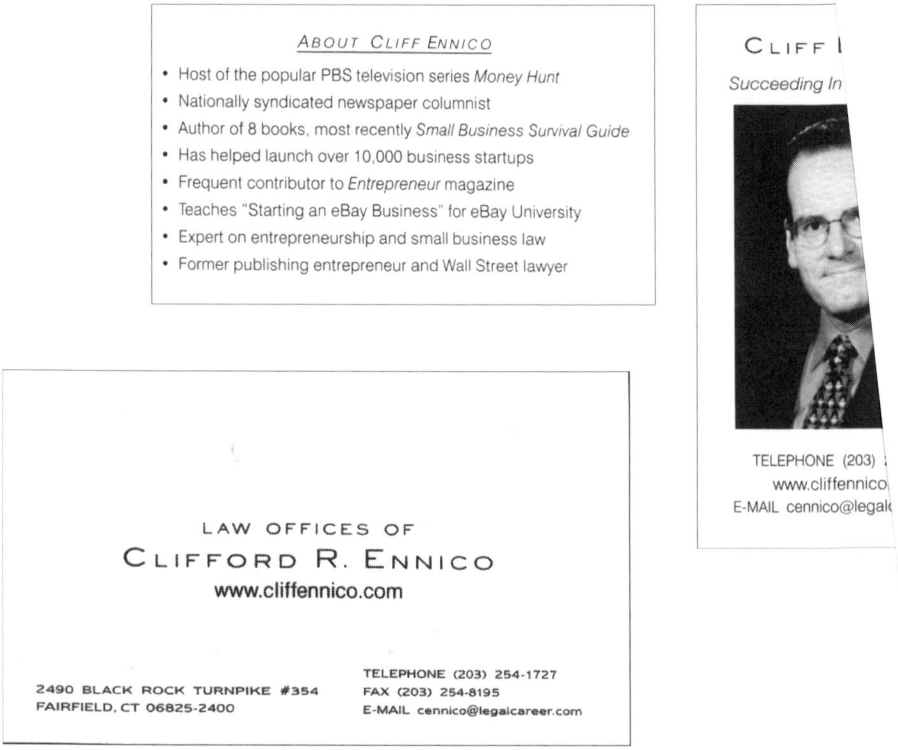

- Host of the popular PBS television series *Money Hunt*
- Nationally syndicated newspaper columnist
- Author of 8 books, most recently *Small Business Survival Guide*
- Has helped launch over 10,000 business startups
- Frequent contributor to *Entrepreneur* magazine
- Teaches "Starting an eBay Business" for eBay University
- Expert on entrepreneurship and small business law
- Former publishing entrepreneur and Wall Street lawyer

CLIFF I

Succeeding In

TELEPHONE (203)
www.cliffennico
E-MAIL cennico@legal

LAW OFFICES OF

CLIFFORD R. ENNICO

www.cliffennico.com

2490 BLACK ROCK TURNPIKE #354
FAIRFIELD, CT 06825-2400

TELEPHONE (203) 254-1727
FAX (203) 254-8195
E-MAIL cennico@legalcareer.com

FIGURE 5.2 Cliff Ennico's "rock star" business card, both front and back. When Cliff make speaking appearance, he hands this card to the person introducing him from the podium, who has to read the text on the back rather than memorize a long-winded biography.

- A list of the typical inventory you carry
- A message, slogan, or "pithy quotation from somebody famous your tomers would find interesting or amusing"
- A 15 percent and 20 percent tipping chart
- Your brick-and-mortar store hours ("a lot of eBay businesses are offsho of brick-and-mortar businesses that have excess inventory—you're go to want to market both at the same time," Randye points out)
- A calendar of dates that are important to people in your business
- If you take consignments (and you should), your consignment terms
- A discount offer on the customer's next purchase

What Should Your Flyer Contain?

Your flyer should contain all of your contact information, of course. But Randye cautions that "your flyer or handout shouldn't just be a big 'business card.' " These are some of the things Randye suggests putting on your flyers and handouts:

- **A photo of your brick-and-mortar store,** if you have one.

- **A "thank you" for the order.**

- **The time zone in which you are located** (especially if you are selling internationally—you don't want to get calls from overseas customers at 4 a.m.).

- **Your website URL or brick-and-mortar store address.** Because of new eBay rules restricting you from promoting an off-eBay website, this may soon be the only way you can permissibly let your eBay customers know you are selling merchandise elsewhere on the Internet.

- **An invitation to an in-store promotion, event, or demonstration,** if you have a brick-and-mortar store. Make it an outing for friends, and serve tea, wine, or whatever is appropriate for your business. (You'll be surprised how well this can work.)

- **A sign-up for a special deal or a short survey** that customers can fill out with feedback about the service they received from you.

- **Testimonials from satisfied customers.** ("This is especially important for eBay sellers," Randye points out, "because their inventory changes over time—the testimonials will speak to the quality of their service, not necessarily their merchandise.")

- **An offer of some kind.** For example, list some additional merchandise and then say "order by [*date*] to get a discount on shipping."

Randye emphasizes that your handout or flyer should always contain an offer like this. For example, if you are selling sports collectibles and memorabilia on eBay, you could include a short questionnaire with a 10 percent discount on the next purchase to anyone who fills it out and sends it back. Here are the types of questions you might ask:

- What do you collect?

- Do you specialize in a particular sport? If so, which one?

- Do you specialize in a particular area, such as female sports figures?

- Are you looking for particular items, and would you like to be notified if I can find them for you?

- Do you want to be notified when I put listings up on eBay that I think you would be interested in?

- Would you be willing to sign up for my free e-mail newsletter and any other communications I send to my customers?

By doing this, Randye says, you are accomplishing a number of goals:

- You are showing a personal interest in your customers, making it likely they will consider you a "preferred" source or list you as one of their Favorite Sellers on eBay.

- You are gathering information about their collecting passions, which will help you focus your product sourcing more effectively.

- Most important, you are getting the customers' permission to include them on your house list for future mailings and correspondence.

Your flyer or handout needs to specify how customers should respond to your offer: Do they visit a website? Do they respond to an e-mail address? Or should they send their response via the U.S. Postal Service? If the latter, it probably is wise to enclose a return stamped envelope or postcard to make it easier for people to respond, but keep in mind that this will drive up your costs.

For a discussion of some other packing-and-shipping marketing techniques commonly used by eBayers, see "Marketing Doesn't Stop Once You Make the Sale," in Chapter 3.

Where Should Your Handouts and Flyers Go?

First and foremost, flyers and handouts should be included in every package you ship to your eBay customers.

Second, they should be distributed wherever your customers are likely to see them. Randye tells the following story, showing how a little creativity—and knowledge of your market—can go a long way.

"A friend of mine recently set up a business doing electrolysis—removal of unwanted body hair. She put together a terrific flyer but couldn't figure out what to do with it. I told her to hire some young people—making sure they were over the age of twenty-one—and have them drive around town putting her flyers on people's windshields in parking lots. But not just all parking lots. I told her to concentrate on parking lots outside of three very particular types of establishment: gay bars, topless bars, and strip clubs. My friend asked why, and I told her to think carefully and name some groups of people who were likely to need lots of electrolysis on a regular basis. Gay people (especially gay men), strippers, and exotic dancers would be fairly high on the list, wouldn't they? Let me tell you, my friend was *inundated* with business!"

Of course, we can't think of anyone selling electrolysis services on eBay, but the point is still valid: Sometimes a flyer alerts people to a buying opportunity on eBay they're not aware of. So, for example:

- If you sell baseball cards and other sports memorabilia, place flyers on windshields outside of local sporting events.

- If you sell music items or rock-and-roll paraphernalia, place flyers on windshields outside arenas where rock concerts are taking place.

A word of caution: You really have to know your markets. A lot of people think that sticking flyers on people's windshields is a tacky way to promote any business. If your clients are likely to react that way, then don't do it. Also, avoid handing out flyers on rainy or snowy days. Have you ever gone to the supermarket and returned to your car with six bags of groceries and, as you are fumbling for your keys and trying not to get soaked, you notice somebody's handbill in your windshield that's now a piece of mush? Yecch.

Extras to Throw into the Box

A lot of people selling baseball cards on eBay throw one or two cheap cards into their shipments, which is nice, but customers often throw them away because they don't collect them.

A better strategy is for the seller to create a giveaway—such as a coffee mug or a pen—with the company name, logo, website URL, and eBay Store address inscribed. If it's really cool and eye-catching, you can be sure customers will keep it, use it, and put it in a place where other people can see it.

Or . . . they might just sell them on eBay ☺.

Still, a free gift can be a very useful way to promote your business. For example, the authors know a retired small business owner who is now supplementing her income by selling new and used sewing patterns on eBay. She often has sewing patterns—what she refers to as "orphans"—that she doesn't feel comfortable charging for, so she tosses them into her packages as freebies for her customers. Her eBay feedback is full of comments from buyers about how wonderful these little gifts are.

When picking a specialty ad item for your business, be sure to take into account the weight of an object—a coffee mug might add a pound or two to your package weight, which will increase your shipping fees.

Coupon Promotions, or "Val-Paks"

A number of coupon companies offer you the opportunity to blanket your community with discount coupons. This can be an effective way to build community awareness if you take consignments of merchandise or offer a unique service on eBay, but Randye offers two cautions:

1. Make sure you have enough inventory in stock to satisfy the demand these coupons will create.

2. Inspect the coupon company's mailing list carefully before hiring them. "Most coupon companies have very limited zones in which they are legally allowed to operate—if you are selling swimming pool supplies and the vast majority of people on the company's mailing list live in apartment houses or condominium developments, most of your coupons will end up in the trash."

It doesn't hurt to ask for *category exclusivity,* either. Sometimes the coupon company will allow it, although you might have to pay a small premium for it. If you are going to invest in this method of marketing, you don't want to be in the same envelope with your competitors. If that is the case, you are better off doing business with a different company or doing a solo mailing yourself to alleviate consumer confusion.

Your Packaging Materials

Every time you ship merchandise to an eBay customer, it's an opportunity for marketing. Sellers on eBay love to use recycled boxes and other packaging materials, but it can send confusing signals to customers. Have you ever ordered something on eBay, and the merchandise arrived in a recycled Amazon box? It's happened to one of the authors of this book—twice from the same seller!

If you must use recycled boxes, use a box cutter to slice the box open, turn it inside out, and reassemble it so there's no writing or printed material on the outside. That way, it looks like a new box, or at least one of your own, until the customer opens it.

More important than the box itself is the address label. "You should always have address labels printed up at the same time you have your business cards done; they're not very expensive, they impress your name and logo in the customer's brain, and they really make you look like a professional," Randye says. Many sellers quickly learn that printing their own labels, driving to the post office, and standing in line take up an enormous part of the day. The logical next step is to use the PayPal shipping service. The only drawback is that, you'll notice, the label advertises PayPal—not you!

Why not customize your address label with a photo of yourself or some other logo that people will immediately recognize? Companies like Endicia.com and Stamps.com integrate with your eBay Store as easily as PayPal and allow you to brand your shipping label by putting your logo and a branded message on it. For a small monthly fee, these services pay for themselves with the extra name exposure your company receives.

Yellow Pages and Other Directory Listings

Although it's unlikely most customers will find your eBay business through the Yellow Pages or another telephone directory, there is one group of people who go to the Yellow Pages first when they think eBay: people who are looking to clean out their houses (or those of a recently deceased relative) and who want to consign all of the household items to someone for sale on eBay.

If you are taking consignments of merchandise for sale on eBay, a listing in the Yellow Pages can be a wise investment. There probably won't be a category for eBay sellers in your local directory, but Randye advises calling the directory publisher and asking whether such a category can be created. "Believe it or not, they will create a new category if they think there's sufficient demand for it, because it doesn't cost them anything," Randye says. If your local publisher won't create a new category, consider listing under "consignment shops," "antiques stores," or the type of merchandise you sell (for example, "sporting goods stores," "jewelry stores").

Another tip from Randye: Go to www.yellowpages.com and type in "eBay," followed by the type of merchandise you sell. With a few mouse clicks you can see where other eBay sellers and consignment shops around the country are listed, and you can follow suit with your local directory.

Your Automobile or Minivan

One of the most overlooked direct-marketing tools—because most people associate it with building contractors and plumbers—is your automobile or minivan. In most states, you can put the name of your business, along with a telephone number or website URL, on your vehicle without obtaining any sort of permission from your state department of motor vehicles. (Be careful, however; in a number of states, you may be required to apply for a commercial motor vehicle permit if you do this. Check with your local DMV and find out the rules before you call the detail shop.)

Your business name, logo, and URL should appear prominently on both the sides and the back of your car or van. A big mistake people make is to have just the sides of their van or truck detailed—that means the only people who see it are people you pass at an intersection, and they won't have time to digest the information. A lot more people are going to be stuck in traffic behind you than next to you, so make sure the back of your van is detailed.

Randye suggests using your URL rather than your telephone number on your car, truck, or van: "When they see your van, most people won't have a pen handy to write it down, and people will remember Web addresses much longer than they will a telephone number, unless, of course, your phone number is very easy to remember, such as 1–800-ILUVJNK."

Charity Events, Silent Auctions, and Local Events

In every local newspaper, there's a section listing all the charity events that will be taking place in the next few weeks. Most of these events have silent auctions, raffles, and other promotions where merchandise from local businesses is sold to raise money. You should call every one of them and offer to give them some merchandise for their next sale—along with a stack of your business cards, handouts, and flyers to give to the attendees! Nonprofit organizations rarely say no to this approach as long as the sales pitch is not too blatant and you demonstrate a sincere desire to promote the purposes of the organization.

Also peruse your local newspaper for listings of street fairs and other, similar events where people rent booths to sell merchandise. You might not be interested in renting a booth yourself, but you can always call the organization and get a list of vendors who have rented them. If there are any vendors offering merchandise with which yours is compatible, you might be able to cut a deal with them whereby they sublet a portion of their booth to you—you pay a portion of their rental fee, and they put a bunch of your flyers and business cards in a place where people can easily pick them up.

Mini-Billboards

Outdoor billboard advertising was discussed previously, but one type of billboard deserves mention here: the mini-billboard. For example:

- Those little placards on the backs of grocery shopping carts that list local realtors. Why couldn't they also advertise an eBay seller who's taking consignments?

- The place mats that diners use.

- Ads on the insides of restaurant bathroom doors (or directly above the urinals in the men's rooms—hey, where else do *you* look?).

These generally don't cost very much, and, especially for eBay sellers who are taking consignments, they can be great ways to build brand awareness. We guarantee your competition won't be thinking about these, unless, of course, they also have read this book.

Look for Centers of Influence

When marketing offline, focus your attention on what Randye calls "centers of influence"—people who are in a position to purchase and/or market your merchandise to their customers and clients.

"A big mistake people make when they sell antiques is to sell only to the collectors," says Randye. "That's great, but if someone has just built a new house and wants to decorate it using antiques, they don't often do it themselves—they hire an interior designer who goes out and buys the antiques as part of the decoration strategy. So if you're selling antiques on eBay, wouldn't you want the local designers to know who you are?"

Another great center of influence, especially for eBay sellers taking consignments, is local estate and divorce attorneys. When households are being dissolved, especially in an emotional context (the death of a parent, a nasty marital breakup), the parties often want someone else to come in and clean out all the household goods. Most estate and divorce attorneys refer their clients to local estate auction houses and liquidators (if you can find these folks anymore—they're all on eBay!). But shouldn't they also recommend the services of a local eBay consignment operation? They probably will (all attorneys want to look resourceful in the eyes of their clients) . . . if they know who you are. Offer to speak to your local county bar association on the topic "Using eBay and Other E-Commerce Platforms to Help Your Clients Liquidate Their Estate." We are pretty sure you will attract a full house of local attorneys who will be interested in what you have to say.

Yet another center of influence can be your local declutter person. These people help businesspeople and individuals who have too much stuff in their lives. Oftentimes the declutter person is called into homes that are stuffed full to the brim, and the items must be removed. The declutterer may have his or her hands full with the psychological aspect of hand-holding their clients and teaching them how to let go of their stuff, and thus might be looking for a partner to help sell off the items. Look for a local declutterer/home organizer.

Others might include the local 1–800-GOT-JUNK franchisee and, as long as the economy continues to stumble, mortgage/bank lenders who hire services to clean out foreclosures.

Coordinating Your Online and Offline Strategies

No matter what else you do when planning an offline marketing strategy, according to Randye, it is extremely important that your online and offline efforts be coordinated. "I once saw a pair of boots in a *New York Times* ad that I was really interested in," Randye recalls. "They had a website URL where you could order the boots, but when I went to the website I couldn't find that pair of boots anywhere on the site! There was no 'order number,' or even a reference to the *New York Times* ad. Needless to say, I was ticked off at this company for wasting my time, and I've never been back to that site."

If you are doing offline marketing, be sure to code responses so you can tell where orders and inquiries are coming from, and be sure to update your website, your eBay Store, and your other online platforms so that people who receive your direct-mail pieces can easily and quickly find the merchandise they are looking for.

Developing an E-Commerce Empire

Building Synergy Among Multiple Marketing Channels

Now that you've built a solid presence on eBay, using the tools and information to market your eBay both online and offline, there is only one thing to do: build an e-commerce empire by establishing outposts elsewhere on the Internet where you can sell merchandise.

As we stated in the introduction to this book, the world of eBay is changing rapidly and dynamically—in ways that often don't benefit smaller sellers or that force them to spend lots of time catching up with the latest rules and requirements eBay imposes on its sellers if they want to continue selling on the site. As a result of these changes, a growing number of eBay sellers are looking to hedge their bets by selling elsewhere on the Internet, whether through their own websites or on e-commerce platforms that compete with eBay, such as Yahoo! and Amazon.com. Then they link everything together so that customers who see them in one place can easily find them elsewhere if they like what they see and want to buy some more.

Chapter 6 of *The eBay Marketing Bible* gives you some advice and tools for doing just that.

Building an "Octopus" Online

An octopus is exactly what you should strive to build when you create your e-commerce empire on the Internet. The octopus basically has two parts: a combination head and digestive system and a bunch of tentacles that spread out from the head into the surrounding water. The tentacles of the octopus contain numerous suckers, which catch prey in the open water and then feed the prey to the mouth of the octopus, which then digests the prey. (See Figure 6.1.)

The Head of the Octopus: Your Website

The head of your online octopus is your business website.

Five years ago, we would have conceded that there are at least some businesses that don't need a website to be successful. Not anymore. These days, every small business, whether it does business primarily online or offline, needs to have its own website.

Why? For two reasons.

First, people these days expect that you have a website if you are in business. When someone hands us a business card at a speaking engagement or networking event, the first thing we look for is a Web address so that we can find out more about the person (assuming, of course, that we want to). If we don't see a Web address, or if it's written by hand on the back of the business card, the person instantly loses credibility in our eyes.

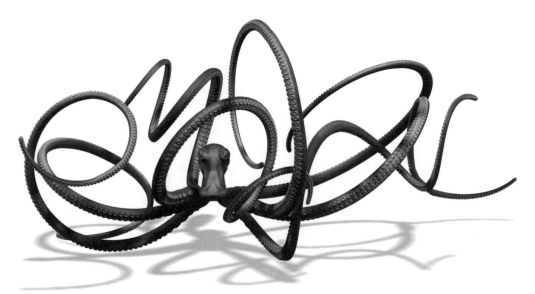

FIGURE 6.1 Your e-commerce empire should look something like an octopus—your website is the head, while your blogs, social networking profiles, eBay Store, and Amazon affiliates page are tentacles that hook the customers and feed them to your website.

Second, and more important, there is one place—and only one—on the entire Internet where you can sell merchandise and keep 100 percent of the proceeds of each sale. That place is your website. Whenever you list merchandise for sale on a platform other than your own website, you have to pay a fee for the privilege—either a listing fee, a "success" fee (a percentage of the sale amount or winning bid), or some combination of the two. When you sell stuff from your website, you don't have to pay anything to anybody.

The Tentacles of the Octopus: Your Presence on eBay, Amazon, Yahoo!, and Other Platforms

The head of the octopus is your website, but it needs tentacles as well. Presences on the eBay, Yahoo!, and Amazon platforms are all examples of the tentacles you put out in the e-commerce ocean once you've established your own website.

What exactly do tentacles do? According to the nature documentaries we see on TV, the tentacles on an octopus serve two basic functions:

1. They use their sticky suction cups (or whatever they're really called) to ensnare prey that swim by.

2. Once they have caught prey, the tentacles use their suckers to pass the prey backward toward the mouth, located in the head, where the prey is consumed and digested.

Your e-commerce tentacles serve much the same goal. Your presences on eBay, Yahoo!, Amazon, and some of the other online platforms we discuss in the next few sections, serve to attract customers surfing the Web who would otherwise not find you in a million years. People search for things on eBay, Yahoo!, and Amazon every day, but only rarely do people search specifically for your website—at least not until you are so well established that your business is a household word (and we hope that happens someday).

Your Goal Is to Feed the Octopus

Here's a pop quiz question: When selling merchandise online, where do you want the bulk of your sales to come from? Answer: Your Website, of course!

Once customers buy a few things from you on eBay and become hooked on your merchandise and service, they will want more, more, more. That's when your tentacles should be feeding them to the mouth of your e-commerce empire—your website, where you can sell lots of stuff to these customers and keep 100 percent of what you make.

Now, the folks at eBay don't make this easy, as we discuss in the next few sections. They don't like to lose revenue, and you can't really blame them. They offer a lot of tools to sellers to help them build real businesses on eBay, and they want you to return those favors by selling exclusively, or mostly, on the eBay site. Integrating an eBay presence with a website outside eBay can be a bit tricky, and the rules keep changing just about every month. But there are a few things you can do to integrate the tentacles of your e-commerce empire with the head, and we describe them in the next few sections.

Make Your Website the Center of It All

Having your own website is the only place on the entire Internet where you can sell things to people and keep 100 percent of the proceeds without having to share them with anyone else.

Having a website with a shopping cart and secure encryption is beyond the realm of most sellers. Avoiding that sort of complexity is probably one of the reasons you choose to sell your wares on eBay. The massive amount of buyers who regularly visit eBay lulls most sellers into thinking they don't need a stand-alone website outside of eBay. However, there are many more marketing techniques available to website owners that will send buyers to your eBay listings, make you money through the referral credit, and build your e-mail list. Having a stand-alone website away from eBay is an excellent way to communicate with your customers. It gives you additional freedom to:

- Collect e-mail addresses.

- Provide links to more information on products you're selling.

- Partner with other vendors to cross-promote.

- Strengthen the bond with your customers.

Your website is the head of your e-commerce octopus, and all of your other online efforts are tentacles whose primary mission in life is to drive customers, sales, and profits to your website.

As the center of your e-commerce empire, your website needs to be both a meeting place and a signpost:

- **A meeting place** for your target customers, who will visit this site to indulge in their passions, hopes, and dreams and find solutions for their problems, whether directly from you or from people who share those passions, problems, hopes, and dreams

- **A signpost** that directs customers to the tentacles of your e-commerce empire and to other venues affiliated with your business, where they can find additional resources for indulging in their passions, hopes, and dreams or solutions for their problems. One point should already be crystal clear: You establish an e-commerce website for the primary purpose of selling things to people. Therefore, your website is not and cannot be about you or your business, although you certainly can have an About Us page to satisfy the occasional customer who is curious about your history.

What Should Be on Your Website?

Your website should be first and foremost about your target customers and their passions, problems, hopes, and dreams. That is what will make them buy things from you.

Cool, Compelling Content

People frequently go online with the specific goal of finding merchandise for sale, of course, but more often they go online to do research or look for information. The Internet is the most amazing research tool ever invented, with billions of online resources on just about every topic in the known universe. Often people who are looking for information online don't even know there are products or services they can buy that are somehow related to that information or that can help them reach the goals that drove them to look for the information in the first place.

For example, search online for information about "outdoor billboard advertising," and your search results page will list several websites of companies that offer (for a fee, of course) to design, print, and place your outdoor billboard advertisement.

So your website should not just list the items of inventory you have to sell. There should be information—lots and lots of information—about:

- The merchandise you sell

- The customers you are trying to attract

- Most important, the passions, hopes, and dreams or solutions for their problems that will drive them to buy merchandise on your website

It is not sufficient that you have information on your website. The information must be cool and compelling—designed to generate an emotional response in your customers that will keep them coming back for more.

Your website should carry your branding. To continue building trust with your customers and help them identify you, be sure to use the same colors and logos that your eBay store has.

From a marketer's perspective, what other components does your website need to help build a tribe of qualified buyers? Although every Web design is dif-

---

THE KING OF COOL, COMPELLING CONTENT

Jim was an English teacher in one of the local high schools, but like many teachers, he moonlighted at several part-time jobs to supplement his income. Among other things, Jim worked as a carpet cleaner.

He promoted his business by sending flyers to his customers four times a year (at the beginning of each season). But Jim did not just send out a flyer listing his prices for various services. Oh, no.—Jim sent out *The Cleaning News.*

The Cleaning News consisted of a single page, printed on both sides. When you opened the envelope, you saw a masthead very similar to that of *The New York Times* (using the same Gothic script), saying, "*The Cleaning News*: All the Dirt That's Fit to Print."

And what did you see directly below the masthead? A screaming headline in fourteen-point type, saying, "IT'S DUST MITE SEASON AGAIN!!!" followed by a half-page electron microscope photo of a dust mite blown up about ten thousand times. Have you ever seen a dust mite up close and personal? Trust us, it is one ugly bug.

The caption below the photo would say, "Save your family and pets from these voracious creatures, at least 10,000 of which are in the carpet below your bare feet right now!" Talk about marketing a solution to people's problems . . . in a way that actually makes them laugh.

The Cleaning News was not junk mail. It was a work of literature (Jim *was* an English teacher, after all), and his customers actually looked forward to receiving it four times a year. Jim's customers even saved their copies of *The Cleaning News,* and gave them to people who moved into the neighborhood—viral marketing at its best.

ferent, there are a few features that are necessary for all. Here is a checklist of items to incorporate into your website.

- **Links to your eBay Store.** This is a no-brainer, but don't forget the refid code so you can collect the 75 percent referral discount.

- **Newsletter sign-up box.** Although, technically, you could link back to the eBay page where viewers can subscribe to your eBay Store newsletter, we recommend building a list outside eBay.

- **Articles.** These are a must. You need to give your customer a reason for coming to your website, and the easiest way to do that is quality content. It's also important for the search engine spiders. This is a great way to present additional information about using your website. Articles can include how-to demos (embed a YouTube video), projects your buyers have completed using your product, and additional uses for your product.

- **Links.** Create a links page. It could be to manufacturers' websites, popular bloggers in your field, or favorite articles you've read. The search engines rank a site on authority. How do they consider authority? They judge it by the number of qualified sites that are linking to you as well as links from your website to outside sites. The algorithms have changed over time. Once it only mattered who was linking to your site; now the spiders consider both incoming links and outgoing links.

- **A search box.** If your site consists of more than one page, it must be easy to navigate. If visitors must pause to ponder your site navigation for more than a few seconds, they'll leave. One easy way to simplify navigation is to have a search box available. Then users need only type in a word or phrase to find what they are looking for. Search boxes used to be complicated, but Google has now made creating one pretty simple: You supply some brief information, then they generate the code for you to cut and paste into the site. Your visitors are already familiar with Google searches, so partnering with Google on your site transfers a bit of Google's prestige to your website while it helps direct your customers.

Interactivity

As we said in Chapter 3, there are four things people look for when they surf the Web, and your website should have as many of these as possible:

1. Cool, compelling, content and relevant information that people will be searching for online

2. Merchandise that people cannot find locally

3. Terrific deals on merchandise that people *can* find locally

4. People who are like themselves in important ways

There are other ways to engage your customers using a website. If you look at this endeavor as a way to build a community, it opens up a whole new world of uses for a website. Here is a quick list of possible uses for your website:

- **Create a membership site.** You could offer your customers access to an exclusive area that only buyers can access. Provide them with something unique such as buyer discounts, bonus information, or additional training.

- **Have contests.** If you sell photo supplies, have a regular photo contest with prizes. If you sell garden supplies, have a garden-of-the-month contest or a biggest-pumpkin-grown contest. You could have an essay contest involving your product—if you sell dance shoes, how about asking customers to write about the most interesting dance the buyer and shoes attended.

- **Ask customers questions.** There are sites such as SurveyMonkey.com that make hosting a survey simple. Use your website as a gateway to the questionnaire, and learn what's on your buyers' minds.

- **Showcase customers.** Have a customer-of-the-month section. If you sold garden equipment, you could showcase customers' gardens with photos and an interview. You could interview customers who had the earliest-ripening tomato or who had the most fragrant roses.

- **If you are taking consignments, provide information about your services** along with links to their existing auctions and testimonials from previous consignment clients.

- **Create a website where customers can rate and remark on your products or services.** You may take a few lumps, but this is one of the best ways to build trust with your clients. They can give you direct feedback, you'll know how to improve, and, given the chance, most people love telling about their experiences. Don't try to control the discussion. Let buyers have their say. But do keep things on topic and damp down flame wars before they start.

- **Build your credibility by displaying awards and honors your business has received.** Provide links and information about associations your business is affiliated with.

- **Humanize your business by showing photos of yourself or staff and writing bios about them.**

- **Create comparison tables about your products to showcase them.** Let buyers know why your product is better than others, by building up your brand, not tearing down others.

- **If you are an eBay Education Specialist, create a website specifically about teaching.** You can include a list of classes, biographical information, affiliate links to products you suggest, and testimonials from students. An Education Specialist often refers students to products and services. With a website, you can send your students to a page that has URLs of recommended resources. Some services give you an affiliate commission for sending customers their way. (See Figure 6.2.)

With the advent of so-called Web 2.0 social networking websites, where people around the world can find people who share their common interests (or, ahem, their passions, problems, hopes, and dreams), you would be crazy not to have some sort of social networking opportunity available on your website.

Setting up a blog or an interactive area where your customers can communicate with you and with each other serves a number of very useful marketing functions:

- You can see at a glance what their passions, problems, hopes, and dreams are (because they will be talking about them), and how they are changing.

- You can ask your customers questions and get answers that are likely to be close to the truth (since your customers don't know you, they aren't as likely to tell you what you want to hear because they're afraid of offending you).

- Most important, you can promote your new stuff in an informal, conversational way that won't come across as cold calling or hard selling.

FIGURE 6.2   Grandpa's Trading Company has a simple webpage that informs readers about classes and has links to the eBay Store (http://grandpastradingcompany.com).

What Should Be Kept off Your Website?

Basically, keep anything off your website that your customers are *not* interested in, even though you think it should be there (see Figure 6.3).

Lawyers and accountants are the worst offenders when it comes to setting up websites (we know, we know, lawyers and accountants don't offer their services on eBay, but we couldn't think of a good eBay example). Look at the typical lawyer's or accountant's website, and here's what you will see:

- A photo of the lawyer or accountant (tell us honestly—do you really care whether your lawyer or accountant is gorgeous or plug-ugly as long as he or she can do the job you need done?)

- A biography of the lawyer or accountant (again, do you really care whether your lawyer went to Harvard or State U., especially if it was more than ten years ago?)

- Links to articles the lawyer or accountant has written in professional journals demonstrating his or her expertise (do you really need to read a five-thousand-word article on the double jeopardy clause of the U.S. Constitution to figure out whether a lawyer can get your kid out from under a drunken driving charge?)

All interesting information, of course, but totally useless when it comes to helping you figure out whether or not to hire the person as your lawyer or accountant.

FIGURE 6.3 The home page of Cliff Ennico's law practice at www.cliffennico.com. Note that Cliff doesn't waste lots of space talking about himself—he focuses on what he does for his clients, what he doesn't do, and how much he charges, which are all most prospective law clients will care about. He does put his photo on the home page, but so far he hasn't lost too much business as a result ☺.

When designing a website, it's very tempting to put up information that satisfies your ego or that you think is entertaining, cute, or important. But when marketing your business, it isn't what you care about, it's what your customers care about that counts. Your website should not contain any information or tool that your customers don't care about. Everything on your website is there to satisfy one, and only one, primary objective: to help you sell merchandise. If you've got anything on your website that isn't helping you do that, take it down.

The lists we've provided here will help you create a website that engages your customers and builds a relationship with them. Keep your website fresh, provide new content, and ask your shoppers questions. You'll start noticing traffic stopping by your website and following links into your eBay Store.

The benefits from having a website are many and worth the extra time and effort. It's one of the first steps in building a source of traffic and tapping the loyalty of existing customers.

Reaching Out with Yahoo!, Amazon, and Other E-Commerce Platforms

Now that you've built a killer website for your e-commerce business, it's time to assemble the octopus's tentacles—outposts elsewhere on the Internet—that will attract customers, get them interested in your merchandise, and gradually move them closer and closer to your website, where your best stuff lives and from which you can sell things without having to decrease your margins because of high listing fees.

The Major E-Commerce Platforms

For the past decade, the world of e-commerce has been dominated by three giant selling platforms: eBay, Amazon, and Yahoo! Once you have an eBay Store, you should at least consider whether you should have a similar retail outlet on Amazon or Yahoo!

Amazon.com

Once upon a time, Amazon (also known as "The River") was the place to go if you wanted to buy books, music CDs, movies, and other information products.

Amazon is still the market leader for these types of products. But Amazon's marketplace has grown far beyond that and is now giving eBay a run for its money by expanding its e-commerce solutions focused at online sellers.

One advantage of selling on Amazon is that you can create a "me too" listing, (where sellers can sell their items alongside Amazon's on the same catalog page) in its expanding catalog of goods without paying any upfront fees. You pay fees only if the item sells. This makes Amazon a wonderful place to dip your toes into the water before subscribing to become a Pro Merchant.

Once you subscribe to become an Amazon Pro Merchant (much like an eBay store subscription), you can create listings for products that are not in Amazon's catalog. As massive as Amazon's inventory selection is, there are still many items missing from its catalog. This is a chance to sell products that are not directly competing with the giant itself.

Amazon continues to create services catering to third-party vendors (that's us folks who aren't Amazon). These services are what have made many eBay sellers stand up and take notice. Among them are:

- **Fulfillment by Amazon (FBA).** This service allows Pro Merchants to send their inventory to the Amazon warehouses. Amazon stores and ships the inventory for the seller. Two great advantages to this are (1) you can have a clean living room with no storage unit fees, and (2) when Amazon handles the shipping, the items are eligible for free shipping.

- **Webstores by Amazon.** These stand-alone websites are supersimple to set up, and sellers do not need to learn complex shopping cart functions to use them. When customers check out, a page tells them the merchant has partnered with Amazon. You, the seller, don't have to worry about invoicing or shopping carts, and your customers experience security and confidence when they buy from you. That's because they know and trust Amazon. Other features of the Webstores subscription include the following:

  - You can automatically insert Amazon's customer reviews for your products. Testimonials are a beautiful thing!

  - You may use Amazon's own inventory to fill in your inventory gaps. This allows you to focus your purchasing power on the items you get the best deals on and receive an affiliate spiff for selling items Amazon carries. Meanwhile, your customers see your store as fully stocked.

  - You can have as many niche stores as you like for one subscription fee.

- **Drop Ship by Amazon.** Yep, that's right, you can sell Amazon merchandise and they will ship it to your customer.

- **Amazon Associates.** This program allows you to collect commissions on sales on Amazon generated by your recommendations. Amazon offers a full range of linking strategies for website owners, including a webstore-type widget for your website.

Yahoo! Stores

The Yahoo! Stores are created for sellers who desire their own stand-alone e-commerce websites but really don't want the headache of learning how to manage shopping cart software or don't have any technological knowledge of Web design. Because this is part of the Yahoo! family, you will be listed for free in the Yahoo directory.

This solution is good for a seller just starting out, but you may outgrow it as your sales increase. For sellers looking for a basic e-commerce site, a small up-front fee plus a transaction fee equal to a small percentage of the purchase price of each item sold gives you the following:

- A simple-to-set-up stand-alone website with inventory

- Easy-to-set-up templates that allow you to customize the color scheme and inventory layout.

- The ability to accept credit and debit cards using your merchant account and PayPal checkout

Other Platforms

The three major platforms (eBay, Amazon, and Yahoo!) continue to innovate and compel buyers and sellers to their sites, but a number of other players have thrown their hats into the ring. These platforms are growing in terms of both the number of users and the variety of merchandise offered there. Sellers looking to branch out on the Web are well advised to consider these, because they generally offer lower fees in an attempt to attract sellers away from the major platforms.

ProStores

ProStores is owned by eBay, so it integrates with your Selling Manager software. That makes it easier to track your shipping and inventory duties. Like

Yahoo! Stores, it has simple-to-set-up templates that are somewhat customizable, and the fees are extremely reasonable.

You can choose from a number of predesigned templates or hire a designer to create your custom store branding. Which templates and how many individual SKUs you can list through your ProStore depends on which subscription level you join.

Cindy Shebley subscribed to a ProStore during a free promotion recently. She found it to be somewhat easy to set up, but the entry-level store really restricted growth. The entry-level ProStore allows only twenty individual SKU's. To make a viable store, the seller must upgrade to one of the higher levels.

Here are some of the benefits of using ProStores:

- As an eBay Store owner, you receive 30 percent off your monthly subscription fees.

- You can import your eBay Store products from your eBay Store to the ProStores easily.

- You have your own unique URL, or you can use a ProStores extension.

- You can get a one-month free trial to see whether it fits your needs.

- Many eBay designers understand ProStores, so cobranding your eBay and ProStore is easier.

Using ProStores is a natural move for those who are ready to expand their reach into the online e-commerce world. But before you plunk down your money out of loyalty to eBay, check prices and features to be sure that ProStores is the right fit for your inventory.

Google Base

Not so much a stand-alone website, Google Base is certainly a feasible alternative or an addition to selling online. Google Base listings are set up much the same way an eBay listing is done. On Google Base you can sell your wares, advertise classes, promote services, and even post personal ads.

Using this service is free. Buyers use Google Checkout to purchase their items from your listings. Google Checkout works much the same way as PayPal, but it is owned by a different company. Your buyers can use a credit card or debit card for the transaction. Having an alternative checkout has its advantages. Cindy has made a few sales to individuals who, for one reason or another, will *not* use PayPal. Cindy will not sell to someone who asks this of her through eBay, but she does have her own stand-alone website and when a customer is uncomfortable using PayPal, it is very easy for Cindy to set up a Google Base listing for that buyer.

Another feature of Google Base is the Store Connector, a free piece of software that sits on your computer desktop. With the push of a button, the Store Connector transfers all your eBay Store listings to Google Base.

Here are the advantages of listing on Google Base:

- It's free.

- Google Base items are automatically listed on Google's Froogle shopping site.

- It offers an alternative checkout system.

- It uses API and XML protocols for larger-inventory sellers.

- You can list inventory without a stand-alone website.

Craigslist

Craigslist.org is a venerable shopping site where people can list items for sale in a classified ad format.

The advantages of using Craigslist are:

- The site reaches 450 different communities around the globe.

- Listing ads is free.

The disadvantages of using Craigslist are:

- Site visitors are distributed among 450 different locations. You have to search each one separately, and you are not supposed to post your ad in more than one location at a time.

- Because of the classified ad format, there is no protection for sellers against unscrupulous buyers, and vice versa. It's *caveat venditor* ("let the seller beware") when you list items for sale on Craigslist.

- In addition to merchandise, Craigslist offers "personal" ads, ads for local services and professionals (lawyers and accountants frequently list on

Craigslist), and basically every other type of ad you would see in the classified section of your local newspaper. This has led some critics to comment that Craigslist is trying to be all things to all people and has spread itself too thin.

Interestingly, a search on Amazon.com reveals that the only book ever published on how to do business on Craigslist has been out of print for several years. This may be because the site is so easy to use that such a book is not necessary. But then again, maybe not . . .

Overstock.com

Overstock.com is, as the name implies, a site where companies and retailers can dump—er, we mean *sell*—excess inventory.

The advantages of selling on Overstock.com are:

- Lower fees

- Strong name recognition backed by a national television advertising campaign

Some of the disadvantages of listing on Overstock.com are:

- The site's (unfortunate) reputation as an "elephant's burial ground" of unsaleable inventory.

- The fact that many of the site's customers are "bottom-feeders" looking for the best possible deals at all costs—meaning low profit margins.

- The site's focus on current consumer goods or merchandise and bulk lots of identical goods—antiques and collectibles won't do well here.

Specialty Websites

Many other online retailers are jumping into allowing third-party sellers on their sites, and it's still early days when it comes to figuring out which partnerships will be most effective. Here's a short list of retailers that have joined the ranks and are welcoming partnerships with you:

- Buy.com

- Half.com

- RubyLane.com (for collectors)

- Etsy.com (for all things handmade)

- Bonanzle.com

- Wagglepop.com

- eCrater.com

- Blujay.com

- Ebid.com

- Webidz.com

- Bidz.com

The major advantage of selling on lesser-known websites is lower fees. The major disadvantage of selling on lesser-known websites is fewer customers.

Still, listing on these sites can't hurt, and you might reach some disgruntled customers who will shop anywhere but eBay (or Amazon, or whatever). However, your time is money. Test these sites out and if they don't provide results, keep looking for your targeted group of consumers. Some of these sites have some real potential and are growing like crazy (but that's a topic for another book . . .).

Micro-Sites

This is a word the authors have invented especially for this book. You can say you saw it here first! A *micro-site* is a website that offers merchandise for sale in a narrow market niche (sometimes an extremely narrow niche) and that is extremely well known among buyers in that niche.

The following are examples of micro-sites:

- **www.penbid.com:** For collectors of antique pens, writing instruments, and inkwells

- **www.mechanicalbanks.org:** The website of the Mechanical Bank Collectors of America, for collectors of antique mechanical banks (banks that do something cute when you put your penny in the slot)

- **www.stillbankclub.org:** The website of the Still Bank Collectors of America, for collectors of (you guessed it) antique still banks (banks that don't do anything but sit there when you put your penny in the slot)

The advantages of listing your merchandise on micro-sites are:

- They have extremely low fees. Some sites allow you to list your merchandise absolutely free for life as long as you write articles every once in a while for the site.

- Most of these sites will keep your listings up for months or years without any additional fees.

- Everybody who visits the site—every single visitor—is interested in the merchandise you have to offer and is therefore a potential customer.

The disadvantages of listing on micro-sites are:

- There is an extremely small (although highly motivated) number of visitors to the site.

- You may be required to become a member of the organization sponsoring the site in order to list items for sale there and pay dues to that organization in order to stay on the site.

- These sites have high volatility—they stay alive only as long as somebody is willing to pay the bills, and they sometimes disappear without warning as membership declines, collecting tastes change, or somebody forgets to pay the renewal fee for the website's domain name.

For eBay sellers specializing in antiques and collectibles, however, micro-sites are a terrific way to build your brand and attract highly motivated buyers to your eBay listings or eBay Store at extremely low cost.

Tips on Linking It All Together

Now that you've built a killer website and have established your octopus's tentacles on eBay, Amazon, Yahoo!, and perhaps also a few of the specialty websites mentioned in the previous section, there's just one thing to do: tie everything together, or, if you prefer, connect your tentacles to the head so that your octopus functions the way you want it to.

Creating Links from Your Website to Your Tentacles

The home page of your website should contain banner ads or buttons linking your site to each of the e-commerce tentacles you have established online. For example, by putting a button on your home page that says "Looking for more? Check out our eBay Store!" with a link to your eBay Store, you will drive traffic to your eBay Store.

You would also do this for your Yahoo! Store, your Amazon Affiliate site, or anywhere else that you are actively selling online. Thus, a click-through button saying "Collect antique mechanical banks? Click here," with links to the items you are currently selling on the Mechanical Bank Collectors of America website (www.mechanicalbanks.org) will take your viewers there.

Generally, eBay doesn't object when you link an outside website to your eBay listings or eBay Store—they actually like it and will offer you guidance and support to help you do just that.

Creating Links from Your Tentacles to Your Website

Likewise, to the extent that online platforms allow you to do so, you should create links to your website in your Yahoo! Store, your Amazon Affiliate site, and anywhere else you sell online. You should also put a similar link in every blog entry, on your Squidoo lens, and anywhere else you post content online to promote your business. Remember always that the goal of having an e-commerce octopus online is to direct traffic to your website—the only place on the entire Internet where you can sell stuff and not have to share the proceeds with anyone. If you're not telling everyone you encounter online where your website is located, they won't know where you are, or even that you have a website at all.

The one exception to this rule, unfortunately, is eBay. They really don't like it when you promote your website or Yahoo! Store on the eBay site. This is probably one of the easiest ways to get your individual listings or eBay Store booted off the eBay site, as will be discussed later.

Find Affiliates and Link to Them

One of the most effective ways to spread your tentacles online is through an affiliate program. An affiliate program works as follows:

- Someone with their own website—usually one that generates much higher traffic volume than yours—agrees to put a link to your website on their website.

- If anyone clicks on that link and is directed to your website (and, hopefully, buys something once they are there), you pay your affiliate—the owner of the other website—a commission or *referral fee.*

Many affiliate relationships are mutual—not only does the other website promote your stuff, but you agree to put a link on your website to their website as well, earning referral fees whenever someone clicks on your link and buys something on the other website.

As you can see, affiliate programs that are based on actual sales taking place on each site are to some extent based on mutual trust—it may be difficult for you to tell whether someone you referred to another website actually bought something there, and vice versa. For that reason, many affiliate relationships are based on *click-through fees* or *pay-per-click fees,* whereby each website pays a small fee to the other website each time someone clicks on the affiliate link, regardless of whether an actual purchase takes place.

Here are some basic rules for creating an effective affiliate program:

- Your commission rate should be generous, at least 20 percent, to encourage affiliates to sign up.

- Be careful whom you affiliate with. Look at any affiliate's website first, and make sure this is a club you actually want to join.

- Offer your affiliates a choice of banners, buttons, and other graphics so that they can pick the one that's most appropriate for their websites.

- Invest in a solid traffic tracking and analytics software program so that you know in real time exactly who's clicking from one affiliate website to the other.

- Make sure there's a clear understanding (preferably in writing or via e-mail) with the other website about when pay-per-click payments will be made and a method for easily dumping an affiliate who doesn't pay on time.

For more information on affiliate marketing programs and tips on developing one for your website, check out the following books: *A Practical Guide to Affiliate Marketing: Quick Reference for Affiliate Managers and Merchants* by Evgenii Prussakov (AM Navigator LL, 2007) and *Internet Riches: The Simple Money-Making Secrets of Online Millionaires* by Scott Fox (AMACOM, 2006).

Using eBay's HTML Builder to Link Outside Websites to Your eBay Store

eBay encourages you to link your website, and other online pages, to your eBay Store and has created a number of tools to help you do that, most important of which is the HTML Builder. To find this feature, go to your eBay Store and then to your Manage My Store area; you will notice a link for the HTML Builder on the left-hand side under Store Design. Once you are on the HTML Builder page, click on the Build Off-eBay Links to Items link near the bottom of the page, and eBay's software will walk you through the process fairly simply.

By using eBay's HTML Builder you can do the following:

- Create links and showcase items inside your eBay listings.

- Create links to cross-promote inventory in other listings.

- Create links for webpages outside of eBay.

This is a very easy way to send traffic to eBay. Let's say you are selling a book. You could write a review about it and then create a link that includes the gallery photo directly into your store. (See Figure 6.4.) Another use for this tool might be to showcase a whole category of items. Maybe you just received a new shipment of china in that special pattern everyone loves. You could create a webpage about the china and below have the category items. This allows buyers to shop through a trusted source—eBay—and you won't have the hassle and expense of processing orders.

Also, the HTML Builder automatically codes in the information necessary for you to obtain a referral fee credit (see Chapter 3) each time somebody links to

FIGURE 6.4   eBay has a customizable tool called the HTML Builder to help you create product links to your eBay listings. Here's a sample of a link, created using HTML Builder, that promotes an eBay listing for a single item.

your eBay Store from your website, so you don't have to worry about adding it each time you post inventory to your eBay Store.

Do you want to list just one eBay Store inventory item on your website? The entire inventory of your store (see Figure 6.5)? Just items in a specific eBay category? Just items that are "Ending Soon" or that have the "Highest Price"? There are many customizable ways to list your eBay Store inventory on your website using HTML Builder. You can also customize your eBay Store link with your store logo and colors. Once you have selected what you want, eBay will create a bit of HTML that you simply cut and paste into your webpage.

eBay Linking Rules

There are some special rules you need to follow when you have your own website and an eBay presence operating at the same time:

- You absolutely *can* link your website to your eBay Store and individual listings on eBay. Not only won't this get you into trouble, but eBay actually *wants* you to do this and makes tools available for you to create these links, free of charge (such as HTML Builder, described previously).

- You absolutely *can* link your individual eBay listings to your eBay Store, and vice versa (in fact, you are crazy not to do that).

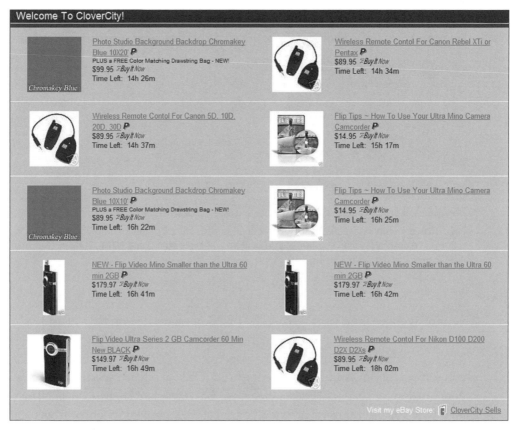

FIGURE 6.5   With the eBay HTML Builder you can showcase all of your store inventory on one page.

For more information about the tools eBay provides to help you advertise and promote your eBay presence on other Internet locations, go to the eBay site, click on the Help tab in the upper right-hand corner of the home page, and type "Promoting Your eBay Store" in the search dialog box. You will be directed to eBay's "Promoting Your eBay Store (On Both eBay and External Sites)" policy.

But . . .

- Except for your About Me page (for an eBay Store, this is called the About the Seller page), you absolutely *cannot* link your individual eBay listings or eBay Store to your website or any other location off of eBay. This violates one of eBay's strictest policies (discussed in the box).

- If you are using eBay to send newsletters to your frequent buyers, you *cannot* mention your website URL in your newsletters.

YOUR WEBSITE URL ON eBAY: NOW YOU SEE IT, NOW YOU DON'T

eBay has never been wild about people using the site to promote their websites and other selling venues outside eBay. Their time-honored explanation for this is that transactions off of eBay aren't as safe as transactions on eBay. But c'mon, folks, we all know the real reason—eBay doesn't want people building their reputation there only to skim off business to their own websites or brick-and-mortar stores. They lose a ton of money in fees when that happens, and (to be fair, like all businesses) they do not want to lose money that they feel rightfully belongs to eBay. Also, eBay doesn't want to be seen as training its competition.

Up until 2008, eBay sellers were allowed to mention their website URLs in one place and one place only: a single mention on their About Me page (or, in the case of an eBay Store, the About the Seller page). Then, in early 2008, eBay changed the rules and prohibited even that one reference.

The outcry from eBay sellers worldwide to this rule change (and others adopted at the same time as well) was so great that eBay backtracked and went back to allowing eBay sellers one website URL reference in the About Me or About the Seller page.

But at the time this book is going to press, eBay hasn't updated all the versions of the policy that appear on its site. Go to the Help section on eBay and type in "Links Policy" (for individual listings) or "Links From an eBay Store" (for eBay Stores), and you will see that eBay's stated policy is that you cannot mention a website URL from an off-eBay site anywhere on eBay . . . period. Go to this page, however—pages.ebay.com/help/policies/listing-aboutme.html—and you will see the current policy stated correctly.

So what do you do? Can you list your website URL on your About Me page or not? The bottom line is that you will have to check eBay's Community section for the latest information on this issue, as it has become something of a political football within the eBay community. Clearly, eBay's goal over the long haul is to eliminate all references to outside websites on the eBay site (except for websites with which eBay has a business relationship, such as Buy.com). So when in doubt, leave it out.

Ubiquity Is the Ultimate Marketing Goal

Picture a sheet of graph paper—you know, the kind with all the little squares like a tic-tac-toe board. (See Figure 6.6.)

In your mind's eye, start placing the letter X in the boxes on the sheet of graph paper, but don't do it in any sort of order—do it randomly.

Now pretend that lightning is striking this sheet of paper and, as with the placing of your X's, it is striking the boxes in random sequence, without any sort of preordained order or logic.

When you have only a few X's placed in the boxes on the sheet of graph paper,

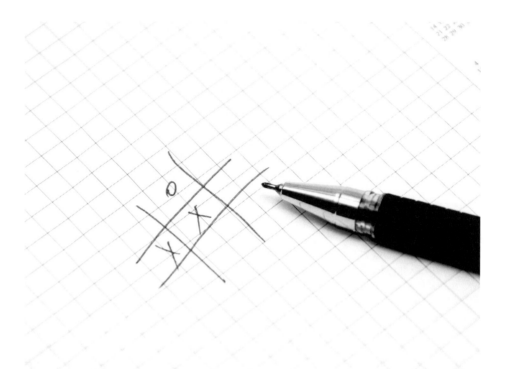

FIGURE 6.6   Fill in the boxes, one customer at a time, and sooner or later everybody knows who you are.

what is the likelihood that the lightning will strike in one of the boxes where an X has been placed? Probably slim to none.

But as you continue to place X's in the boxes, the likelihood increases—in fact, it increases dramatically—that lightning will strike one of the boxes that has your X on it. Once the sheet of graph paper has been completely filled in with X's, the probability that lightning will strike a box with an X in it is 100 percent—a dead certainty.

When you are marketing a business, whether on eBay or anywhere else, the sheet of graph paper is the universe of marketing venues: people who may become customers (we call them *prospects*), people who refer you and your business to other people who become customers (we call them *referral sources* or *centers of influence*), and places where people will hear about your online presence and go out of their way to try to find you (these are the tentacles of your online octopus that will draw business to your website).

Your marketing efforts, both online and offline, are the equivalent of putting X's in the boxes on the sheet of graph paper—you stake a claim on a certain piece of online or offline territory and put an X in a box every time you do something to get your marketing message out.

The "lightning" that is striking the sheet of graph paper is marketing opportunities—people using search engines to find merchandise online, people looking for online sources for a certain type of merchandise, organizations looking for drop-dead speakers on the history of the bobble-head doll in America for their next monthly meeting, and so on.

When you have gotten your marketing message out to only a few people, or when your octopus has only a few tentacles, you aren't likely to attract huge volumes of customers, either online or offline. But as you build more tentacles—you establish an online presence in more places, you advertise and promote your eBay selling business in more places offline, there are more people who know about your business and want to help you—the likelihood increases dramatically that lightning will strike and someone will get in touch with you.

Your goal is *ubiquity*—getting your marketing message across to all the people who matter, everywhere that counts, all the time—an X in every box on the tic-tac-toe board that is your marketplace.

There's nothing magic about achieving ubiquity, but it takes time and a dedicated effort.

Now, we can hear some of you saying, "All of this marketing stuff sounds great, but I don't have time to write a blog or a custom page or a Squidoo lens, because I spend all my time listing. Is there any way I can market my eBay Store and individual listings without investing a lot of time?"

This is perhaps one of the biggest mistakes any small business owner (not just eBayers) can make. Marketing is the one essential activity when you run your own business. Stop doing it, and sooner or later your sales wither and die. If you're in business for yourself, at least 20 to 25 percent of the total time you spend on your business should be spent on marketing activities. If you devote any less time than that (and we know it's difficult to do when you are up to your ears trying to post eBay listings and ship packages to Lower Slobbovia), you are not giving your marketing efforts the time and attention they deserve.

Look at it another way: Your marketing efforts are not designed to generate sales today. Instead, they are setting the stage for sales three, six, nine, or twelve months down the road. By keeping up your marketing efforts, no matter how busy you are, you are creating a pipeline of business that will keep you going months and, perhaps, years into the future.

Cliff Ennico has been marketing his law practice every day for the past twenty years. It's gotten to the point that if you should contact anyone in the small business or entrepreneurship community in Connecticut and ask for a referral of a good small business attorney, Cliff's will almost certainly be one of the names, if not the only name, your contact mentions. That's ubiquity at work—when everyone who's trying to find the merchandise you have finds you via several different routes, that gives them the confidence to think: "This person is a player and has an in-depth knowledge of what I'm looking for; I will have a good experience." Or, as one new client told Cliff recently, "Gee, I think I'm going to *have* to hire you as my attorney, because three different people who don't know each other all said you were the 'go to' person for this type of work."

Building a ubiquitous marketing presence online takes time and patience, but it definitely pays off. Get out that pencil, put that X in the first box, and don't stop until you are eBay's top seller of the merchandise your customers are screaming for.

APPENDIX A

Marketing Resources for eBay Sellers

Books

1. *5 Steps to Success: Sell Your Product on the Internet,* by Cindy L. Shebley (Ghost Leg Media, 2007).

2. *Blogging With WordPress, How to Set Up Your Blog for Maximum Traffic,* by Dany Byrne (Ghost Leg Media, 2008).

3. *Building Your eBay Traffic the Smart Way: Use Froogle, Datafeeds, Cross-Selling, Advanced Listing Strategies, and More to Boost Your Sales on the Web's #1 Auction Site,* by Joseph T. Sinclair (AMACOM, 2005).

4. *Duct Tape Marketing: The World's Most Practical Small Business Marketing Guide,* by John Jantsch (Thomas Nelson, 2007).

5. *The eBay Business Answer Book: The 350 Most Frequently Asked Questions About Making Big Money on eBay,* by Cliff Ennico (AMACOM, 2008).

6. *The eBay Seller's Tax and Legal Answer Book: Everything You Need to Know to Keep the Government Off Your Back and Out of Your Wallet,* by Cliff Ennico (AMACOM, 2007).

7. *Easy Auction Photography: A Product Photography Guide for Everyone Who Sells on the Internet,* by Cindy L. Shebley (Ghost Leg Media, 2006).

8. *eBay Performance! Selling Success with Market Research and Product Sourcing,* by Robin Cowie and Jen Cano (Independent Publisher Services, 2007).

9. *Facebook Marketing: Leverage Social Media to Grow Your Business,* by Steven Holzner (Que, 2009).

10. *Go Google! 20 Ways to Reach More Customers and Build Revenue with Google Business Tools,* by Greg Holden (AMACOM, 2008).

11. *Guerrilla Marketing on the Internet: The Definitive Guide from the Father of Guerrilla Marketing,* by Jay Conrad Levinson, et al. (Entrepreneur Press, 2008).

12. *How to Make Money with Your Blog: The Ultimate Reference Guide for Building, Optimizing, and Monetizing Your Blog,* by Duane Forrester and Gavin Powell (McGraw-Hill, 2007).

13. *How to Win Sales and Influence Spiders: Boosting Your Business and Buzz on the Web,* by Catherine Seda (New Riders, 2007).

14. *Launching Your Yahoo! Business: Set Up, Launch, and Manage a Successful Yahoo! Store,* by Frank Fiore and Linh Tang (Que, 2006).

15. *Marketing Metrics: 50+ Metrics Every Executive Should Master,* by Paul W. Ferris et al. (Wharton School Publishing, 2006).

16. *Mastering LinkedIn in Seven Days,* by Jan B. Wallen (self-published by author, 2009, available at www.janwallen.com).

17. *Podcasting for Profit: A Proven 7-Step Plan to Help Individuals and Businesses Generate Income Through Audio and Video Podcasting,* by Leesa Barnes (Maximum Press, 2007).

18. *Publish and Prosper: Blogging for Your Business,* by D.L. Byron and Steve Broback (New Riders, 2006).

19. *Search Engine Advertising: Buying Your Way to the Top to Increase Sales,* by Catherine Seda (New Riders, 2004).

20. *Selling Beyond eBay: Foolproof Ways to Reach More Customers and Make Big Money on Rival Online Marketplaces,* by Greg Holden (AMACOM, 2006).

21. *Selling on "The River": The eBay Sellers Guide to Amazon.com,* by Steve Lindhorst (self-published by author, available at www.genuineseller.com).

22. *The Unofficial Guide to Building Your Business in the Second Life Virtual World,* by Sue Martin Mahar and Jay Mahar (AMACOM, 2009).

23. *The Seven Essential Steps to Successful eBay Marketing,* by Janelle Elms, Phil Dunn, and Amy Balsbaugh (McGraw-Hill/Osborn, 2005).

24. *Web Analytics for Dummies: Analyze Your Site Traffic to Boost Sales,* by Pedro Sostre and Jennifer LeClaire (Wiley, 2007).

25. *YouTube for Business: Online Video Marketing for Any Business,* by Michael Miller (Que, 2008).

Audio and Video Products, DVDs, and e-Courses

1. *Add Video to eBay Auctions,* CD-ROM, by Cindy L. Shebley (available at http://www.ezauctionphotos.com.)

2. *Amazon 101: Starter's Guide to Selling on the River,* CD-ROM, by Cindy L. Shebley (available at www.ghostleg.com).

3. eBay Boot Camp DVD series, with Skip McGrath, Jen Cano, Lynn Dralle, and Cindy Shebley (available at www.clovercitysells.com/internetsellerspackage.htm).

4. Success Training CDs, CD-ROM, OSI Success Library–(complete series available at www.osiSuccessLibrary.com):

    Profitable Keywords: 4 Hours of Step-by-Step Training on HOW Your Buyers Are Finding You! (Don't You WANT Them to Find You?).

    Profitable Blogging: Have a Blog Up and Running in Less Than 60 Minutes!

Classes and One-on-One Instruction

If you are looking for one-on-one instruction on running an eBay business, consider the following resources.

- *eBay Education Specialists.* These people are usually (but not always) eBay PowerSellers who give adult education classes on eBay at local high schools, community colleges, and other adult education venues. To find one near you, go to http://www.poweru.net/ebay/student/searchIndex.asp and type in your city, state, and zip code. Be sure to ask local specialists what level of experience they have on eBay; you're looking for someone who doesn't just "talk the talk" but "walks the walk" as well.

- *eBay Certified Business Consultants.* These people have been trained by eBay in how to teach buying and selling on eBay and in the basics of running an e-commerce business. To find one near you, go to http://www.poweru.net/ebay/student/bizCons.asp and type in your city, state, and zip code. The Certified Business Consultant program is relatively new, and there are only a handful of people around the country who have passed eBay's rigorous training requirements. Be prepared to travel some distance (or pay the consultant's travel and lodging expenses to visit your business). However, these people are probably the best resource for an existing brick-and-mortar retail business looking to add eBay as a distribution channel.

Online Instruction

- *OSI Rock Stars* (www.osiRockStars.com). This site offers over 250 hours of eBay and online education for your business success, including podcasts and webinars by some of the top experts in the e-commerce world such as Seth Godin, Terapeak, Andy Sernovitz, WorldWide-Brands, John Jantsch, search engine marketing guru Catherine Seda, and more. Topics include sourcing, taxes, research, eBay Stores, and more.

- *Web Sellers Circle* (www.websellerscircle.com). This resource is for sellers who want to create multiple streams of income using the Internet. Resources include Internet retailing, affiliate marketing, producing your own products, and the multitude of other ways to diversify online.

Graphic Designers Who Understand eBay

Look for an eBay Certified Store Designer at pages.ebay.com/storefronts/designdirectory.html. Award-winning designers represented in this book include:

- *Dandelion Consulting* (http://www.dandelionconsulting.com)

- SittingBoo Productions (www.sittingboo.com).

- *Somersault Media* (http://www.somersaultmedia.com).

Here are some other great eBay store and listing designers:

- *Pixclinic*–(www.pixclinic.com)

- *Proimpulse*–(www.proimpulse.com)

- *Meepworks*–(www.meepworks.com)

Other People You Should Know About

- *D. Byrne Associates.* WordPress experts who understand how to set up a blog to drive traffic to your eBay store (http://www.dbyrneassociates.com/).

- *Peter Shankman's "Tell a Friend."* Get on this mailing list to watch for opportunities to talk to local and national reporters (www.helpareporter.com).

- *WebSellersCircle.com* is an online resource for sellers who wish to learn more about alternative methods of creating income online.

Index

About the Authors

CLIFF ENNICO (www.cliffennico.com) is widely regarded as one of America's leading small business and e-commerce experts. He is best known as the former host of *MoneyHunt,* the fast-paced PBS reality television series on which entrepreneurs defended their business plans before America's toughest panel of experts. His weekly business advice column, *Succeeding in Your Business,* called the "Ann Landers of the business world," is syndicated nationally by Creators Syndicate (www.creators.com) and appears in dozens of major newspapers and on small business websites throughout the United States and Canada. Cliff also contributes frequently to *Entrepreneur* and other magazines, has written ten books on small business law and management, and is the legal editor of the Small Business Television Network (www.sbtv.com).

An eBay Certified Education Specialist and former eBay University instructor, Cliff talks to thousands of eBay entrepreneurs each year about the legal, tax, accounting, staffing, and international business issues involved in running a business on eBay. He hosts frequent eBay Community Workshops on legal and tax topics on the eBay website and is the author of *The eBay Seller's Tax and Legal Answer Book* and *The eBay Business Answer Book.*

CINDY SHEBLEY (www.clovercity.com) is an eBay Certified Business Consultant, Education Specialist, and author who teaches throughout the northwestern United States.

Cindy's eBay career started in the late 1990s as a way to liquidate inventory from her bricks-and-mortar store. Today Cindy is an eBay PowerSeller who sells photography and video equipment, and supplies for eBay sellers. As an eBay Certified Business Consultant, Cindy helps clients grow their businesses and teaches them the marketing techniques needed to stay competitive in today's quickly changing online world. Cindy is also a leading instructor online at www .websellerscircle.com, a resource for Internet entrepreneurs.

Cindy is the author of several books including *Easy Auction Photography, How to Squidoo,* and *5 Steps to Success: Sell Your Product on the Internet.* Cindy also hosts two CD-ROM instructional courses for online merchants: *Add Video to eBay Auctions* and *Amazon 101: Starter's Guide to Selling on the River,* both of which are produced by Ghost Leg Media (www.ghostlegmedia.com).